TWENTIETH-CENTURY EUROPE

TWENTIETH-CENTURY EUROPE

EUROPE

PATHS TO UNITY

RICHARD VAUGHAN

CROOM HELM   LONDON

BARNES & NOBLE BOOKS · NEW YORK
(a division of Harper & Row Publishers, Inc.)

© 1979 Richard Vaughan
Croom Helm Ltd, 2-10 St John's Road, London SW11

British Library Cataloguing in Publication Data

Vaughan, Richard, b.1927
   Twentieth century Europe.
   1. European federation — History
   I. Title
   321'.04   D1060

ISBN 0-85664-846-9

Published in the USA 1979 by
HARPER & ROW PUBLISHERS, INC.
BARNES & NOBLE IMPORT DIVISION

Library of Congress Cataloging in Publication Data

Vaughan, Richard, 1927-
   Twentieth-century Europe.

   Includes index.
   1. European federation.   I. Title.
D1060.V37   341.24'2   78-13007
ISBN 0-06-497172-4

Printed and bound in Great Britain

CONTENTS

ACKNOWLEDGEMENTS

This book owes its existence to the generous help the author has received from persons and institutions too numerous for each one to be mentioned individually: I thank them all. In some cases, however, the help has been too substantial *not* to be specifically acknowledged. My special gratitude is due to David Croom for his encouragement and helpful advice; to the British Academy, which awarded me a European Exchange Grant, the Deutscher Akademischer Austauschdienst or German Academic Exchange Service, and the University of Hull, for financial assistance; and to Inter Nationes, the Gesamtdeutsches Institut and the Bundeszentrale für politische Bildung, all at Bonn, for gifts of books.

Although I have made no attempt whatsoever to speak to all the right people on the subject of European integration, I would like to thank the following for giving me the opportunity to discuss certain aspects of this subject with them and for answering my questions: Hendrik Brugmans, formerly Rector of the College of Europe at Bruges; Henk Aben, Dutch journalist; Tom Westergård of the secretariat of the Nordic Council of Ministers; Odd Medbø, director of public relations of the Scandinavian Airlines System (SAS) for Norway; Gerhard Arnesen, administrative director of Foreningen Norden (the Norden Association of Norway); and Godvin Låder Ve, Secretary-General of the Norwegian delegation to the Nordic Council.

Apart from the special thanks naturally owing to my own university library and its staff (especially the staff of the inter-library loan department, Wendy Mann and John Morris) at Hull, I am most grateful to the authorities and staff of the following libraries, where I have been given every possible assistance: the library of the College of Europe at Bruges, especially Leons L. Paklons; the Press Library of the Royal Institute of International Affairs at Chatham House, London, especially Susan Boyde; the library of the Norwegian Nobel Institute in Oslo, especially Anne Kjelling; and the Dokumentationstelle of the Research Institute of the German Society for Foreign Affairs (Deutsche Gesellschaft für Auswärtige Politik) in Bonn, Gisela Gottwald. I should also like to thank various members of staff of the offices of the Commission of the EEC in London, The Hague (G.J.N. Wijnand), Bonn (Holger Mirek) and Rome (Gerardo Mombelli), and of the European Movement at The Hague, Oslo and Copenhagen; and, last but certainly not least, the institutes where I have been permitted to work and where I have profited from conversations with experts. I am particularly grateful to the Rector of the College of Europe at Bruges, Jerzy Lukaszewski, for allowing me to reside in the

College for a week, and to Marie Joseph Lory; to John Sanness and his colleagues Arne Olav Brundtland and Martin Saeter at the Norsk Utenrikspolitisk Institutt (NUPI) in Oslo, where I was given office accommodation, the run of the library and much help; to J.L. Heldring and Henriette C. van Dijk of the Netherlands Institute of Foreign Affairs (Nederlands Genootschap voor Internationale Zaken) in The Hague; to the authorities of the German Society for Foreign Affairs' research insitute in Bonn, where I was again given office accommodation, and to Eberhard Schulz there; to Cesare Merlini and the Istituto Affari Internazionali in Rome; and to Edmondo Paolini, editor of the journal *Comuni d'Europa,* organ of the Italian section of the CCE, who allowed me to work in his office, likewise in Rome.

For their valuable comments and suggestions, and for reading through the manuscript of this work, I am indebted to Dr Philip R. Jones of the Department of Economics, University of Hull, Dr Richard Mayne, director of the London Office of the EEC Commission, and Professor Geoffrey Warner of the Department of History, University of Leicester.

To Mrs Alwyn Thurlow I owe much for her expert typing of the entire manuscript; and, once more, I thank my wife and children for help, encouragement and forbearance.

March 1978   Richard Vaughan

ABBREVIATIONS

ACP	African, Caribbean and Pacific countries, signatories of the 1975 Lomé Convention
AEF	Action Centre of European Federalists (1956)
ASEAN	Association of South-East Asian Nations
ATIC	Association Technique de l'Importation Charbonnière
Belux	Customs or Economic Union of Belgium and Luxembourg (1922)
Benelux	Customs or Economic Union of Belgium, the Netherlands and Luxembourg
BP	British Petroleum Ltd
CAP	Common agricultural policy of the Common Market
CCE	Conseil des communes d'Europe or Council of European Municipalities
CDU	Christian Democratic Union Party of the Federal German Republic
CEEC	Committee of European Economic Cooperation (1947-8)
CEMT	Conference of European Ministers of Transport
CEPTA	Conference of European Postal and Telecommunications Administrations
CGIL	Confederazione Generale Italiana del Lavoro
CGT	Confédération Générale du Travail
CIEC	Conference on International Economic Cooperation
CMEA or Comecon	Council for Mutual Economic Assistance, Moscow
COPA	Committee of Professional Agricultural Organizations
COREPER	Committee of Permanent Representatives, Brussels
COST	Committee on European Cooperation in the Field of Scientific and Technical Research
CSCE	Conference on Security and Cooperation in Europe
CSU	Christian Social Union Party of the Federal German Republic
DGB	Deutsche Gewerkschaftsbund
EAGGF	European Agricultural Guidance and Guarantee Fund, also called the Farm Fund or the Agricultural Fund, of the EEC
ECA	Economic Cooperation Administration
ECE	United Nations Economic Commission for Europe, Geneva
ECITO	European Central Inland Transport Organization (1941)

ECO	European Coal Organization (1945)
ECSC	European Coal and Steel Community
EDC	European Defence Community, projected
EEB	European Environmental Bureau
EEC	European Economic Community or Common Market
EFTA	European Free Trade Association, Geneva
ELEC	European League for Economic Cooperation
ENEA	European Nuclear Energy Agency
ENI	Ente Nazionale Idrocarburi
EPC	European Political Community (also used for European Political Cooperation under the Davignon formula)
EPP	European People's Party
EPU	European Payments Union (1950)
ERP	European Recovery Programme
ETUC	European Trade Union Confederation
EUCD	European Union of Christian Democrats
Euratom	European Atomic Energy Community
FAO	Food and Agriculture Organization of the United Nations, Rome
FIFA	Fédération Internationale de Football Associations
Francital	Projected customs union between France and Italy (1947)
GATT	General Agreement on Tariffs and Trade, Geneva
GDR	German Democratic Republic
Georg	Gemeinschaftsorganisation Ruhrkohle
GSP	Generalized system of preferences
IAR	International Authority for the Ruhr
IBM	International Business Machines Corporation
ICFTU	International Confederation of Free Trade Unions
ILO	International Labour Organization, Geneva
IMF	International Monetary Fund, Washington, DC
IRI	Istituto per la Ricostruzione Industriale
ITT	International Telephone and Telegraph Corporation
JET	Joint European Torus, Culham
MCA	Monetary compensatory amount
MFE	Movimento Federalista Europeo
MP	Member of Parliament
NATO	North Atlantic Treaty Organization
NEI	Nouvelles Equipes Internationales, Rome
OEEC, OECD	Organization for European Economic Cooperation, later Organization for Economic Cooperation and Development, Paris
OPEC	Organization of Petroleum Exporting Countries
PEP	Political and Economic Planning, London

RPF	Rassemblement du Peuple Français
SAS	Scandinavian Airlines System
SED	Sozialistische Einheitspartei of the German Democratic Republic
SHAEF	Supreme Headquarters Allied Expeditionary Forces
SHAPE	Supreme Headquarters Allied Powers Europe
SPD	Social Democratic Party of the Federal German Republic
TUC	Trades Union Congress
UEF	Union of European Federalists
UEFA	Union of European Football Associations, Bern
UNCTAD	United Nations Conference on Trade and Development
UNESCO	United Nations Educational Scientific and Cultural Organization, Paris
UNICE	Union of Industries of the European Community
Uniscan	Economic cooperation between the United Kingdom and the Scandinavian countries (1950)
UNO	United Nations Organization
UNRRA	United Nations Rehabilitation and Relief Administration
URPE	Union des Résistants Pour une Europe Unie (1952)
US	United States of America
USSR	Union of Soviet Socialist Republics
WEU	Western European Union
WFTU	World Federation of Trade Unions

1 BEFORE 1918: A RECURRING IDEA

Has real progress been made towards some kind of a United States of Europe or is the concept of a united Europe merely an idle dream? In seeking an answer to this question we shall begin by ranging over the myth of European unity from Rome to the First World War. But we must beware of asserting that European unity in some past epoch, or proposals for European unity, could have any direct connection with the Europe of today. We shall not even attempt to establish a causal connection between the nineteenth-century German customs union and the twentieth-century Common Market, still less a link between early writers on European unity like Pierre Dubois and modern statesmen such as Aristide Briand or Robert Schuman. On the other hand, there is no hard and fast chronological frontier between nineteenth-century internationalism and developments after the Second World War: witness the long history, from 1816, of the Central Commission for Navigation on the Rhine, still flourishing now. Who, in any case, can say exactly when the history of integration in present-day Europe, which is perforce the principal subject-matter of this book, begins? The customs union between France and Monaco dates from 1865. The background sketched out in this chapter is thus by no means irrelevant.

European unity should not be read into situations which had little or nothing to do with it. Rome may have contributed to Europe's cultural unity but there was little European about her Empire, which was mainly Mediterranean. Charlemagne's Empire, which has been compared, territorially, to the Six of the original EEC, because its boundaries did more or less embrace the area now occupied by France, Germany, Italy, Belgium, the Netherlands and Luxembourg, was by no means European in spite of the Carolingian court poet Angilbert's application to its ruler of the epithet 'father of Europe'; whatever unity it may have had was Christian or Western, not truly European. Naturally we cannot pretend that Napoleon's Europe was anything but a French hegemony, nor Hitler's other than a German one. As to the 'recurring idea' of European unity, it must be emphasised that its protagonists, almost to a man, were interested, not in Europe, but in peace: their federal schemes, their dreams of European union, were not dictated in the first place by a vision of unity, but by a desire to avoid war. Moreover, they were mere schemes.

In this chapter, consideration of these theorists of a European union of some kind and, in the nineteenth century, of the peace movements and congresses which formed a backcloth to their activities, will be followed by a brief mention of three historical phenomena which have contributed in varying degree to twentieth-century developments: federations, customs unions and 'internationalism'.

Early Theorists of a United Europe

Many of the early exponents of a European league or union were inspired by the urge to create peace between the warring states of the West so that an effective crusade, or common defence, could be organised against the infidels or Turks of the East. The somewhat muddle-headed French lawyer Pierre Dubois wrote a book *On the recovery of the Holy Land* soon after 1300 — the last crusading foothold there, Acre, had been lost shortly before, in 1291. He pleaded, among other things, for shorter wars and shorter legal cases, education for girls, and uniforms and bands for crusaders. He proposed the convocation by the Pope of a council of lay and ecclesiastical princes to meet at Toulouse under the control of the king of France. Apart from organising the crusade, employing sanctions against the recalcitrant, this Council would also act as an international court of justice in the arbitration of disputes. All very modern-sounding; Dubois, however, was no federalist but more of a French nationalist, advocate of French hegemony in Europe.

In the fifteenth century another Frenchman, Antoine Marini or Marigny, drew up a draft treaty for a league or perpetual union of Christian princes on behalf of his royal master George Podiebrad, king of Bohemia. This League was to have some quite sophisticated institutions: a court of justice to arbitrate disputes, a common army, seal, emblem and functionaries; and a federal assembly which was to consist of ambassadors from all the member states. This was to remain in permanent, uninterrupted session for five years from 26 February 1465, at Basel 'in Germany', and to constitute 'a true body, community or college'. Thereafter it would sit in a French town for five years, then in an Italian town, and so on; its decisions would be made by majority voting. Members of the League were to renounce the resort to war against one another. This elaborate scheme came no nearer to reality than that of Pierre Dubois.

Yet another Frenchman, Emeric Crucé, described rather similar institutions — a standing assembly of ambassadors voting by majority, this time at Venice — in his *Le Nouveau Cynée*, published in 1623; but his was a world federation, the aim was peace, and the Turk was to belong. The 'Grand Design' of Maximilien de Béthune, Duc de Sully, comprised a fifteen-state Christian league against the Turk, but it was also aimed against Russia and designed to diminish Habsburg power. Its text exists only in fragmentary form in Sully's *Memoirs,* but it has enjoyed considerable influence none the less. It lies behind two famous later schemes for a league of European powers, in both of which, as the titles imply, the primary aim was the maintenance of peace: William Penn's *Essay towards the present and future peace of Europe,* published in 1693, and Charles de Saint-Pierre's *Perpetual peace* of 1712. The influence of Sully's 'Grand Design' reached even further: on 7 May 1948, at the Congress of The Hague, Winston Churchill invoked it, suggesting that Sully and his royal master King Henry IV of France were the prime originators of the idea of a united Europe, and even that the Council of Europe, shortly to be set up, would be a successor or continuation of their 'Grand Design'.

Towards the end of the eighteenth century the idea of a union of states was taken up by the philosophers; again, the emphasis was on the maintenance of peace. Rousseau discussed Saint-Pierre's plan, and dismissed it as unrealistic, in his two treatises on perpetual peace, and Kant elaborated a theory of international relations maintained by the rule of law in his *Thoughts on perpetual peace* of 1795. Neither Rousseau nor Kant was concerned with the United States of Europe, a phrase which was perhaps first coined in the 1780s by George Washington, in a land where the theory and practice of modern federalism had just been born. But the dramatic events of the French Revolution, from 1789 on and, especially, the rise and fall of Napoleon between 1798 and 1815, concentrated people's attention on Europe and her problems. It is hardly surprising that the Congress of Vienna, which inaugurated the so-called 'Concert of Europe', and prompted the composition of Beethoven's cantata *The glorious moment* with its 'European' theme, was accompanied, in 1813-15, by a gush of treatises on European unity which urgently discussed why and how it should be achieved and maintained. The Austrian statesman, Metternich, was jokingly referred to in 1815 as the secretary-general of Europe. It was in October 1814 that Henri de Saint-Simon published the most influential and profound plea for an institutionalised European unity so far devised, entitled *On the reorganization of European society, or on the need to bring the peoples of Europe into a single body politic while conserving the national independence of each of them.* Many nineteenth-century writers took their cue from Saint-Simon, who proposed a single federal government headed by a king of Europe, and a European parliament.

The Nineteenth Century

As the forces of nationalism, liberalism and revolution worked their way through the nineteenth century, so the idea of a European union or federation was repeatedly advanced by theorists as the only effective means towards peace and stability. Prominent in the first half of the century, it receded into the background towards the end, partly because the energies and attention of Europeans were then increasingly absorbed in imperialism. These nineteenth-century theorists of European unity were divided on whether they wanted a federation of states (properly speaking a confederation) or a single federal European state; but they were nearly united in wishing to include Britain and exclude Russia from their calculations. Few of them believed in the practicality of their projects; all were dreamers. Deriving their ideas very largely from Saint-Simon, their inspiration was socialist and radical, and many of them belonged to the peace movement which embodied a mainly British and American religious and moral reaction to the Napoleonic wars. This peace movement became a prominent feature of nineteenth-century intellectual life.

The Geneva Peace Society was founded in 1830 to cooperate with existing British and American societies. The first Universal Peace Congress was held in London in 1843, but it was at the third Congress of the Friends of Peace in Paris in 1849 that the idea of European unity was proclaimed as a central aim of the movement by the president of the Congress, the French romantic poet Victor Hugo. In his opening speech to the assembled delegates — 670 from Britain (among them Richard Cobden), 20 from the United States, 130 from France and Belgium and 30 from the rest of Europe — Hugo predicted that the day would come

> when cannonballs and bombs will give way to votes, with universal suffrage of the peoples, with true arbitration by a great sovereign senate which will be to Europe what parliament is to England, what the diet is to Germany, what the legislative assembly is to France!. . . A day will come when those two immense communities, the United States of America and the United States of Europe will be seen holding hands across the sea.

Later in the congress the celebrated American pacifist and 'learned blacksmith', Elihu Burritt, pleaded for a 'Congress of Nations' and the delegates went home resolved to support this idea in their respective countries, without however having made the least attempt to decide what it meant.

In May 1867 the Congress of the Friends of Peace reopened at Geneva. This time there were some 6,000 participants and the president was Giuseppe Garibaldi. Little emerged from its rowdy sessions save a periodical called *The United States of Europe* which survived until 1888: the editors were a Swiss, a German and a Frenchman. It was not, however, the first 'European' periodical: that had been edited in Paris and printed in Frankfurt between 1803 and 1805 with the title *Europa*. As to the Universal Peace Congresses, they continued into the twentieth century and their work was crowned, as it were, in 1899, when the Peace Conference of The Hague set up a Court of International Arbitration to settle disputes.

Many others besides Victor Hugo the Frenchman were urging a European federation in the middle years of the nineteenth century. The Italian writer, Carlo Cattaneo, who led the 1848 revolution in Milan, proposed, in that same year, a union of free peoples to form the United States of Europe. The Scottish journalist Charles Mackay outlined a similar plan in two articles published in the spring of 1848. The Prussian official Konstantin Frantz published his book on federalism in 1879; he advocated a central European federation comprising Germany, Austria, Switzerland, the Scandinavian countries, Belgium and Holland. A Swiss academic,

Johann Kaspar Bluntschli, wrote *The organization of a league of European states* in 1878; his was a confederation controlled by a Federal Council and a popularly elected senate. None of these schemes, nor any other indeed, was as penetrating and significant as the ideas advanced by the socialist thinker Pierre Joseph Proudhon in his classic work *Du principe fédératif* published in 1863, two years before his death. He dismissed the notion of a confederation of sovereign states, which could be no more than a mere coalition, and insisted instead on a thoroughgoing federation at the level of regions and even cities.

After the turn of the century the theorists of European unity continued to write; in 1905 Tullio Martello published a work with the suggestive title *The Franco-Italian Zollverein and the United States of Europe*. But an important new development occurred in 1913 when the European Unity League was founded in London. It was the first organised society or pressure group created specifically to work for European unity: the twentieth century had arrived.

Federations

Alongside the occasional puffs of hot air and the often rather eccentric visions mentioned thus far, there were important historical developments prior to 1918 which are relevant in different ways to European unity. One of them, federalism, although not wholly absent from European history, has, as a political structure, been for the most part anomalous and unimportant. The Greeks made use of it in its confederal form – their leagues had common assemblies which did not, however, impinge on the sovereignty of their city-state members. The medieval Hanseatic League, comprising over a hundred city-state members at its peak around 1400, was federal in a sense. It possessed a constitution in the shape of a diet or assembly, which usually met in Lübeck, but no army and no flag. It still managed to fight wars against monarchies like Denmark, and defeat them; but it crumbled in the sixteenth century.

Germany, a patchwork quilt of large and small political units – principalities, archbishoprics, county palatines, free cities, even kingdoms – in early modern times, which had constituted a sort of federation in the shape of the Holy Roman Empire, became an authentic confederation in 1815. The Deutsche Bund established in that year, ruled by an ineffective diet, hamstrung in any event by the requirement of unanimity for all important decisions, was eventually replaced by Bismarck's Empire in 1871. After the First World War the short-lived Weimar Republic was a genuine federal state and, since 1945, both West Germany and Austria have flourished as federal states; nor should we forget the theoretically federal states of Eastern Europe – Yugoslavia, Czechoslovakia and the Union of Soviet Socialist Republics. In the case of West Germany, the federal structure was specifically designed to weaken the central power of the state, a fact which reminds us that, behind the federal idea, as also behind much of the ideology of European union, lies a far-reaching dissatisfaction with the nation state and with the European states system.

Switzerland is described in two of her official languages as a confederation (Confédération Suisse, Confederazione Svizzera); but in German she is known by her earliest collective name, the Schweizerische Eidgenossenschaft, which could be translated 'sworn association'. Frequently held up as a sort of microcosm or even model of European unity, she is really nothing of the sort. Like the United States of America, she was put together by force of arms; historically, she is more of an aggregation than a true union. Her present-day constitution, modified in 1874 and again in 1947 to give more power to the federal government, is essentially that of 1848; it was modelled on that of the United States.

Customs Unions and Free-trade Areas

If Europe's federations have had little impact on integration in the twentieth century, the same is by no means true of her customs unions. Originating in the first half of the nineteenth century, these are still with us today: the EEC itself has scarcely yet grown out of its original customs union clothes. Alongside customs unions, attempts have been made, both in this century and the last, to create free-trade areas or low-tariff zones. Although in both a customs union and a free-trade area tariffs are lowered, there is an important difference between the two. The member states of a customs union join together in a single unified tariff area with, ideally, no customs duties on goods circulating inside it, and around their common external frontier a common external tariff is levied. Each of the member states of a free-trade area, on the other hand, is allowed to maintain whatever tariff rates it chooses against non-members: there is no common external tariff, only reduced or abolished internal tariffs.

Europe's first and most famous customs union was the German Zollverein, which came into force on 1 January 1843 and survived until its member states, all of whom belonged to the Deutsche Bund, were unified in Bismarck's German Empire of 1871. The Zollverein was built up step by step, starting in 1819, as various territories forming enclaves within Prussia were gradually incorporated into the Prussian tariff system, which had been thoroughly reformed the year before. In 1828 Prussia concluded a customs union treaty with Hesse; only a few weeks beforehand, a South German Customs Union had been set up by Bavaria and Württemberg. It was the merger of these two unions, and the accession of various other states, which brought the Zollverein into existence. Hanover and Brunswick and other north-east German states stayed outside it and formed their own customs union later in 1834, the North German Tax Union (Steuerverein). But many of its members, persuaded of the advantages of the Prussian system, went over to the Zollverein, Brunswick in 1844,

Hanover in 1851; eventually, only Hamburg and Bremen were left outside the Zollverein.

The Zollverein, like most customs unions, including the EEC, was never complete. Some categories of goods were always excluded from it and some countries, notably Austria. It was the creation of Prussian civil servants, and since they regarded it as a German national institution all non-German countries were automatically excluded, with the solitary exception of partly French-speaking Luxembourg: the German-Luxembourg customs union was created in 1842 and survived until dismantled by the victorious allies at the end of the First World War. The member states of the Zollverein did their utmost to hold on to their much-prized individual national sovereignties and every member enjoyed the right of veto in the General Congress; at times they even made war on one another! The creation of the Zollverein probably promoted trade; it was claimed in the eighteenth century that if one's hat blew off in Germany one might well have to cross a national frontier to recover it, and that there were then some 1,800 customs frontiers in Germany. The Zollverein also promoted German railway-building which started in 1835 and was probably soon thereafter promoting trade even more than did the Zollverein. Although the creation of the Zollverein made a profound impression on contemporary Europe, it was unpopular in England, the Netherlands, France and Austria; it was, not unnaturally, mainly protectionist as against the outside world of non-members.

The great theorist and protagonist of the Zollverein was the economist Friedrich List, whose horizons extended to the whole of Europe, for he also advocated the creation of a Continental Union by six countries — Germany, France, Belgium, the Netherlands, Denmark and Switzerland — which he hoped Britain might ultimately join. Another nineteenth-century customs union theorist was the Danish economist Viggo Rothe. The first volume of his *Denmark's industrial situation considered especially in relation to the question of concluding customs and commercial unions* appeared in 1843; the second in 1845. Impressed by the Zollverein, Rothe argued that, if Denmark was unable to join it, she should proceed forthwith to create a Scandinavian customs union. As a matter of fact, Norway and Sweden had been struggling, since their political union in 1814, to create such a union. The 1825 trade agreement freed the major part of land trade between the two countries from tolls; but it was only in 1874, after the opening of the Oslo-Stockholm railway in 1871, that sea as well as land trade was included. In the decades that followed, Norway made increasing use of fiscal tolls, which were allowed under the treaty, while Sweden became increasingly protectionist. Undermined also by political difficulties, the customs union broke down completely in 1897, and the rupture of economic links between Sweden and Norway was followed in 1905 by their political separation. The Scandinavian Monetary Union, based on the crown of 100 ore, was scarcely more successful. It was inaugurated in 1873 by Denmark and Sweden; in the Norwegian Parliament or Storting the future Prime Minister Johan Sverdrup opposed it, explaining, 'I vote against it because it is a foreign growth without root in our domestic situation'; but Norway joined in 1875. It collapsed in the First World War, mainly because of inflation.

The only one of the nineteenth-century customs unions so far mentioned which was established between wholly independent states was that of Luxembourg and the Zollverein. But it cannot be taken very seriously, for it amounted only to the absorption of a state so small as to find it difficult to maintain a customs service of its own, into a larger neighbour's tariff system. The same is true of the other two nineteenth-century customs unions: Liechtenstein joined Austria in 1852 and Monaco France in 1865. Other customs unions were mere projects. France, Belgium, Switzerland and Spain planned a Union du Midi in 1837; there was a Franco-Belgian project in 1836-42 which was opposed by the British and others. Still other schemes date from 1879 and 1880 — just the time when tariffs began to be raised all over Europe, ushering in an age of protectionism which is still not entirely at an end.

The free-trade area tradition was just as firmly established in the nineteenth century as the idea of a customs union; but attempts to create such an area enjoyed only short-lived success. An economic historian has called the Anglo-French commercial treaty of 1860 'a landmark in European history'; Gladstone called it 'a great European operation'. The chief negotiators were the renowned internationalists and free-traders Richard Cobden and Michel Chevalier, and the thrust of the treaty was towards general trade expansion and the creation of a low-tariff area. The arrangement was outward- not inward-looking and there was no exchange of exclusive privileges. Instead, the treaty contained a 'most favoured nation clause', embodying a principle dear to present-day GATT, in which the contracting parties agreed to extend automatically to each other any tariff reductions which either of them might in future grant to any other country. Since both Britain and France were soon busy negotiating similar treaties with other powers, and the other powers were soon doing the same with each other, and including 'most favoured nation' clauses in their treaties, a quickly expanding low-tariff area was created comprising England, France, Belgium, the Zollverein, Switzerland, Italy, Sweden, Norway, Spain, the Netherlands and Austria. But this network became gradually more protectionist in the 1880s, as more and more treaties were renegotiated, and finally collapsed altogether in 1892.

Internationalism

Although the political scene in nineteenth-century Europe was one of fiercely competitive, mutually exclusive, often warring nation states, none the less this universal nationalism was accompanied here and there by quite definite signs and expressions of an internationalism which was a response to the growing economic interdependence of the different nations. The static rural world of agricultural economies was being transformed by industrialisation, by railways and other developments in transport, and by the revolution in written and verbal communications, into a moving, rapidly changing complex of activities and exchanges, all interlinked. Wherever national institutions failed to cope with the demands of the new situation, international ones, taking the form of organisations or conventions, were set up. Few of those founded in the nineteenth century survived into the twentieth, but they still form part of the history of European economic integration and therefore take their place in a chapter designed to show that, prior to 1918, certain ideas and occurrences from time to time pointed the way towards European unity.

The Universal Postal Union of 1874 and 1878 is perhaps the best-known product of nineteenth-century internationalism. Within ten years of Britain's penny post of 1840, the Austro-Prussian postal union was created, at a time when there were seventeen different postal systems in Germany alone. But if the actual history of the later Universal Postal Union began thus in Europe, it was from outside Europe that the main stimulus came: in 1862 the United States postmaster-general circulated a plea for a world postal union to all countries in diplomatic contact with his government. Fourteen or fifteen states conferred on this project in 1863 in Paris, but these efforts only bore fruit in 1873, after an initiative by the head of the Prussian Postal Service, Dr von Stephan, when a successful union was formed at Bern by 21 states. Its headquarters are still there, at No.4, Weltpoststrasse. It has rightly been pointed out that the creation of the Universal Postal Union 'marked a successful invasion of the jealously guarded territory of national sovereignty'. The convention declares that the members of the Union form 'a single postal territory for the reciprocal exchange of correspondence between their post offices', and the Union's congresses can alter the convention — and thus vary postal rates — by a simple majority vote binding on all the member states of the Union. The International Telegraph Union (now the International Telecommunication Union) pre-dated the postal union; it was founded in Paris in 1865 and became a United Nations Specialized Agency in 1947.

In the field of transport, too, international action was found to be essential as the volume of waterway traffic increased and railways were constructed all over Europe after 1830. We have already mentioned that venerable institution, the Central Commission for the Navigation of the Rhine, a standing diplomatic conference of plenipotentiaries with headquarters at Strasbourg. It was set up in 1816 to implement the decisions of the Congress of Vienna, which had accepted the principle of freedom of navigation on Europe's principal international rivers first proclaimed by the French revolutionaries and taken up thereafter by Napoleon. But navigation on the Rhine remained obstructed by Dutch tolls and the staple rights of Cologne and other towns until the Prussians intervened in 1831 and the Mainz Convention was signed. Article 1 of its successor, the 1868 Mannheim Convention, proudly proclaimed the principle that 'The navigation of the Rhine and its mouths, from Basel to the open sea, in either ascending or descending, shall be free to the ships of all nations for the transport of merchandize and passengers.' But was it free? In fact, the regulations of these conventions discriminated against non-riparian states; worse still, they did not prohibit 'internal' national restrictions on traffic within the frontiers of one country, which was known as *cabotage*. Thus traffic on the Rhine from one German town to another was still restricted to German carriers; indeed Germany, France and Italy still to this day reserve the 'internal' waterway carriage of freight for their own nationals. On the Danube, the principle of free navigation was affirmed in 1856 in the Treaty of Paris which ended the Crimean War and set up two international bodies to supervise the river traffic. One of them, the European Danube Commission, survived until 1914 and administered the lower reaches of the river 'in complete independence of the territorial authority' of Romania.

International cooperation was even more essential for the smooth running of the rapidly growing European railways. As early as 1846 the Prussians had set up a Union of German Railway Authorities to try to achieve uniformity in the goods traffic of the various German states. In 1890 ten European countries signed an International Convention on Railway Freight Traffic after Swiss initiatives; a central office was set up in Bern and arrangements were made for the mutual settlement of accounts and disputes and for the introduction of standardised procedures for dealing with freight and for insurance. International timetabling was evolved between the first timetable conference at Munich in 1860 and the first European Timetable Conference in 1891; international express trains began in the 1880s: the Orient Express from Paris to Istanbul was one of the first (1883); there were 28 by 1907. Meanwhile, the Compagnie Internationale des Wagons-Lits had come into existence in 1876. Remarkable, too, was the fact that in all European countries trains were driven on the left and all Continental countries save Spain (and Portugal) and Russia (and Finland) were using the same standard gauge track derived from the existing tramways, which George Stephenson had used for all his railways, of 4 feet 8½ inches. Curiously, the only serious clashes between rival gauges occurred within the United Kingdom, where the Great Western Railway held on to Brunel's seven-foot gauge until, after an 1869 decision of the directors, the narrower gauge was gradually adopted. In Ireland there were at first two gauges, each of them different from the gauges in use in England, but the Irish still have a gauge to themselves!

Few nineteenth-century international organisations made any inroads on the power of the state. Many were simple matters of common convenience – for example, the Metric Union in the 1870s, the aim of which was to authenticate and standardise the existing prototypes of the metre and kilogramme, and the Geneva Convention of 1864 which set up the Red Cross. More worthy of note, perhaps, because of the tension it produced between nationalism and internationalism, was an institution which, though short-lived, did exercise real but limited powers over its members: the Sugar Union. This body was eventually brought into existence in 1902 by the Brussels Sugar Convention after at least two unsuccessful attempts had been made to set up an organisation to promote sugar consumption and equalise conditions of competition as between cane and beet sugar. The Sugar Union had the avowed aim of ending the system of export bounties practised by many European countries. A Permanent Commission was established at Brussels consisting of a delegate from each member state. Voting by a simple majority, this institution was successful in its war on 'bounty-fed' sugar, but it collapsed in 1920, Britain having left it in 1913, after criticising the Permanent Commission for acting like a police court.

Countless other examples of internationalism could be cited from the years before 1918. The Rothschilds, the richest bankers in Europe, who were a main source of investment both for governments and for private industry, constituted a truly international institution in themselves – if not supranational, for they certainly enjoyed substantial political influence – especially in the years up to about 1860, when the five brothers Rothschild were based respectively in Frankfurt, Vienna, London, Paris and Naples. A field in which rapid progress was made prior to the First World War was international labour legislation. In 1904 France and Italy signed a treaty granting the same rights and benefits to 'immigrant' workers from the other country as were enjoyed by their own workers, and by 1914 27 similar labour treaties had been signed. The search for an international language also perhaps ought to be mentioned here. In the night of 31 March 1879, at Constance in Germany, Martin Schleyer, who was alleged to have 'known' over fifty languages, suddenly thought of Volapuk. In spite of the extraordinarily complicated conjugations of its verbs, Volapuk could soon boast textbooks, conferences, even an academy. But by the 1890s it was being overtaken by Esperanto, which, after the turn of the century, had a Lingua Komitato and a Centra Oficejo in Paris. Neither, nor any other of the many artificial languages, has enjoyed more than a passing vogue. Finally, besides international scientific collaboration, international churches like the 1875 World Presbyterian Alliance, and international congresses of all kinds, important international events took place in the world of sport: in 1893 French crews were allowed to compete in the Henley regatta, and in 1896 the first modern

Olympic Games were celebrated in Athens.

On the question of whether or not there was a significant quantitative increase in international organisations in the years leading up to the First World War, historians have given the following numbers of new administrative conventions and arrangements between states: in 1870-80, 20; in 1880-90, 31; in 1890-1900, 61; and in 1900-4, 108. It is not, however, suggested that these figures be taken too seriously. On the other hand, we may note that, between 1900 and 1914, at least ten books were published in Germany, France, Italy and Holland with the phrase 'European federation' or 'United States of Europe' in their titles. The 'recurring idea' was recurring faster than ever. United Europe had become a time-honoured tradition; it was a myth which, given the right conditions, could surely become a reality.

2 FALSE STARTS BETWEEN THE TWO WORLD WARS

The First World War and its Aftermath

Revolution, above all in Russia, was just as much a part of the European crisis in the years after 1914 as was the war itself; and this twofold crisis constituted a more or less distinct break in European history, bringing with it precariously wobbling economies, a more unstable balance of power as between France and Germany, a totally new type of political organisation in Russia which marked that country off from the rest of Europe even more radically than had its pre-war Tsarist autocracy, and a counter-revolution in Italy which heralded the rise of Fascism there. This mainly political crisis had economic repercussions. The share of foreign trade in the gross national product of the industrialised European states dropped dramatically during and after the First World War; the rate of population growth slowed; Germany, the economic heart of Europe, was mortified and seriously damaged by pressures from France. Along with this European crisis came the raising everywhere of tariff walls. Between 1913 and 1931 most European countries doubled or more than doubled their tariff rates: France raised hers from 23 to 38 per cent, Germany's increased from 17 to 40 per cent, and some Eastern European countries raised theirs by a factor of three or even more. Almost alone, Sweden lowered her tariffs fractionally in this period. To cap it all, the import quota arrived on the scene in 1930. Then, in 1931-2, the last bastion of multilateral free trade fell when Britain signed the Ottawa Agreements and embarked on the creation of a regional trading bloc out of her erstwhile Empire, based on a system of imperial preference. Germany, Japan and others followed suit. Meanwhile, the League of Nations, which was meant to inaugurate a new era of international peace and cooperation, proved a failure; some powerful countries like the United States never joined it; others, like Germany in 1933, left it; its constitution actually served to *protect* the powers and sovereignty of its constituent members when it ought to have restrained them; nor did it dare take any effective measures when Japan invaded Manchuria in 1931 and Mussolini overran Ethiopia in 1935. A historian tells us that the League dealt with 66 international disputes between members. It failed to settle eleven — which were the most serious ones. Thirty-five were dealt with successfully but only four of these involved hostilities, and all of them certainly would still have been settled even if the League had not existed.

It is perhaps hardly surprising, against this background, that a number of schemes and movements aimed at solving Europe's problems appeared in the 1920s. Although at first, in 1917-22, as a result of the United States becoming a belligerent, which helped to transform the European war into a world war, attention was focused on world problems, and Europeans tended to look outward towards a global solution in the form of a world-wide or universal security organisation, even in these years the European idea had powerful advocates. The League of Nations was criticised in a remarkable book by two Italians, a businessman and a professor of economics, Giovanni Agnelli and Attilio Cabiata, entitled *European federation or League of Nations?* published in Milan, Turin and Rome in 1918 and soon translated into French. Only a closely organised specifically European union could save Europe from further decline, they argued; and the Frenchman Albert Demangeon, in his brilliant analysis of the 'de-Europeanising' of the world published in 1920 – *The decline of Europe* – agreed with them.

Post-war Federalism and Coudenhove's *Pan-Europa*

Nobody took these ideas seriously; all eyes, in the immediate post-war years, were on Versailles, where the peace settlement was thrashed out in 1919, and all hopes were vested in the League, which came into existence on 10 January 1920. It was largely fear of the growing Bolshevik menace among more conservative circles in the West, especially in Germany, as well as French fears of revived militarism in Germany and another war, which caused the extraordinary outpouring of federalist literature in 1922 and the years immediately succeeding. In 1922 at least five writers pleaded in print for a United States of Europe. But the names of Joseph Caillaux, Wilhelm Heile, Richard Baerwald and the Pole Emmanuel Malynski have all been forgotten, while that of the 27-year-old idealistic Austrian aristocrat Richard Coudenhove-Kalergi (died 1972), a Doctor of Philosophy of the University of Vienna, who wrote an article on European unity in summer 1922, is alone remembered.

Not that Coudenhove would have been remembered had he stopped short at this article; it was his book *Pan-Europa,* published in October 1923, and above all the foundation of the Pan-European Union in 1923-4, which made his name and guaranteed his fame. He was a count of the Holy Roman Empire who became a Czech citizen in 1918. The Coudenhoves were Brabantine nobles, the Kalergis claimed descent from the Byzantine imperial dynasty of the Phocae. His father, in the Austrian diplomatic service, was posted to Tokyo and married a Japanese. Coudenhove, born in Tokyo in 1894, was brought up mostly in Vienna; in 1931 he bought a house at Gstaad in Switzerland but became a French citizen in 1939. He had a flair for publicity and substantial private financial resources which were put to good effect from the start. Every copy of his book *Pan-Europa,* many of which were sent out free to prominent public figures all over Europe, contained a postcard with his name and address on one side and the words 'I adhere to the Pan-European Union' and a space for the signature on the other. Within a month there were over 1,000 registered members of the new movement, the emblem of which was a red cross on a golden sun. Its headquarters were in Vienna; the first issue of its journal *Pan-Europa* appeared in April 1924. In 1925, as a result mainly of Coudenhove's personal efforts and contacts, national sections were set up all over Europe and an American Cooperative Committee of the Pan-European Union was established in the United States after his visit there in 1925. In October 1926 the movement's founder could take legitimate pride in the fact that some 2,000 delegates from 24 states attended the first Pan-European Congress in the Konzerthaus in Vienna, and that several of Europe's best-known statesmen were among them.

Eduard Beneš, then Foreign Minister of Czechoslovakia, was perhaps the most influential of Coudenhove's early supporters; others were Aristide Briand and Edouard Herriot, Carlo Sforza and Benedetto Croce, Karl Renner in Austria, and Emile Mayrisch in Luxembourg. Later the net spread much wider and many persons famous at the time or to become famous later belonged to the Pan-European Union: Léon Blum, Georges Pompidou, Maurice Schumann, Fridtjof Nansen, J.L. Mowinckel, Adenauer, Freud, Einstein, Heinrich and Thomas Mann, Ortega y Gasset and numerous others. But this veneer of great names cannot conceal the fact that most of the statesmen members were utterly powerless to take any practical steps whatsoever towards a united Europe. Nor can it conceal an almost equally serious shortcoming – the complete absence of popular support. The movement had no foundations in public opinion. It was unashamedly élitist; its supporters were 'ivory-tower' academics, fashionable politicians, intellectual eccentrics, idealistic visionaries and aristocratic cranks. Nor finally does the list of great names, of which Coudenhove himself was justly proud, conceal the fact that putting together these various and quite discrete elements did not create a unified force of any kind; it was an exercise in pure syncretism – he might just as well have added those whom he himself called 'the Pan-Europeans of the past': Charlemagne, Sully, Saint-Pierre, Kant, Victor Hugo and others. The trouble was that these, and the actual Pan-Europeans, all believed in different Europes.

As the phrase 'Pan-Europa' implies, Coudenhove's inspiration and part-model was the 1922 Pan-American Conference at Santiago, Chile, rather than the traditional dream of a United States of Europe. He was no federalist. The message of the book *Pan-Europa,* and the appeal of the movement, were emotional and propagandist. To avoid a destructive war and to compete economically with the rest of the world and the other great powers, Europe must unite. To the twin evils of poverty and another 'poison-gas' war, Coudenhove added a third: Bolshevism. These could be avoided, he argued, if the European states formed a confederation or union, and organised a supreme court of justice, a military alliance, a customs union, a European currency and common administration of their colonies. The Pan-European Union was against nationalists, militarists, Communists and protectionists. Though not explicitly anti-Fascist, it did become anti-Nazi in the 1930s. Coudenhove's anti-Bolshevism was expounded in his book *Stalin & Co.*, published in 1931. Inside its front cover a map showed a divided Europe on the extreme left, dominated by an enormous, united, bright red Russia. The Soviet economy was alleged to be the world's most powerful; the Soviet Union was the world's largest empire; the Third International was the world's youngest and most dynamic church. Only a European union could resist the growing pressure of the Bolshevik menace. 'The whole European question culminates in the Russian problem. The principal aims of European policy ought to be to hinder a Russian invasion. There is only one way to prevent this – to bind Europe together.' Needless to say, Coudenhove-Kalergi did not want Russia in his European union; nor, incidentally, did he envisage the adherence of Britain.

Other 'European' movements

Historians who assert that the Pan-European Union was the only movement for European unity between the two world wars are mistaken; it was merely the most successful among several. Some of these movements, like the Union for Economic Cooperation founded by Gaston Riou, author of *Europe my country* (1928), Emile Borel and Wilhelm Heile at Geneva in 1926, looked rather like rivals of the Pan-European Union and were composed to some extent of 'Europeans' who disagreed with Coudenhove. In March 1924 another organisation, the European Customs Union Movement, had launched its first 'Appeal to all Europeans'. Founded by Edgar Stern-Rubarth, Charles Gide and others, it was efficient and active; in the 1930s it had nineteen different national sections, two of which published their own journals, and it organised the first Congress for a European Customs Union in Paris in 1930. Political parties also took up the 'European' cause. German socialists believed in a European union, and the last pre-war SPD Basic Programme, agreed to at Heidelberg in 1925, included the statement that the German Social Democratic Party 'is in favour of the creation of European economic unity. . . and. . .the foundation of the United States of Europe'. At the 1927 British Trades Union Congress Ernest Bevin carried a resolution supporting attempts to create a United States of Europe. Other movements which supported European unity were Redressement Français, formed in 1927 by a group of French industrialists and parliamentarians; l'Ordre Nouveau, which published a journal of the same name in 1933-8, and consisted of a group of intellectuals, all convinced federalists, among them Alexandre Marc, Robert Aron and Denis de Rougemont; Europa-Union, a Swiss organisation founded at Basel in 1933 to promote European unity and to oppose Hitler; and the New Commonwealth movement of 1932 (global rather than European) and Federal Union of 1938, both London-based and English. Even this has not exhausted the list of pre-war movements devoted to the cause of European unity.

The Literature of European Unity

Between 1922 and 1930 literally hundreds of works in every conceivable European language were published on the theme of a European federation or a European customs union. One of the most interesting was written by a Danish ophthalmologist, C.J. Heerfordt. His book, published in Copenhagen in 1924, was entitled *A new Europe. On the ways and means towards cooperation and political peace in our part of the world.* Although he insisted that every member state of what he called *Europa communis* must be free to conduct its own affairs as it liked, Heerfordt equally insisted that there must be a common defence administration and army, a common foreign office and policy, common transport and communications, and a single monetary system. All internal barriers to trade must go. The principal federal institutions would be a Praesidium or Council, a Supreme Court, and a Federal Assembly. Britain was somehow to be persuaded to join. The new European federation could only be successfully established through the building up of a popular 'European' movement in each European country, a Europa Association or Europaeisk Forening on the lines of the Norden Associations which had been set up in 1919 to promote cooperation between the Scandinavian countries. But Heerfordt's determined efforts to found movements of this kind and to enlist interest among statesmen and others for his scheme, especially in Scandinavia, were totally unavailing; not a single Danish political party showed the slightest interest. Now he is forgotten in spite of the fact that his book was translated into French and English (*A new Europe*) in 1925, and German in 1926.

The literature of European unity reached a climax in 1929-30 – the years of the Briand Plan, which we shall discuss shortly – and then declined. It was in March 1929 that the editor of the *Revue des Vivants* opened a competition for the best project for a United States of Europe: within a year, 502 entries had been submitted! In the same year the past and future Foreign Minister of Italy, Carlo Sforza, then living in exile in Belgium because of his opposition to Mussolini and Fascism, published his *The United States of Europe* in Brussels in French. Another work by an even better-known statesman, Edouard Herriot, entitled *Europe,* followed it in 1930. The title of the German and English translations of this book, which came out in the same year, was *The United States of Europe.* Herriot argued for a European union or confederation to include Britain and indeed all European states, within the framework of the League of Nations, and for the lowering of tariff barriers. He had already established for himself a reputation as a 'European'; as President of the Council of Ministers, he had declared on 25 January 1925 in the Chamber of Deputies: 'My greatest desire is one day to see appear the United States of Europe.' Unfortunately his government collapsed three months later. A more profound analysis of Europe's needs than most of those so far mentioned also appeared in 1930: Andreas Fleissig's *Plan-Europe. The social and economic future of Europe.* This German author criticised Coudenhove-Kalergi and others for being too political and argued that the United States of Europe was just a pipe-dream. Even if it were a practical political possibility it would be used to create an Anglo-Saxon-free French-dominated Continental bloc. Much more practicable than Pan-Europa would be a planned international capitalist economy — a 'Plan-Europe' or general, Continental economic community, to include Britain; and, with some prescience, Fleissig suggested that a start should be made with the rationalisation and reorganisation of European agriculture on a multinational basis.

The Briand Plan

Thus far we have considered theoretical schemes only; ideas and movements which pointed more or less vaguely toward some kind of European unity. But in examining the 'Briand Plan' we come to a scheme put forward as a practical proposition by a national government; suddenly, we are much nearer reality.

Coudenhove-Kalergi seems to have naïvely assumed, as he sat in the diplomats' gallery while French Foreign Minister Aristide Briand proposed on 5 September 1929 in the Assembly of the League of Nations at Geneva 'some kind of confederal bond', *une sort de lien confédéral,* between the peoples of Europe, that at last his Pan-European Union was to be transformed into public policy; after all, Briand had listened to him sympathetically when he met him early in 1926. Perhaps one can forgive Coudenhove and his wife for being, on this occasion, 'as happy as two children under a Christmas Tree', but Briand's initiative was far more a product of French foreign policy thinking and the changing international relations of the day, than of Coudenhove's Pan-European Union.

The French Foreign Minister had already declared in the National Assembly at the end of 1928 that his aim was 'the final, universal, liquidation of war'. The signature of the Pact of Locarno in 1925 by France, Germany, Britain, Belgium and Italy, by which frontiers were guaranteed, the *status quo* accepted, and war renounced, seemed to inaugurate a new era of international collaboration and consultation in the interests of Europe as a whole. Germany was welcomed into the League of Nations, and Cologne was evacuated by the allied occupying forces. Having thus begun the abandonment of their harsh anti-German policy of the immediate post-war years, which had culminated in the occupation of the Ruhr in January 1923, and taken important steps towards reconciliation with Germany, the French now cast around for some effective system of collective security. The League seemed inadequate; the fifteen-power renunciation of war enshrined in the Kellogg-Briand Pact of 27 August 1928 had finally confirmed that the United States of America was not prepared to guarantee the security of Europe. A 'European' solution was called for. It was this, in the form of a European Union, that Briand proposed to the German Chancellor Gustav Stresemann, in Madrid on 11 June 1929, when the two statesmen were there for a meeting of the Council of the League of Nations. And it was this that Briand proposed in his 5 September speech at Geneva. He followed it up on 9 September by inviting the delegates of the 27 European member states of the League to a private luncheon party, a kind of 'Pan-European breakfast' as it was called at the time; and they invited him to circulate a memorandum setting out his project in more detail.

The Briand Memorandum, *On the organization of a system of European Federal Union,* dated Paris, 1 May 1930, was handed over to the European governments by the French ambassadors on 17 May. Unlike the Schuman declaration of May 1950, it had been long awaited. Instead of the 'confederal bond' between peoples, mentioned by Briand the previous autumn, the proposed union was to be between governments, and it was to be firmly situated within the framework of the League of Nations. Political first, and economic only in the second place, 'in no case and in no degree' would the 'Federal Union. . .affect in any way any of the sovereign rights of the states which are members of such an association'. It would be brought into being by a treaty binding the signatories to accept the general principle of European Union, and its institutions would be limited to a European Conference, a permanent political committee and a secretariat. Its aims were not too closely defined, but they would include the liquidation of war and an onslaught on the '20,000 kilometres of customs barriers' created by the peace treaties through 'the establishment of a common market which will raise to the maximum the standard of human well-being in all the territories of the European community' and achieve the 'progressive liberation and the methodical simplification of the circulation of goods, capital and individuals'. The reader will recognise here the same phraseology and ideas which were enlisted on behalf of the Treaty of Rome just over a quarter of a century later.

The European governments had been invited to send their comments on this French proposal to the Quai d'Orsay by 15 July; all 26 of them did so, though not all of them as punctually as they were asked; Britain, perhaps predictably, was a day late. Most expressed approval in the vaguest and most guarded possible terms; nearly all argued that economic matters must have priority over political, and many rejected the proposed secretariat as unnecessary. The great powers were the most doubtful about the project;

only lesser powers like Albania, Czechoslovakia, Greece, Luxembourg and Romania expressed general unqualified approval of the memorandum as a basis for discussion, and several of these relative enthusiasts insisted that economic problems must have priority over political questions. While Fascist Italy insisted on preserving the absolute sovereignty and political independence of the member states, the Dutch argued that it would be impossible to establish any kind of union, economic or moral, without limitations on national sovereignty. They were not convinced of the need for a separate European organisation, nor were the British. Both stressed the danger of increasing inter-Continental rivalries by the formation of a European bloc. The British, naturally emphasising the 'special considerations' required by their membership of the Commonwealth, concluded that the whole affair should be referred to and dealt with by the League of Nations (whose non-European members had already successfully blocked several European schemes); the Dutch concluded with a plea for the general lowering of tariffs. The Germans were noticeably cool, and implied, somewhat obliquely, that equality of rights and revision of the peace treaties in their favour were a pre-requisite of their support for the plan.

Behind this smokescreen of ambiguously sympathetic official verbiage the Briand Memorandum was greeted with considerable scepticism and hostility. A British document of 30 May for internal consumption in the Foreign Office advised caution, though 'cordial caution', in responding to the French proposal: on no account should His Majesty's Government approve any moves which might weaken or harm the interests either of the British Commonwealth or the League of Nations. In Europe as a whole, the right-wing press was opposed to the plan; the left, apart from the Communists, was sympathetic. In France Léon Blum criticised it for insisting on the maintenance of national sovereignties; in the Netherlands and Belgium it was criticised for giving priority to political, instead of economic, questions. The Fascist press in Italy was universally hostile. In Britain all were agreed that the Commonwealth connection precluded joining a Continental union, but there was disagreement on whether or not Britain should favour a Continental union without herself. In a *Saturday Evening Post* article on 15 February 1930 entitled 'The United States of Europe', Winston Churchill, insisting that Britain was 'With Europe but not of it', eloquently urged Europe to unite: 'every stride towards European cohesion which is beneficial to the general welfare will make us a partner in their good fortune'. Russian attitudes were predictably negative. In a speech to the sixteenth Congress of the Soviet Communist Party, on 26 June 1930, Stalin dismissed moves towards European cooperation as part of a 'bourgeois movement for intervention against the Soviet Union'.

The coolness of the replies to the Briand Memorandum led the French government to modify its proposals slightly in the report it submitted in September 1930 to the eleventh Assembly of the League of Nations. Briand now pressed for a Study Commission for a European Union or Commission of Enquiry for European Union, and this was duly set up, meeting for the first time on 17 September. Briand was elected President; the Secretary was Sir Eric Drummond, the Secretary-General of the League. It was the British and German members who insisted on the above-mentioned title for the Commission, against the French proposal of 'Commission for the European Union'. Three further sessions were held in 1931, before the next meeting of the League Assembly; during them a great deal of time was taken up discussing whether or not the Commission could make decisions or only recommendations, condemning the proposed Austro-German customs union, and considering various recommendations on economic matters which were mostly rejected as a result of British opposition. Much criticism of the Commission was voiced at the twelfth Assembly of the League in September 1931; it had absolutely no political recommendations to make and was accused of trying to find European solutions to economic problems which were global in extent. It survived to organise two economic conferences in 1932; its last meeting was in September 1932.

What killed the Briand Plan? It simply is not good enough to dismiss the problem of its failure by asserting that it was impracticable – a mere castle in the air; nor by pointing out that it was too vague and that nobody was enthusiastic anyhow. It failed partly because of Britain's lack of enthusiasm for it, partly because contemporary circumstances conspired against it. Right at the outset it suffered two disastrous blows: early in October 1929 the German statesman whom Briand had consulted in the early stages and who would probably have championed his plan, Gustav Stresemann, died; and at the end of that same month the economic optimism of the years after 1925 was shattered by the Wall Street crash, which dramatically ushered in the great Depression of 1929-33 and radically altered the entire situation of Europe. It reawakened Franco-German distrust, which had been dormant for some years, by helping to hoist the Nazis to power in Germany: in the German elections of September 1930 the National Socialists gained over 100 seats, becoming the second-largest party in the Reichstag, and this put paid to any serious possibility of implementing any kind of European union. Meanwhile, the author of the project, Aristide Briand, was himself slipping from power in France; in 1931 he was in fast physical decline and he lost much of his political prestige in May of that year when he failed in his bid to become President of the Republic; he died on 7 March 1932.

Two weaknesses of the Briand Plan contributed to its failure. First, departing in this from its author's original intentions, it envisaged only a loose association or confederation of states which differed very little from the League of Nations itself and represented no improvement on that organisation. Second, in the eyes of the Germans especially, but also in those of the other powers dissatisfied with the peace treaties of 1919, namely Italy, Austria, Bulgaria and Hungary, the French plan was seen, at worst, as an attempt to establish a French hegemony in Europe in the national interests of France, and at best as a move to further consolidate the *status quo* of the 1919 peace treaties. As was pointed out to the German ambassador in Moscow, 'In Briand's intent, Pan-Europa means in the first place, Pan-Versailles.'

Regional Customs Unions

Was the Briand Plan a customs union? First and foremost, no, it was a political union, among the aims of which was the lowering of customs duties. But there were a number of attempts between the two world wars to create regional customs unions, a product in part of the reaction against the increased protectionism of the post-war years: we have already mentioned the European Customs Union Movement, founded in 1924. By that time one of the only two successful customs unions of this period had already been created – the fifty-year Belgian-Luxembourgeoise Economic Union came into force on 6 March 1922; it was prolonged for a further ten years in 1971 and still exists. But the creation of 'Belux' was no epoch-making event. It did not even entail the absorption of the Luxembourg customs service into the Belgian because, though it was laid down that 'The personnel of the Luxembourgeois customs shall adopt the uniform, cockade excepted, the equipment and the arms of the Belgian customs service', it was also stated that 'Each Member State of the Union shall recruit its customs and excise personnel exclusively from its own nationals'. The supreme authority of this two-power Union was the Superior Council of the Union, consisting of representatives of the two countries making decisions by unanimous vote. Just as it had been the First World War that had brought Belux into existence by detaching Luxembourg from its previous arrangement with Germany, so the same events persuaded Liechtenstein to cut its links with Austria, which dated from 1852, and to form a customs union with Switzerland which came into existence on 1 January 1924. The only other customs unions in this period seem to have been the union which was forced on conquered Albania by victorious Italy in the treaty of 20 April 1939, and the absorption of diminutive San Marino into the Italian tariff system, which likewise dates from 1939.

As in the nineteenth century, so in the twentieth, far more customs unions were proposed than were actually created. Latvia and Estonia signed a series of treaties starting on 1 November 1923 and culminating in a 1927 plan which provided for the integration of transport and communications as well as the creation of a common external tariff and the abolition of internal ones in one and a half years. Nothing came of it, though a Treaty of Friendship and Cooperation between Estonia, Latvia and Lithuania was signed in 1934.

The projected Austro-German Customs Union of 1931, like the project enshrined in the Oslo Convention and the more generalised, political scheme considered at the first Balkan Conference, both dating from 1930 and to be discussed shortly, were largely results of the general activation of public opinion and government policies which discussion of the Briand Plan brought about. The idea of an Austro-German union was an old one: it had been proposed during the First World War, and in February 1925 Stresemann had expressed his hope that the customs barriers between the two countries would be torn down; 'we want to form a single country and a single economic community'. When they drew up and published their projected customs union treaty in March 1931, Julius Curtius, German Foreign Minister, and the Austrian Vice-Chancellor and Foreign Minister Dr Schober, presented it in the form of a regional pact on a purely economic basis which might serve as a practical start towards the European union then under discussion at Geneva. 'The treaty is destined to mark the beginning of a new order of European economic conditions on lines of regional agreements', their first article optimistically proclaimed; and both parties declared their willingness 'to enter into negotiations for a similar agreement with any other country expressing such a desire'.

The draft treaty's specious wording could not hide the possibility that the proposed customs union was an attempt at the much-dreaded *Anschluss* or incorporation of Austria within Germany; moreover, the fact that its publication on 21 March 1931 took Europe completely by surprise helped to ensure its hostile reception, especially in England and France. It was killed in just the same way as the Briand Plan had been killed: by referral to the Study Commission for a European Union at Geneva; as well as by strong French pressure on Austria. Just to be on the safe side, it was also referred to the Permanent Court of International Justice at The Hague, whose judges condemned it by eight votes to seven as incompatible with Austria's post-war treaty obligations, which bound her 'to abstain from any act which might directly or indirectly. . .compromise her independence'. Both the British and French governments put forward alternatives: the British suggested that a group of European countries, including Britain, should lower tariffs between each other by 25 per cent. We shall come across this British tactic, of offering a wider free-trade area in lieu of a customs union, again after the war. There is little doubt that contemporary fear of an Austro-German *Anschluss* was well founded; the German Foreign Ministry certainly had this in immediate view and was not in the least bit interested in lowering customs duties nor in Briand's European union. The real aim was to extend German economic power by virtually taking over Austria, and to disrupt the Little Entente, an alliance of Balkan powers aimed in part against Germany.

Quite different was the line of thought which maintained the desirability of 'open-ended' regional customs unions as a more practicable and effective answer to Europe's problems than the Briand Plan. This approach was particularly apparent in Scandinavia, most of all in Norway. The Norwegians had perhaps suffered more than their fair share of post-1918 trade warfare. Between 1919 and 1923 France, Spain and Portugal had raised tariff barriers against Norwegian fish and other goods in retaliation for the Norwegian prohibition of alcohol consumption; they had forced the Norwegians to accept a certain quantity of imported wine, and eventually driven them to abolish prohibition. Not unnaturally, Norway became a leading proponent of the 'customs truce' idea, which had been suggested in the League of Nations Assembly in September 1929, and had found expression in the International Convention for Economic Rapprochement opened for signature at Geneva on 24 March 1930. Norway was the first to sign this extremely mild treaty, which only called for the mutual reporting of tariff increases and a one-year moratorium on the unilateral denunciation of trade treaties. Belgium and one or two others followed, but, since there was no prospect of gaining sufficient signatures for ratification, the Norwegian Foreign Minister, J.L. Mowinckel, took the initiative in the September 1930 League of Nations Assembly of proposing a separate treaty which, in line with the views of a 1929 meeting in Copenhagen of Scandinavian and Low Countries trade experts, would bring together a group of small states interested in lowering customs duties. The result of this Norwegian initiative was the Oslo Convention of 22 December 1930, signed by Belgium-Luxembourg, Denmark-Iceland, Norway, Sweden and the Netherlands, each of which bound itself to give the others fifteen days' notice of any new tariff or increase in tariff rates. Anyone might join them. The treaty only came into force on 7 February 1932; Finland signed in 1933. It did, in fact, lead to the dropping of certain proposed tariffs: in 1932 the Norwegian Storting, yielding to pressure from Belgium and the Netherlands, resolved against a duty on imported tyres; in 1937, on receiving a remonstration from Belgium, the Norwegian government withdrew a proposal for raising the duty on celery.

While the very limited Oslo Convention did at least continue in being through the 1930s, an attempt to intensify and consolidate it by some of the signatories in 1932 came to nothing. The Ouchy Convention, signed in June and July 1932 at Ouchy near Lausanne in Switzerland and at Geneva, by Belgium-Luxembourg and Holland, was radical enough to embody totally new principles of cooperation between states; too radical indeed for the Scandinavian governments, which refused to join their Oslo partners in this new venture. The signatories agreed not to introduce any new protectionist tariffs or other restrictions, and to reduce existing tariff rates by 10 per cent per annum over a five-year period so that tariffs would be halved; but the treaty was never ratified, mainly because of the opposition of Britain and the refusal of any other powers to sign.

The Balkans

In the Balkans the regional pact idea was much more to the fore than customs unions. A first Balkan Conference was held in Athens in October 1930 as a direct result of the Briand initiative. Albania, Bulgaria, Greece, Yugoslavia, Romania and Turkey took part in the talks, which were repeated in the following years. There was much discussion of economic questions, particularly by the Conference's Economic Affairs Commission, but only 9 per cent of Balkan trade was 'internal' and there was thought to be no real possibility of or need for economic integration along customs union lines.

The so-called Little Entente had come into existence before the Balkan Conference, on 21 May 1929, in the shape of a general Act of Conciliation, Arbitration and Judicial Settlement between Czechoslovakia, Romania and Yugoslavia; the bilateral alliances out of which it emerged had been signed in 1920-3. This association of Balkan powers was a political one; its aim was the maintenance of the *status quo*. A statute signed on 16 February 1933 transformed the Little Entente into a 'unified international organization' governed by 'a Permanent Council of the states of the Little Entente, composed of the ministers of foreign affairs of the three countries'; its decisions had to be unanimous and it was to meet at least three times a year. In 1934 a parallel organisation was created by Greece, Romania, Yugoslavia and Turkey, called the Balkan Entente, which also had a Permanent Council meeting three times a year; on occasions joint meetings of the two Permanent Councils were held. But these treaty organisations, like nearly all the other steps towards unity in this period, did not survive the Second World War.

Nordic Cooperation

More far-reaching and infinitely more sophisticated than the limited inter-state cooperation in the Balkans between the wars were the numerous initiatives towards each other made by the Scandinavian states at this time. Of course it is scarcely fair to compare the two regions. The Balkans had been and still were bitterly divided between nations, languages and cultures; Denmark, Sweden and Norway shared a common cultural heritage, their languages scarcely differed, and they had a long history of unions starting with the Kalmar Union of 1397 and ending with the peaceful dissolution in 1905 of the union of Sweden and Norway which dated from 1814. On the other hand, a certain tendency to disintegration (rather than integration) into separate national units has been apparent in northern Europe in the fairly recent past and may not be over yet: Norway became independent in 1905; Finland split off from Russia in

1917; Iceland acquired 'home rule' in 1918 and complete independence in 1944; and The Faeroes and Greenland are evidently following suit. Linguistically, too, the tendency towards divergence was often more apparent than attempts at uniformity, especially in the late nineteenth century and the first half of the twentieth. Dialect differences in the Scandinavian language area were once no greater than those in Germany; yet a standard German has evolved but no common Scandinavian language. Instead, in spite of the 'Scandinavianism' of the mid-nineteenth century, the Nordic languages diverged rapidly and were still diverging at least until around the Second World War, when a movement for the promotion of Scandinavian language unity at last got under way. Particularly striking was the way three different orthographies emerged, partly as a result of national spelling reforms: thus the word for man, pronounced identically, came to be spelt in three different ways − Danish *mand,* Swedish *man,* Norwegian *mann* − and quite recently a Norwegian law unilaterally laid down spellings of foreign loan words like *stasjon, sjef* and *garasje.*

No sooner had Norway made the long-debated and historic 1905 decision, to split off finally from Sweden and become a quite independent state; no sooner had Sweden resolved to let her go, than the two countries, encouraged by Denmark, who provided Norway with a king from her royal family, began serious attempts at cooperation. The presence of the Swedes in 1907 at a Scandinavian Agricultural Congress in Oslo sponsored by the Norwegian government was perhaps of small moment; but the formation of a separate section for Norden of the Inter-Parliamentary Union, in the same year, 1907, was to be of far-reaching significance in the history of Nordic cooperation. It was the Danes who brought the Nordic Inter-Parliamentary Union into being; among its aims was the promotion of goodwill among the Scandinavian countries and the preparation of joint legislation in certain fields, especially social and economic affairs. As we shall see, the Nordic Inter-Parliamentary Union was the distant precursor of the Nordic Council.

The onset of the First World War made a profound impact on Scandinavian cooperation, which it promoted in almost every possible way − in foreign policy, in trade, and militarily: in 1915 joint minesweeping units were formed by the three countries. Already as war loomed the three governments had taken up a common stance on neutrality and peace. Beginning with unilateral proclamations of intent to remain neutral in case of war by the Danish and Swedish governments in 1912, this Nordic solidarity culminated in the early autumn of 1914, when all three governments issued declarations of neutrality and signed an entente guaranteeing to keep the peace. It was at this time that a memorial stone was set up on the border between Norway and Sweden engraved with words King Oscar I of Sweden originally pronounced in 1856: 'Henceforth a war between Scandinavian brothers is an impossibility.' In November 1914 the Nordic

Inter-Parliamentary Union gave its support to the policy of neutrality and on 12 November the three governments sent identical protests on behalf of neutral shipping to the belligerent powers. A new era in Scandinavian cooperation seemed to have opened. In December 1914 at Malmö in Sweden a conference of the three Scandinavian kings and their Foreign Ministers issued a communiqué asserting that

> The discussions between the kings and their foreign ministers have served not only to strengthen the good and friendly relations between the three northern countries but. . .it has been agreed to continue the collaboration which has been so happily inaugurated, and with this in view to let representatives of the three governments meet again when circumstances make this advisable.

They did meet again: the kings and Foreign Ministers in 1917; the Foreign Ministers alone on several occasions up to 1920; the Prime Ministers and Foreign Ministers in 1916; the Ministers of Social Affairs in 1926 and annually from 1928. Particularly striking was the near-unanimity attained in the immediate post-war years by the Scandinavian powers in relation to the Versailles peace settlement and the League of Nations. Partly as a result of the work of the Nordic Inter-Parliamentary Union, a Scandinavian plan for a league of nations and Scandinavian amendments to the League of Nations Covenant were submitted to the peace conference and first Assembly of the League respectively. Later, in 1920, a Scandinavian programme or policy in the League was formulated by the Nordic Inter-Parliamentary Union and more or less implemented at Geneva. This Nordic collaboration, which amounted almost to a joint foreign policy, was even more successful and apparent in the early years of the International Labour Organization. At home, the Scandinavian Foreign Ministers, after a break between 1920 and 1932, again began to meet regularly; and these meetings became Nordic after 1934 when the Finnish Foreign Minister joined them. This progress towards unified policies was typified in 1931 when, following Britain and after discussions between their central banks, the three Scandinavian countries simultaneously abandoned the gold standard, Finland following fourteen days later. But the impact of the Second World War was quite different from that of the first; it drove wedges between the Nordic countries, the effects of which remain to this day: Finland was isolated, and Sweden was separated from Norway and Denmark, which both suffered Nazi occupation.

Any discussion of Nordic collaboration between the wars must include mention of the Norden Associations, which originated partly in response to C.J. Heerfordt's wartime pleas for Nordic cooperation. They were a post-war development of the Letterstedt Association founded in 1873 to promote goodwill and collaboration among the Scandinavian states in

industry, science and the arts. It had launched its periodical, *Nordisk Tidskrift*, in 1878, and after 1925 this was published jointly with the Norden Associations. The nature and structure of these organisations nicely illustrates the positive and negative aspects of Nordic collaboration. On the positive side, in 1919 a national association for Nordic cooperation, called the Norden Association, was set up in each of the three Scandinavian countries; sister organisations were later established in Iceland (1922) and Finland (1924). The one and only aim was to promote Nordic cooperation yet, on the negative side, it must be emphasised that each Norden Association was and is quite independent. Only in 1965 was a League of Norden Associations set up; but this gave the entire organisation what at best can only be described as a loose *con*federal constitution. However, though Heerfordt's federalism was a voice crying in the Nordic wilderness, none the less the Nordic countries had already, before 1919, taken mere collaboration between governments and other institutions (for example in 1919 the Nordic Administrative Union of senior civil servants came into existence) much further than any other group of nations and, from then on, the Norden Associations must be awarded a large part of the credit for further developments.

Usefully for a chapter discussing events between the two world wars, the president of the Swedish Norden Association wrote an article in 1938 reviewing the Associations' achievements to date, namely in their first twenty years. They had published a Nordic yearbook, a Nordic economic handbook, and a Nordic songbook (at a reduced price for members); held conferences, organised exchanges of schoolchildren, made representations of all kinds to the Nordic governments, and undertaken the revision of school history books. The necessary funds for these activities had not only come from members' subscriptions: an annual income for the three Scandinavian Associations of 150,000 Swedish crowns was provided in 1920 in the will of the Danish-born Clara Lachmann, who had married a Swedish industrialist.

The reader will perhaps forgive a historian for paying special attention to the revision of history textbooks; indubitably, however, national attitudes and national rivalries have been vigorously fostered by national histories as presented in the schools. Moreover, it is not perhaps sufficiently appreciated that the Nordic countries were the first in this field: the Norwegian Norden Association set the ball rolling by initiating an examination of Norwegian history school-books in November 1919; the French and Germans only got under way in 1935-7; the Americans and Canadians only set up a joint committee in 1947; the Italians and Austrians are still at it. Meanwhile an International Conference on History Teaching, held at The Hague in 1932, condemned school-books which contained 'evident manifestations of nationalist propaganda', omitted important facts, applied a 'double morality', or used opprobrious language or disparaging remarks. Plenty of examples of these faults were found by the members of the different Norden Associations as they examined each other's history books in the 1920s and 1930s. A Norwegian textbook claimed that the Swedes behaved like 'savages' when they invaded Norway during the 1563-70 war, even stabling their horses in Trondheim Cathedral; but the author failed to point out that the famous Norwegian national shrine, which was totally reconstructed in the nineteenth century, was in ruins at the time! The Danes objected to the phrase 'but the Old Norwegians were not easily frightened' in a Norwegian elementary school textbook, and to the statement in a Swedish book that 'As usual, the Danes proved to be superior in trapping their opponents with cunning negotiations, but on the field of battle the Swedes held their own.' The Norwegians complained that Swedish textbooks, in referring to the rulers of the united kingdoms of Denmark and Norway in the period 1380-1814, invariably used the phrase 'king of Denmark' rather than correctly 'king of Denmark and Norway', and that the Viking leader Rollo or Rolf the Ganger was wrongly described in some Danish books as a Dane.

While this cultural collaboration was pursued by the Nordic historians, economic cooperation was by no means neglected: in 1934 each of the five Nordic governments set up a Delegation for Nordic Economic Cooperation; these were the so-called Nabolands Boards, or neighbouring countries boards, originally proposed by the Norden Associations. They held four joint meetings in 1935-8, but much of their activity seems to have been devoted to making it possible for the Nordic countries to grant preferential tariffs or other commercial advantages to each other, in spite of the principle of the 'most favoured nation' clause.

Mayrisch and the Steel Cartel

Most of the initiatives and activities described in this chapter proved to be without immediate sequel; nor were they necessarily cut short or inter-rupted by the Second World War. They were 'false starts' which often, like the Briand Plan, died a natural death. Yet many of them were forerunners of post-war developments. The Pan-European Union was followed by the European Movement; the Briand Plan by the Schuman Plan; Belux by Benelux; and Nordic cooperation eventually gave birth to the Nordic Council and the Nordic Council of Ministers. The same is true of one further inter-war phenomenon which remains to be mentioned: Emile Mayrisch and the International Steel Cartel or Entente Internationale de l'Acier, which was in some senses a precursor of the ECSC.

Born at Esch in Luxembourg, Emile Mayrisch was a convinced 'Euro-pean' who played a part in the formation of Belux in 1921. As creator and head of the United Steelworks of Burbach, Esch and Dudelange, he was largely responsible for convening a meeting in 1926 which led to the setting up of the International Steel Cartel, the agreement for which was signed in Luxembourg on 30 September 1926. Mayrisch became the President of this organisation, which was a private arrangement between French, German, Luxembourgeois and Belgian steel-producers for the control of production. It restricted their total annual crude steel production to 25.5 million tons and allocated this between firms in the four countries and the Saar. Any country which exceeded its quota had to pay a fine, and quotas could only be altered by a unanimous vote. The cartel collapsed in 1929 but was revived on a different basis in 1933; it was joined by Polish and English firms and survived till the outbreak of war.

Meanwhile, Emile Mayrisch had been partly instrumental in founding the Franco-German Committee for Information and Documentation which began life in July 1926 with offices and reading rooms in Paris and Berlin; its aim was to improve Franco-German understanding but it collapsed in 1932. Its founder Mayrisch, who was also President of the Luxembourg section of the Pan-European Union, was an early motoring enthusiast. His big yellow car, known as 'The Yellow Peril' — *Die Gelbe Gefahr* — was well known on the Luxembourg-Paris road, and it was there that he met his untimely death in a motor accident on 5 March 1928.

3 THE WAR NO INTERRUPTION?

The Second World War interrupted nothing; it was a natural continuation of the First, and the years between the two wars, the years of the League of Nations, were a mere interlude. The peace settlement of Versailles had left Germany and Italy dissatisfied and the French anxious and insecure; the Americans soon abandoned Europe to her own devices; and the economic crisis of unparalleled severity in 1929-33 was followed by the collapse of the post-war international system in Europe, such as it was. On 30 January 1933 Adolf Hitler, the Nazi Führer, became Chancellor of Germany, which withdrew from the League of Nations later that year. In 1935-6 universal compulsory military service was reintroduced in Germany, Mussolini's troops invaded Ethiopia, Hitler remilitarised the Rhineland and the German-Italian alliance or Axis was formed. At the same time the collapse of League of Nations sanctions against Italy was accompanied by the retreat of the smaller European powers into neutrality and away from collective security. In 1938 Hitler grabbed Austria, in March 1939 he annexed Czechoslovakia, and in September 1939 he precipitated the Second World War by invading and conquering Poland. Then, between 9 April 1940, when Denmark and Norway were attacked, and the summer of 1941, when Yugoslavia and Greece were overrun, most of the Continent of Europe — excepting only Spain, Portugal, Switzerland, Italy, Sweden, part of France, Albania and parts of Russia — was occupied, and subsequently more or less administered, by Germany.

In the chaotic and disastrous years that followed, of Nazi occupation and oppression, Britain, alone unconquered, became throughout Europe a symbol of resistance and a hope for the future; and, partly because of the personal prestige of her wartime coalition leader Winston Churchill, she came to wield an important influence throughout Continental Europe. She soon found herself at the point of interaction, as it were, of some of the ideas and activities which were to mould the shape of post-war Europe and, in particular, of those which were to contribute most to the post-war moves towards integration. It is these ideas and activities which form the subject of this chapter: Allied plans for the future of Europe after the war, the projects of the Resistance movements on the Continent of Europe, the activities of the governments-in-exile in London, and the programme of wartime aid provided by the United States of America, and its distribution and administration. In this context we should note that, in encouraging the Resistance, the British government was encouraging radicalism, subversion, revolution, not to mention federalism; while in harbouring the refugee governments of countries overrun by Hitler —

Belgium, Norway, Yugoslavia and the rest — she was committing herself to the restoration of the pre-war *status quo*. However, before embarking on an examination of these phenomena, which point the way forwards to the future, we ought at any rate briefly to look back at an empire and an ideology without a future, namely the Nazis and their concept of Europe's 'New Order' or *Neuordnung*.

The Europe of the Nazis

Hitler himself was not interested in uniting Europe; not interested in anything which was neither Nazi nor German. In his scheme of things, the Europe of the future would consist of a powerful and extended German heartland. In the East a massive programme of deportation and colonisation would enable Germany's frontiers to include the Balkans, Poland, Czechoslovakia and even the Ukraine; Italy, Spain and Portugal would be controlled by the Reich; and the Belgians, Dutch, Danes, Norwegians and Swedes would enjoy the privilege of belonging fully to it. None the less, the 'united Europe' theme was often prominent in Nazi propaganda, especially when, after 1941, it could be enlisted in support of the anti-Bolshevik crusade. When a 'European Congress' of Axis powers and their associates was held in Berlin on 25 November 1941 to renew the anti-Comintern pact, German radio stations broadcast a new 'European song' and the Berlin post office stamped letters with the legend 'European United Front against Bolshevism'. On 29 November the *Deutsche Allgemeine Zeitung* proclaimed that 'born out of discord, struggle and misery the United States of Europe has at last become a reality'. Only a handful of 'collaborators' in occupied countries were taken in by this nonsense.

The Nazi 'New Order' in Europe was not designed merely as a united front against Russia. It was administrative and economic as well as ideological. Walter Funk, Hitler's Minister of Commerce, stated in January 1942 that one of Germany's war aims was the creation of 'a profitable and permanent European economic community'. The prototype of the system envisaged, with Germany in control at the industrialised centre surrounded by a predominantly agricultural periphery, the whole based on the 'international division of labour', had already been constructed before the War in the Balkans by the German banker Hjalmar Schacht. The foundations of this pre-war Nazi economic empire were laid in 1934, when Hungary and Yugoslavia both concluded bilateral trade agreements with Germany. The subsequent development of a network of bilateral trade treaties, which provided for the export of food and raw materials from the Balkans to Germany in return for German manufactured goods, was accompanied by a forceful German economic penetration, especially in Yugoslavia and Bulgaria. The same pattern was to be repeated by Russia after the war, using ex-Nazi economic experts like Dr Karl Klodius, at the expense of the same East European countries; there was certainly no interruption here.

Peace Plans and Federalism Among the Allies

Of far more consequence, in view of the unconditional surrender of Nazi Germany in May 1945, than the 'New Order' as conceived by the Nazis, were the peace aims and plans of the Allies; and here we are referring chiefly to the United States of America, the Soviet Union and Britain. Why was it that these three powers, two of them themselves federations, never seriously proposed a federal arrangement of some kind in Europe? And this in spite of the fact that, especially in Britain, neither statesmen nor writers were lacking to promote the idea.

Among the statesmen, two influential leaders repeatedly proclaimed their support for a post-war United States of Europe. The South African Prime Minister, Jan Christiaan Smuts, made a moving appeal, in a speech to the Empire Parliamentary Association on 25 November 1943 at the House of Commons, for the creation after the war of a European federation with Britain as a leading member and initiator; only in this way would Britain be able to maintain herself alongside Russia and America as a major world power. Winston Churchill was already well known before the war for his support for a United States of Europe; on 21 March 1943 he outlined his plan for a post-war Council of Europe in a radio broadcast. The details, such as they were, were filled in more privately at a luncheon party in the British Embassy at Washington on 22 May 1943, when Churchill explained to his American allies that, after the war, Europe 'might consist of some twelve states or confederations'; each would 'appoint a representative to the European Regional Council, thus creating a form of United States of Europe'. Nor was Churchill the only English political leader to come out in support of the United States of Europe; on 8 November 1939 Clement Attlee, leader of the Labour Party, in outlining his party's peace aims, used the phrase, 'Europe must federate or perish'.

As to the writers, the trickle of English-language federalist literature in the 1930s became a steady stream as war loomed, and broke into spate in 1940. No single spring produced this eventual flood, but the English civil servant and League of Nations official Arthur Salter, who was a close associate in these years of Jean Monnet, has as good a claim as any to be its originator. A few days before Briand announced his plan in September 1929, Salter circulated privately a memorandum entitled *The 'United States of Europe' idea*, in which he proposed a European Council of Ministers, one of whose main tasks would be to make sure that the principle of the 'most favoured nation' clause was accepted by all members. This plan for an early version of EFTA became known to the public when it was reprinted in Salter's book, *The United States of Europe,* published in 1933; it was followed in 1935 by Philip H. Kerr's pamphlet *Pacifism is not enough (nor patriotism either)*, in which the British ambassador in Washington (alias Lord Lothian) criticised the League of Nations and argued for a world federation. In 1937 David Davies pleaded in a lecture at Swansea for a 'Federal Commonwealth of Nations'; but such occasional pamphlets scarcely impinged on the public conscience, no more than did the Professor of Economics at London University, Lionel Robbins, in his *Economic planning and the international order* of that same year. It was the American journalist Clarence K. Streit who, under the immediate threat of war, gave the federal idea real popular appeal, especially in the English-speaking world.

Union now was, in the author's own words, printed in September 1938 'at my own expense for free distribution to influential leaders when I could find no publisher who would bring it out'. Harper and Brothers and Jonathan Cape took the plunge and published it in 1939; it was translated into French and Swedish in that year and sold 300,000 copies in ten years. Streit was an ex-First World War soldier who studied at Paris and Oxford, worked for the *Philadelphia Public Ledger* and the *New York Times* and lived at Geneva from 1929 to 1939. Inspired very largely by an almost hysterical fear of war, the author proposed a Union of North Atlantic Democracies, to include the United States, Britain and her 'white' Dominions, Canada, Australia, New Zealand and South Africa, and the non-Axis West European powers. He calculated that his fifteen founding democracies could together muster 3.6 million tons of naval armaments against the 1.8 million tons of Germany, Italy and Japan. The tone of the new version of the book published in New York in 1941 entitled *Union now with Britain* was even more hysterical. One map was captioned 'Control of the Sea Keeps the World Free'; another, which bore the legend 'Where We Are Without the British Fleet', showed North and Central America black, as defensible by the American fleet, and the rest of the world grey, as likely to fall to the Axis if they gained control of or obliterated the British navy. Diagrams explained 'How Nationalism leaves you out on the rim' and 'How the Union makes you the hub of the world'. This 'Union of the Free' could now, of course, only comprise the United States and Britain with her white Dominions: by 1941 virtually the whole of Continental Europe was under the sway of dictators.

The torrent of federalist literature which followed *Union now* in 1939-41 was mostly influenced by it. Leonard Woolf's *The future of international government,* published by the Labour Party in 1939 for one penny, advocated limitations on the sovereignty of states and, more realistically than *Union now* perhaps, proposed a Franco-English federation after the war. W.I. Jennings, in *A federation for Western Europe,* William Beveridge in *Peace by federation?* and R.W.G. Mackay's *Federal Europe,* all three published in 1940, followed Streit's original plan except in leaving out the United States; two of them included a rough draft of their proposed federal constitution. By 1941 everyone had jumped on to the federal bandwagon — H.G. Wells, C.E.M. Joad, Barbara Wootton, D.N. Pritt, Lionel Curtis, K.C. Wheare and numerous others all wrote on the subject at this time.

There was nothing philosophical or profound about most of this Anglo-American federalism and, perhaps for this reason, its impact was popular and short-lived. Smut's appeal had been blatantly nationalistic — Britain should create a federation to maintain her own power. Neither Churchill's, still less Attlee's scheme, were in the least bit carefully thought out; Churchill used the 'United States of Europe' as a convenient catch-phrase. As to the literature, most of the proposals were half-baked and superficial; the aim was the limited one of avoiding international anarchy and war; and few of the authors thought seriously in terms of a possible post-war situation: their projects, created to meet an imminent threat, became irrelevant as soon as that threat disappeared. It is thus scarcely surprising that these outpourings had no influence on Allied policies and very little in post-war Europe, where Britain emerged as profoundly hostile to all forms of federation.

Nevertheless, the Allies did consider various federal proposals during the war, and before Axis aggression brought Russia and America into the war on her side, Britain made a remarkable offer to France. In a draft Declaration of Union which Churchill and the British government sent to the French on 16 June 1940 it was stated that 'The two governments declare that France and Great Britain shall no longer be two nations, but one Franco-British Union.' 'Joint organs of defence, foreign, financial and economic policies' were to be set up and 'Every citizen of France will enjoy immediately citizenship of Great Britain; every British subject will become a citizen of France.' This proposed Anglo-French federation was turned down by the French government, which accepted the resignation of the President of the Council of Ministers, Paul Reynaud, that same day, and then proceeded to make peace with Germany. The idea of the Declaration derived from Jean Monnet, who was with a group of Frenchmen then in London which included his assistant René Pleven. Churchill, who had at first been dubious, confides in his war memoirs that he and Charles de Gaulle had hoped

> that this solemn pledge of union and brotherhood between the two nations and Empires would give the struggling French premier the means to carry his government to Africa with all possible forces and order the French navy to sail for harbours outside impending German control.

In other words, the Declaration of Union was a mere device, and the federal element in it cannot be taken seriously.

More important in any case than this Declaration of Union was the fact that, in the first few months of the war, until the Anglo-French alliance began to break down in the spring of 1940, a serious start had been made in creating an ambitious, elaborate structure of military, economic and political Anglo-French cooperation, and some of its architects or supporters, including Jean Monnet and Paul Reynaud, were already thinking of a post-war Europe based on Anglo-French union when the sudden French defeat of June 1940 brought the entire structure crashing to the ground.

Other federal schemes were proposed or discussed but came to nothing, mainly because of Russian and American opposition. The Russians told the British Foreign Minister Anthony Eden in 1943 that they were against federations, and in the autumn of that year Soviet Foreign Minister Vyacheslav Molotov was quoted in *Izvestia* as expressing in the strongest possible terms his government's opposition to regional federations, which might presage the re-creation of the *cordon sanitaire,* or the start of hostile bloc-building, against Russia. The Americans were also against regional federations; President Franklin D. Roosevelt and Secretary of State Cordell Hull respectively favoured a world policed by an alliance of the 'Big Three' (or Four) powers or a world organised into a global security system. Moreover the State Department's Special Sub-Committee on Problems of European Organization, which met irregularly in 1943-4 to study 'proposals for the organization of Europe on a regional or other group basis', aroused no enthusiasm whatsoever in Washington for European unity. Finally, it should be pointed out that the British, far from making any attempt to assist the Continental governments-in-exile in London to work together, insisted throughout the war on dealing with each of them separately.

American Aid

Although Allied peace plans were hostile to federal schemes, certain aspects of the wartime alliance were of considerable importance in the history of integration in Europe after the war. Indeed, far from constituting an interruption, in some respects the war actually laid the foundations for future developments. Most important of all was the programme of American aid, which really began on 29 December 1940 when President Roosevelt declared (reputedly in Jean Monnet's words) that America 'must be the great arsenal of democracy'. The Lend-Lease Act, authorising the United States administration to manufacture or procure 'any defense article for the government of any country whose defense the President deems vital to the defense of the United States', became law on 11 March 1941, before either the United States or the Soviet Union had become a belligerent. The Mutual Aid programme itself formally began on 23 February 1942 when Great Britain and the United States signed the 'Master Agreement' under the Lend-Lease Act, which was also signed by China, Russia, Belgium, Poland, the Netherlands, Greece, Czechoslovakia, Norway and Yugoslavia before the end of 1942.

The flow of American aid, above all to Britain and the Soviet Union, which followed, though no firm provision was made for it to be paid for, was by no means given unconditionally. The dislike of men like Cordell Hull, and other United States planners, for the trade barriers and discrimination which were typified by the British government's Ottawa Agreements with the Commonwealth, was expressed in Article 7 of the Mutual Aid Agreement. This was of absolutely fundamental importance for the entire perspective of post-war European integration, for it laid down that 'the final determination of the benefits to be provided to the United States of America by the Government' of each of the signatory states in return for the aid furnished under the Mutual Aid programme, should

include provision for agreed action. . .directed to the expansion, by appropriate international and domestic measures, of production, employment, and the exchange and consumption of goods, which are the material foundations of the liberty and welfare of all peoples; to the elimination of all forms of discriminatory treatment in international commerce, and to the reduction of tariffs and other trade barriers.

Here, rather than in post-war events, is the key to an understanding of Marshall Aid and indeed to much of post-war American policy towards Europe. It is remarkable that, already in 1941 (24 September), Cordell Hull referred to the Mutual Aid programme in the following terms:

It seems fantastic today to suggest handing over some of our accumulated gold as a free gift to establish international currency, to let other nations set their house in order, and thereby re-establish trade and normal life. But this may not seem nearly so fantastic a few years hence. It seems impossible today to think of using the enormous resources of the Federal Reserve System as a means of rebuilding the shattered life of another Continent, but when the time actually comes, and we are faced with that contingency, we may find that the idea looks more like an immediate necessity than a gang tale.

Lend-Lease was followed, after a 1943 agreement, by the United Nations Rehabilitation and Relief Administration, and UNRRA funds were soon flowing into Europe from the United States. Meanwhile a remarkable degree of economic integration was achieved in the administration of Mutual Aid under the Lend-Lease Act. Britain first, then Russia, imported quantities of component parts and machinery from the United States, leaving their own labour force free to produce munitions. While the Grand Alliance was thus extremely well concerted economically, the Western section of it provided a notable example of supranational administration in the military field for, especially after the invasion of Normandy on 6 June 1944, the British and American armies fought as one. All this provided useful experience which would contribute to post-war developments, and it is no exaggeration to say that the framework of the post-war relationship of the United States and Europe, including the institutions connected with the Marshall Aid programme and NATO, was based on Anglo-American wartime collaboration in Europe.

There were of course other allies besides the 'Big Three', and some of the governments-in-exile in London from Nazi occupation of their territories were more or less active in the cause of European unity, in spite of British coolness, and more or less successful. Two efforts, in particular, were directed from wartime London; one, Benelux, was successful; the other, the creation of federations in Eastern Europe, was not.

East European Federations?

Poland and Czechoslovakia were the prime movers in working for a post-war central European confederation, and both President Beneš of Czechoslovakia and General Wadyslav Sikorski, the Polish Prime Minister, appear to have thought of the British Commonwealth, rather than the United States, as a model. The two governments made a joint statement on 11 November 1940 in which they declared 'solemnly even now that Poland and Czechoslovakia. . .are determined on the conclusion of this war to enter, as independent and sovereign states, into a closer political and economic association.' Eduard Beneš himself regarded 'the creation of a federal Europe immediately after the war as impossible'; instead he foresaw its gradual formation, step by step, and in a lecture at Aberdeen University on 10 November 1941 he described some of the first steps: a 'decentralized confederation' within Germany; in central Europe, a 'Czechoslovak-Polish Confederation'; and 'the Balkan bloc, which should consist of a confederation between Yugoslavia, Greece, Albania and, possibly, Romania'.

In January 1942 two quite firm steps were taken towards the realisation of these projects. An Agreement for a Polish-Czechoslovak Confederation, dated London, 23 January, which other states were invited to join, comprised a common general staff, a customs and passport union, maintenance of parities between the various national currencies, and close collaboration in transport and communications. A few days before, on 15 January 1942, also in London, the kingdoms of Greece and Yugoslavia had signed their Agreement Concerning the Constitution of a Balkan Union; they envisaged 'the future adhesion to this Agreement of other Balkan states'. This confederation was also to have a common general staff and to become a customs union; and there was to be a Balkan monetary union to go with it. Foreign policy coordination was to be achieved by regular meetings of the Foreign Ministers of member states, and there were to be 'regular meetings between parliamentary delegations of the States of the Union'. But neither this part-successor of the Balkan Entente nor the Polish-Czechoslovak confederation survived the Russian opposition to federations which has already been mentioned.

Benelux

On the other hand, the governments of the Netherlands, Belgium and Luxembourg, likewise in exile in London, were successful in planning a customs union during the war which was actually implemented afterwards, though only with difficulty and after many delays. They enjoyed substantial advantages over their East European fellow-exiles: their countries were small, contiguous and closely interdependent; Belux was already in existence and the 1863 Belgian-Dutch Treaty of Commerce and Navigation was still in force; their scheme was limited to economic affairs and did not even amount to a confederation; and steps in the direction of a customs union had already been taken by their three countries in 1930 and 1932, in the conventions of Oslo and Ouchy respectively.

Joseph Bech for Luxembourg and Paul Henri Spaak for Belgium, both Foreign Ministers, were prominent among the wartime Benelux negotiators; later they both went on to help create the 'Europe' of the Six. A Monetary Agreement was first signed, in October 1943, by the Belgian and Dutch governments, which fixed the Dutch guilder at 16.52 Belgian francs and made arrangements for the facilitation of bilateral payments. Before this agreement came into force at the time of the liberation of Holland from German occupation in May 1945, the London Customs Convention had been signed on 5 September 1944. Somewhat optimistically, as it turned out, the three governments implied in this document that their ultimate aim was the formation of an economic union, and they stated their intention of organising a common external tariff 'on the reinstallation of the Belgian and Dutch governments in their territories'. In fact the economic union still has not been fully realised, nor, as we shall see in a later chapter, could the customs union be begun until long after the close of the Second World War. None the less, these particular governments in exile certainly made their mark on history; they also demonstrated yet another important way in which the war was by no means an interruption in the process of integration.

The Resistance Movement

'Of the twenty-six states in Europe in 1938, seventeen had become authoritarian, and almost half of these Fascist. Democracy survived in only nine.' These are the words of one of the early victims and opponents of Fascism, Altiero Spinelli, who had already been in a Fascist gaol for over a decade when Europe reluctantly took up arms against Hitler in 1939. The Resistance movement, which began in Italy, was not only an opposition, not only anti-Mussolini and anti-Hitler; it was also pro-Europe, revolutionary in many ways, often federalist, and thus immensely positive. The ferment of ideas it produced was perhaps the greatest single intellectual landmark in the history of European integration; it provided Europeans with a 'European' ideology.

How did it come about that the Resistance created and effectively promulgated the idea of 'Europe' and of federation? Was it not, at least in times and in places, for example Norway, where one thinks of the slogan *Alt for Norge!* 'All for Norway!', an intensely patriotic, even narrowly nationalist, struggle to free one's country from the invader? This is true, but it was much more than this. It was always much more than a mere armed struggle; it was an entire mentality, and one which brought people of different countries together in a quite new way. The spirit of the Resistance was typified by the simple act of tuning in to the BBC in London — an activity that was equally illegal in every occupied territory. Everyone shared the same aims, used the same weapons, fought against the same enemy. Thus, as the Dutch federalist and Resistance fighter Hendrik Brugmans has put it, 'Patriotism. . .gained a European dimension.' This solidarity soon developed into the common consideration of post-war aims by men and women who were intensely concerned that their efforts and sacrifices should not be wasted on the restoration of the pre-war European system. Except perhaps in Denmark and Norway, which were always 'Atlanticist' in their outlook, they wanted something more than the empty rhetoric of the Atlantic Charter or the vague promise of the United Nations. To quote Brugmans again: 'Some original thinking had to be done under occupation, since the Western Allies seemed to lack constructive imagination.' In France, Italy, Belgium and the Netherlands especially, this thinking very largely took the form of federalism. And the federalism of the wartime Resistance paved the way for the post-war federalist movements, which in their turn helped to create the Europe of the Six.

The most radical and original element in Resistance federalist thinking was in part a straightforward response to the overruning and destruction of national states by Nazi Germany, in part a reaction to the fact that both Fascism and Nazism were products of the national state. This novel idea was, simply, that Europe should be reconstructed on some other basis; the national state had totally failed in its duty to protect the lives and provide for the welfare of its citizens. Instead of it, a federal arrangement must become the basis for post-war political life. These revolutionary thoughts were set out clearly for the first time in the manifesto of Ventotene of July 1941: 'The problem which must first be solved', it proclaimed, 'is the final abolition of the division of Europe into sovereign national states. Without this, any progress made will be appearance only.'

It is a far cry from the conceptual clarity and trenchant conclusions of the manifesto of Ventotene to the more empirical but much less profound and radical English federalism of 1939-41. Indeed it is surprising to discover that Altiero Spinelli and Ernesto Rossi, authors of the manifesto, and their associates in prison on the island of Ventotene, actually read the leaflets and essays of the English federal unionists; and that the appendix to the collected edition of Luigi Einaudi's writings on the federal unification of Europe, published in 1948, the year he became President of the Italian Republic, under the title *La guerra e l'unità europea*, contained a detailed bibliography of this English federalist literature. Surely the true inspiration of the manifesto of Ventotene was in Italian antecedents: ultimately, Giuseppe Mazzini and Carlo Cattaneo; immediately, Luigi Einaudi himself, and perhaps Benedetto Croce, Silvio Trentin and, above all, Carlo Rosselli? While Spinelli and his friends languished in Mussolini's gaols, Rosselli took refuge in France, where he founded the anti-Fascist association Giustizia e Libertà (Justice and Liberty) and became a convinced supporter of a European federal union. Mussolini contrived his assassination in June 1937. Thus not only did the Resistance originate in Italy but its federalism, its 'Europeanism', found its first clear expression in Italy too.

The ideas set out so lucidly in the manifesto of Ventotene were later taken up by the Resistance as a whole. Smuggled to the Italian mainland, the manifesto was circulated privately in Rome and elsewhere, and later printed in Rome in 1944 during the Nazi occupation. In 1942 Spinelli sent a message to the leading anti-Fascist Carlo Sforza, then in exile in America, urging him to press for a post-war European federation. The message was never delivered, but in the American journal *Foreign Affairs* an article by Sforza appeared in October 1943 arguing for a post-war 'Latin federation' comprising France, Italy and a 'free Spain'. By that time the underground federalist paper *L'Unità Europea* was being published by the ex-prisoner of Ventotene, Eugenio Colorni, and Mussolini had been overthrown by the *coup d'état* of 25 July 1943. Although all political activity was banned, a group of Italian federalists met in Milan on 27 August and founded the Movimento Federalista Europeo, the European Federalist Movement or MFE. They issued a six-point declaration of principle, based on the manifesto of Ventotene, proposing the creation of 'a European Federation to which shall be transferred those sovereign powers which concern the common interest of all Europeans', and appointed a Provisional Committee to contact federalist groups in other countries. Within days many of them found themselves involved in the armed struggle against the Germans, who now occupied northern Italy and reinstated Mussolini there. Some lost their lives at this time, others escaped to the only safe spot available in Nazi-occupied Europe — Switzerland.

Meanwhile other Italian federalists had emerged in Resistance circles and proclaimed their belief in a post-war European federation. In 1941-2 many of them joined to form the Action Party (Partito d'Azione), which in July 1942 included 'a European Federation of free democratic states' among its basic principles and which in 1943 numbered Spinelli and Rossi, as well as Italy's first post-war Prime Minister, Ferrucio Parri, among its federalist members. In September 1942 what remained of the Italian Socialist Party, in the shape of its Secretary-General Ignazio Silone, established at Zürich, declared its faith in a post-war European Federation which would replace 'the old-established and reactionary system of national sovereignties'; and some time between autumn 1942 and 8 September 1943, when both authors joined the Resistance, Tancredi Galimberti and Antonino Repaci drew up their *Costituzione confederale europea ed interna,* which was in fact a scheme for a European federation, rather than a confederation, for Article 5 stated quite unambiguously that 'The European states recognize the complete sovereignty of the confederal organs as regards foreign policy, defence, economic policy and the colonies.' Although Galimberti and Repaci organised some meetings with representatives of the French Resistance, for instance on 22 May 1944 with the Forces Françaises de d'Intérieur, Galimberti was killed and their work remained unpublished until after the war.

It fell to others, and notably to Spinelli and Rossi of Ventotene fame, effectively to link up Italian Resistance federalism with similar movements elsewhere. The already-mentioned Luigi Einaudi, economics professor at Turin University, who had devoted his energies during the Badoglio government's 'forty-five days' to reconstituting the Italian Liberal Party, fled to Switzerland on 8 September 1943 and there proclaimed his membership of the MFE. In Switzerland, too, Ernesto Rossi's essay *The United States of Europe* was translated into French with the title *L'Europe de demain (The Europe of tomorrow)*; 10,000 copies, printed on thin paper, were sent into Nazi-occupied France in May 1944. In it, writing under the pseudonym 'Thelos', Rossi argued that the only way of permanently disarming, without humiliating, the eighty million Germans, was to incorporate them into a federation, which must also include Britain, as a counterweight to them. Rossi's pamphlet was subsequently reprinted, along with other federalist literature of the years 1943-4, in a book called *L'Europe de demain,* published in 1945 by the Action Centre for European Federation at Neuchâtel in Switzerland.

Meanwhile the Italians organised a series of meetings at Geneva with Resistance federalists from France and several other countries which culminated, in July 1944, in an international federalist declaration, or *Draft declaration of the European Resistance movements,* which was approved by the Italian, French, Yugoslavian, Dutch, Polish and Czecho-slovakian representatives but not, apparently, by the Danes and Norwegians. Drafted, just as the manifesto of Ventotene had been drafted, very largely by Altiero Spinelli, it embodied the same philosophy and the same arguments. The proposed post-war Federal Union was to have 'a government responsible not to the governments of the various member states but to their peoples'; there was to be a single federal army and national armies were to be abolished, and a supreme federal court. This and other federalist documents and declarations circulated widely in Continental Europe as the war drew to its close, and on 22-25 March 1945 an international meeting of federalists was held in Paris; once more the indefatigable Spinelli drafted a resolution, this time calling for the 'establishment of close international agreements among all movements, parties and states that advocate a European federalist policy, with the hope of developing a common and coordinated action'. The May 1945 issue of the foreign affairs magazine *Politica Estera* was wholly devoted to the theme of European unity by its editor Roberto Ducci, later a prominent 'European'.

High hopes were thus entertained by many, in 1944 and early 1945, for the early creation of a European federation after the war. Alongside, or following, the thrust of opinion within the Italian Resistance, which has just been briefly described, many other groups and individuals had taken up the federalist idea. In Britain, Federal Union soldiered on. In 1941, year of the manifesto of Ventotene, the French socialist leader Léon Blum and the clandestine opponent of Hitler, Count Helmuth von Moltke, both drew up declarations of their faith in Europe's federal future. In the heart of Nazi Germany, at Munich, a group of students appealed in 1942 to all Germans to rebel against Hitler, stating their belief that 'only a healthy federal organization of states can now breathe new life into sick Europe'. They were decapitated early in 1943. Like the Italian socialists in exile in Switzerland, the German socialists in exile in London proclaimed at Easter 1942 their belief in a Europe organised no longer in nation states, but in a Federal Union.

The Resistance movements in the Netherlands and France were important especially because of their widely read 'underground' newspapers — up to 300,000 copies of individual issues of the French weekly *Combat,* edited by the federalist Henri Frenay, were printed; and the circulation of *Het Parool,* a socialist paper which began life in 1940 as the duplicated *Nieuwsbrief van Pieter 't Hoen,* and has survived to become a major Dutch newspaper, rose to over 50,000 towards the end of the war. As well as many others, both these papers frequently carried federalist articles: in September 1942 *Combat* declared that 'The United States of Europe. . . will soon be the living reality for which we are fighting'; and early in 1944 it advocated the abandonment by all the European nations of part of their sovereignty, in favour of a European federation. It was partly due to the efforts of its editor, Henri Frenay, that a group of French Resistance leaders founded the Comité Français pour la Fédération Européenne at Lyons in June 1944.

What went wrong in 1945? Why was it that the European idea, which emerged spontaneously out of the Resistance and seemed so noble and yet so practical a concept, came to nothing, while the Europe of the national states was reborn?

Altiero Spinelli has pointed out that he and other radical thinkers of the Resistance cherished three all-important aims in their vision of post-war Europe: the establishment everywhere of free democratic states embodying regional autonomies; the universal application of the principles of the planned market economy and social justice; and the creation of a federal European authority for such matters as defence and foreign policy. But in fact the members of the Resistance were bitterly divided between themselves and, from summer 1941 onwards, the Communists among them began everywhere to increase their influence. It was thus only part — to a large extent the socialist part — of the Resistance movement that was in any sense 'European'; beside Spinelli, Brugmans and their associates were more conservative elements, interested primarily in national recovery, and more revolutionary elements, mainly Communists, whose overriding ambition was to seize power for themselves, again on a national basis. These ideological differences within the Resistance movement severely hampered the efforts of the federalists to make their voices heard in post-war politics, which were in any case everywhere dominated by the newly re-created pre-war party systems: there were no effective 'Resistance parties'.

More damaging, perhaps, than the ideological were the geographical divisions of the Resistance movement. Because it was an 'underground' movement it had always been extremely decentralised; only right at the end of hostilities were serious efforts made to merge the various local committees in any one country into a unified national force. And when such a unified force was created, it was in no position to take over political control; this was done piecemeal by the armies of the Allies, who, in most cases, simply installed their own protégés, namely the governments which had been in exile in London. Thus the leader of the Free French, Charles de Gaulle, exploited his control of the French Committee of National Liberation (Comité Français de Libération Nationale) to become head of the Provisional Government of the French Republic, which was recognised by the Allies in October 1944, although he had been in London during the war. Similarly in Belgium, the Netherlands and Norway, existing governments-in-exile were re-established and at once set about the tasks of national recovery and restoration. In any event the Resistance never was in a position to present a sort of international front, in spite of the efforts of the federalists, mainly because the different countries were liberated at different times; a fact which seriously jeopardised even so limited a scheme as Benelux.

The rebirth of the National States

The destiny of Europe in 1945 was in the hands of the 'Big Three'. But Britain, in spite of Churchill's eloquent but intermittent declarations and in spite of the federalist literature already discussed, was not prepared to make any moves to encourage the setting up of federal arrangements of any kind in post-war Europe. The Russians remained opposed to federations, and the Americans were suspicious of regional arrangements, preferring the world-wide security system embodied in the United Nations. France was the only country in 1944-5 which might have been in a position to take some sort of federal initiative. But de Gaulle's foreign policy while he was head of state between October 1944 and January 1946 was quite out of touch with public opinion, which at that time was distinctly federalist — a July 1945 opinion poll recorded 73 per cent of Frenchmen as being favourable to the re-creation of Europe as a federation of states. At first de Gaulle's foreign policy was pro-Russian, which precluded federal proposals; then, when he failed to have France fully accepted into the 'club' of Great Powers, de Gaulle's occasional federalist pronouncements did take on a little more force: though at best only suggestive, they did appear to foresee France initiating a regional, mainly economic, confederation in Western Europe. But this moment was not to come until the Council of Europe and the Schuman Plan in 1948-50. Meanwhile, the hopes of Frenay and Spinelli and others were dashed to the ground; the national state system was re-established in 1945, as near as possible as it had existed in 1939. However, thanks to the war, there was now a flourishing federalist movement in several Continental countries, especially Italy, France and the Netherlands; and a tradition of cooperation, and some experience of integration, among the Western Allies. Thus, during the war certain significant steps had been taken in the general direction of European unity, and a foundation in public opinion had been laid for the subsequent formation of the Europe of the Six.

THE SUPERPOWERS AND POST-WAR EUROPE

The fate of most of Europe, as the Second World War came to an end with the surrender of Germany on 7 May and that of Japan on 14 August 1945, was effectively in the hands of the two superpowers, the United States of America and the Soviet Union; it was thus to be decided by events, circumstances and policies originating to a great extent outside Europe's borders. Mainly as a result of this, the immediate post-war years, besides witnessing some progress towards unity in Western Europe, were years of a growing division of Europe into two parts, East and West, a division which had been prefigured in the Nazi-Soviet Pact of 1939. The purpose of this chapter is to explain how it was that this dichotomy came about, starting with the very first moves in what soon became known as the 'Cold War' between the United States and Russia, and ending with an account of the 'bloc-building' on either side which finally determined that the Europe of today would be a divided, not a united, Europe. In the course of this explanation we shall mention certain topics which form a part of, or are at least relevant to, the history of integration in Europe as a whole, such as the post-war attempts to set up international organs at the global level, and other topics which relate only to one part of Europe or the other: namely, the establishment of the Organization for European Economic Cooperation (OEEC), and of the North Atlantic Treaty Organization (NATO), in 1948-9, and Stalin's post-war reorganisation of Eastern Europe.

The Big Three

During the closing stages of the war everything seemed to be decided and determined by the 'Big Three', represented by their wartime leaders President Roosevelt, Prime Minister Churchill and Marshal Stalin, who met in conference – notably at Tehran towards the end of 1943 and at Yalta in February 1945 – to settle the future of post-war Europe. But one of these 'Big Three' could no longer be accounted a world power, and her political and economic decline at the moment of victory was soon reflected in her rapidly dwindling role in world affairs: Britain took no part, for example, in the Russian-American post-war settlement in the Far East. The change of government after the 26 July 1945 general election deprived her of her only statesman of international stature: half-way through the all-important Potsdam conference, Churchill had to be replaced by Clement Attlee as leader of the British delegation. In spite of American financial aid, the war-weakened British economy refused to upturn, and it was so disastrously damaged by the savage blizzards early in

1947 that the British government was forced to cut short her aid to Greece and Turkey and invite the Americans to take over her responsibilities there. Thus, withdrawing from the eastern Mediterranean as she was to from India and Burma, Britain turned in upon herself, concentrating her attention upon the problems of creating a socialist society.

Her place in world affairs could scarcely have been taken by France, whose vocal and ambitious leader, Charles de Gaulle, having been excluded from the Potsdam conference, refused to accept its decisions. But French attitudes and policies did certainly have an important impact on the Allied treatment of post-war Germany, and it has even been argued that the breakdown of joint four-power control over a still united Germany and the consequent partition of Germany into two parts was due to the French rather than to the Russians. It must in any case be borne in mind that, even as regards the superpowers, the course of events we now have to outline was by no means brought about by consistent, determined or even properly defined policies.

At the end of the war the United States, having more than doubled its industrial production while that of many other countries had been dangerously diminished, having almost doubled its gross national product, and having created for itself – and itself alone – a weapon of extraordinary power in the atom bomb, was determined to reorganise the world to make it free for trade and open to United States capital; but it had worked out no detailed plans for bringing this about. On the other hand, the Russians, with no such global ambitions, were intent on implementing certain specific projects designed in the main to ensure their own security and the future of Communism. Above all, Stalin was determined to incorporate into the Soviet Union, or at least retain or gain control over, those territories which had been taken away from Russia after the First World War, but which the Russians regarded as theirs: the Baltic states and Poland, and perhaps Finland. Evidently, too, the advance of the victorious Red Army would enable Russian influence in the Balkans to be extended and increased, especially in Bulgaria and Romania.

Europe Divided into West and East

The post-war division of Europe into Eastern and Western 'spheres of influence' or 'blocs' really dates from two wartime agreements. As early as January 1943 the Allies agreed on their demand for the unconditional surrender of Germany, thus ensuring the creation of a 'power vacuum' in central Europe after the war which would inevitably be filled by dividing it between Germany's conquerors. The second agreement was made in Moscow, in October 1944, by Churchill and Stalin. In spite of the disapproval of the United States, which was against spheres of influence (except in Latin America), the two wartime leaders then divided the Balkans into post-war spheres of interest, allocating one (mainly Greece) to the British, the other (the rest) to Russia. Nor should it be forgotten that the British and Americans had already brought Italy, as a result of the 1943 armistice, firmly into their sphere of interest.

After Roosevelt's death on 12 April 1945 tension between Russia and her allies perceptibly increased. His successor, Harry S. Truman, right from the start of his presidency, took a much firmer line with the Russians. In January 1945 they had recognised the 'puppet' Provisional Government of Poland at Lublin, in spite of the existence of the Polish government-in-exile in London; at Potsdam in July Churchill complained bitterly to Stalin that the Russians were surrounding parts of Eastern Europe with an 'iron fence'. During the summer of 1945 American 'Lend-Lease' aid to her allies, including Russia, was abruptly wound up. Admittedly it was followed in 1946 by the United Nations Relief and Rehabilitation Agreement funds, three-quarters of them provided by the United States; but this UNRRA programme, which had been agreed in November 1943, was likewise abruptly terminated by the Americans in the first half of 1947. Meanwhile, some of America's allies received loans, notably Britain and France, but Stalin's request, originally made early in 1945, for an American loan to Russia, was turned down, though not finally until March 1946.

As a matter of fact, the Russians had evidently hoped to obtain American aid and at the same time control and exploit Eastern Europe to their own economic and political advantage; failing in the former objective, they concentrated on the latter. One after another the East European countries succumbed to Communist plots and manipulation, which brought them more and more firmly under Russian control; in Poland, Bulgaria, Romania and Hungary non-Communist politicians were eliminated and the peasant parties outmanoeuvred or taken over by Communists. By 1947 all four countries had virtually become Russian satellites, and in February 1948 Czechoslovakia fell victim to a long-prepared Communist *coup*. With the invaluable assistance, Czechoslovakia apart, of the occupying forces of the Red Army, Stalin had constructed an empire of 'People's Democracies' along the eastern borders of Russia. However, in 1948, when the net was closed and tightened, two apparently intended victims were somehow left out and contrived to maintain thereafter a somewhat precarious independence: Finland and Yugoslavia. Their two cases were, of course, entirely different.

The division of Europe was further intensified by the transformation of Germany from a single entity divided into four occupation zones but administered by a central four-power institution, the Allied Control Commission Council in Berlin, as agreed in July 1945 at Potsdam, into two quite distinct political entities, one Western and 'capitalist', the other Communist and Russian-controlled. The Russians accepted this arrangement only after they had failed to persuade their allies to set up a provisional all-German government from which they might hope to exact the massive reparations they had repeatedly demanded, and only after they had settled on the profitable alternative of manufacturing reparations in their own zone of occupation. They had created the Sozialistische Einheitspartei Deutschlands (SED) in April 1946, by merging the Social Democratic and Communist parties in their zone, and this party organisation formed a nucleus for the subsequent creation in October 1949 of the German Democratic Republic. Meanwhile in the West, the British in July 1946 accepted the American suggestion of merging the American and British occupation zones to form a single 'Bizone' for economic purposes, mainly because they could no longer afford the luxury of a zone of their own. In 1947 the Bizonal Agreement came into force and a central Executive Committee with one representative from each *Land* was established at the same time as the Russians set up a central German Economic Council in their zone. Finally, in May 1949 after the Soviet blockade of Berlin, which had begun in June 1948, had shown that the Russians had no interest in a united Germany unless it were entirely under their control, the Basic Law or *Grundgesetz,* which set out the constitution of the new Federal German Republic (Bundesrepublik Deutschland), was promulgated. Thus, in 1949, two new German states came into existence in circumstances of rivalry and confrontation.

The Post-war Organisation of the World

During these very years of the war and its aftermath, when any possibility of creating a united Europe evaporated and instead pre-existing national divisions were restored and a new East-West partition imposed on them, considerable efforts were made, in the main by the United States, to inaugurate a world system by setting up world organs which might help to avoid war and promote cooperation and unity. These efforts, and the international institutions which resulted from them, though they were global and not just European in scope, did, none the less, impinge in an important way on European affairs.

First and foremost among them was the successor to the League of Nations, the United Nations, which was conceived as an international political organisation to maintain world peace and promote harmonious relations between states. It derived from the United Nations Declaration of 1 January 1942 which was signed by 26 nations, all of them at war with either Germany or Japan or both; and it was planned in detail in 1944 at Dumbarton Oaks in Washington by representatives of Russia, Britain, the United States and China. Finally, representatives of fifty countries meeting between April and June 1945 at San Francisco drew up a detailed constitution for the new organisation, signed on 26 June 1945, which became known as the Charter of the United Nations. Provided with an all-powerful executive organ in the Security Council, a General Assembly, an Economic and Social Council and an International Court of Justice, the new organisation was soon linked to existing world institutions like the International Labour Office (ILO), the World Health Organization (1948) and the Universal Postal Union. It also gave birth to offshoots of its own like the Food and Agriculture Organization (FAO), founded in 1945, and the United Nations Educational, Scientific and Cultural Organization (UNESCO) of 1946, with headquarters in Paris. This last especially, but others too, have done much to promote international collaboration in Europe. Nor did the United Nations Charter itself preclude the possibility of regional groupings such as a United States of Europe: Article 52 encourages member states to make regional arrangements for the maintenance of peace and security and the settlement of disputes.

Of outstanding importance for Europe was the Economic Commission for Europe (ECE) at Geneva, a regional commission of the Economic and Social Council of the United Nations, which was set up on 28 March 1947 at the same time as a similar Commission for Asia to 'initiate and participate in measures for facilitating concerted action for the economic reconstruction of Europe, for raising the level of European countries, both among themselves and with other countries of the world'. Much of the importance of the ECE lay, and lies, in the all-European nature of its membership: since its inception it has been virtually the only institution in which representatives of both West and East European countries have met regularly to discuss European affairs. All European members of UNO, as well as the United States, were designated as members, who originally numbered 18, the Byelorussian and Ukrainian Soviet Socialist Republics enjoying separate membership alongside the USSR, as they did in UNO itself. In fact, however, the European non-members of UNO participated in a non-voting capacity almost from the start, namely Albania, Austria, Bulgaria, Finland, Hungary, Ireland, Italy, Portugal, Romania and Switzerland. Thus everyone in practice belonged to the ECE, whose first Executive Secretary was the Swedish economist and politician Gunnar Myrdal.

The ECE was really created as a result of the investigations in Europe of the United Nations Temporary Sub-Commission on the Economic Reconstruction of Devastated Areas. To form it, three organisations were brought together, all of which had been set up by the wartime Allies and all of which are strictly relevant to European unity, for they represent early attempts at integration in the economic field. They were known as the 'E-Organizations'. The European Coal Organization (ECO), successor to the Solid Fuels Section of the Supreme Headquarters Allied Expeditionary Forces (SHAEF), was set up in London in May 1945 with Belgium, Denmark, Luxembourg, the Netherlands, Norway, Turkey, Britain and the United States as original members, with Sweden, Portugal and Finland joining later as associate members, and Poland and Czechoslovakia as subsequent full members. It was taken over by the ECE on

1 January 1948, becoming its Coal Committee. The European Central Inland Transport Organization (ECITO), successor to the Technical Advisory Committee on Inland Transport (TACIT), had been established in London in September 1941 by the Inter-Allied Committee on Post-war Requirements. Its original members were Belgium, France, Greece, Luxembourg, the Netherlands, Norway, Poland, the United Kingdom, the USA, the USSR and Yugoslavia; it was absorbed by the ECE on 1 October 1947. Third, the functions of the Emergency Economic Committee for Europe, which originated in London on 28 May 1945, were transferred to the ECE in 1947-8.

Besides its early work on problems relating to energy supply, transport and the like deriving from these predecessors, the ECE turned in 1948 to consider the question of East-West trade, and a prolonged debate began which was intensified in 1949 when the Russians complained, not without justification, that the United States was practising discriminatory export-licensing policies against them. Thus at a time of growing division and dissension between East and West, the years of the Marshall Plan, the ECE did provide a continuing meeting-point, and thus formed to some extent a bridge between the two halves of Europe. It endeavoured unsuccessfully to transform the system of bilateral trade agreements into a multilateral system, but was opposed by Britain and Russia; and it complained of the intensively nationalistic character of European economic recovery, and argued for much more integration.

While, politically, the United Nations was established, a world organisation to maintain peace and security, economically, a new international system was to be devised and set up to promote the general well-being and ensure economic recovery. Here the Americans were intent on promoting their own interests as much as anybody else's: they were determined to try to create institutions which would maintain stable exchange rates, provide a supply of international long-term capital and abolish or substantially diminish discriminatory and other restrictions to trade. The necessary institutions which it was hoped might achieve these aims were for the most part agreed on at the United Nations conference held at the New Hampshire resort of Bretton Woods in July 1944 in which the Russians participated, though they failed to sign the resultant agreements setting up the International Monetary Fund (IMF) and the International Bank for Reconstruction and Development, or World Bank, partly because of American preponderance in them. At Bretton Woods, 44 countries pledged themselves to support for 25 years a stable international monetary system based on fixed exchange rates.

The IMF was an international currency pool to which members contributed 100,000 dollars for every vote in the Council of Governors: the USA obtained 28 per cent of the votes and Britain 13.4 per cent. It started to function on 6 May 1946, but it failed to provide adequate financial assistance to countries in need, it failed to prevent trade restrictions and, above all, its rules ignored by countries like Britain and France, it failed to stabilise exchange rates. The World Bank, in which the USA possessed 38 per cent of the votes, was somewhat more successful in its aim of providing, or guaranteeing, loans for major projects in undeveloped or needy countries, but it only began operations in 1947.

A third body, the so-called International Trade Organization, was proposed to undertake the task of reducing trade restrictions and discrimination. As a first step in this direction, the General Agreement on Trade and Tariffs (GATT) was signed on 23 October 1947 after a prolonged 23-nation conference which set up a permanent secretariat at Geneva, included a first round of negotiations in which 123 bilateral treaties were made affecting half the world's commerce, and drew up a set of rules for the conduct of international trade. The following winter representatives of 56 countries gathered at Havana and, after the undeveloped countries had bitterly criticised the GATT and proposed over 800 amendments to it, they agreed on the Havana Charter for World Trade, which envisaged the progressive lowering of tariffs, the prohibition of quantitative restrictions (quotas) on industrial goods, and the abolition of discrimination (except in the Commonwealth). But the Havana Charter never came into force; it was never even presented to Congress for ratification by the United States government. Long before 1948 the effects of the East-West division of Europe had made themselves felt: Czechoslovakia was the only East European country to subscribe to the GATT, and she did not participate in the tariff reductions. Other East European countries only joined twenty or more years later.

One further institution in the post-war international system merits brief mention; it illustrates the way in which, after the initial wartime optimism, the growing differences between America and Russia undermined every cooperative effort. The Council of Foreign Ministers, which was agreed to as a permanent institution at Potsdam in July 1945, met first in September 1945. It supposedly comprised the Foreign Ministers of the United States, the United Kingdom, France, Russia and China; but the first four usually managed on their own. The achievements of its sporadic meetings were minimal; the first session did not even contrive a communiqué and the last ended in Paris in June 1949, having provided for the end of four-power occupation in Austria but having achieved no satisfactory settlement of Germany's future. The Foreign Ministers, indeed, had done nothing to prevent the ever-widening division of Europe into two camps, nor to deter either of the superpowers from organising its own camp into an integrated or unified whole. Who started this dangerous but seemingly inevitable game, which will occupy us on one side or the other through the rest of this chapter, it is hard to say. For the sake of convenience only we shall begin with America and the West.

America and a United Europe

At the end of the war much of Europe was in America's pocket. Her armed forces had invaded and occupied the territories of European states, most of which owed her large sums of money that they could not hope to repay. No wonder she felt like throwing her weight around, attaching strings, for instance, to her 1946 loans to Britain and France. Her foreign policy at this time was indeed anti-imperialist, anti-British to an extent, and anti-protectionist (though the 1933 Buy American Act remained in force!), rather than anti-Communist. But, so far as Western Europe was concerned, it went further than this: it had swung from its traditional isolationism to something approaching interventionism; namely, intervention in favour of a European federation, or of some measure at least of European unification. After all, America herself was a federation; she herself, with more Irish than in Ireland, and cities like New York inhabited by Italians and Cleveland by Poles, was 'a vast and continuous unification of Europe'; and she had an intense, almost doctrinal attachment to the 'larger market', to which she very largely attributed her astonishing economic success. Add to all this the impact on leading United States politicians of the 'Pan-European' ideas of Richard Coudenhove-Kalergi, who, while spending the war years as a refugee from Hitler in America, had promoted himself, as it were, from being a count, by becoming a professor of history at New York University in August 1944. He claimed to have won President Truman over to his ideas, and certainly he discussed Pan-Europa with John Foster Dulles, Dean Acheson and George Kennan before he left the United States in June 1946. Later, he was convinced that Marshall Aid came about partly because of his influence; in fact, however, the indefatigable but unassuming Jean Monnet may have been more effective in persuading Washington's top officials of the virtues of European unification during his wartime stay there.

American hopes, and even pressure, for a United States of Europe, became prominent early in 1947 as hopes of an East-West agreement over Germany receded. The Republican Party's adviser on foreign affairs, and American representative at UNO, John Foster Dulles, delivered a speech at a dinner of the National Publishers' Association in New York on 17 January 1947. He said:

> Whoever deals with Europe deals with the world's worst fire hazard. Repeatedly it bursts into flames. Twice within the last thirty years the edifice has virtually been burned to the ground. The human and material losses have been colossal and irreparable. After each past conflagration, the structure has been rebuilt substantially as before.

He advocated a German settlement within a framework of European unity and deprecated the rebuilding of 'independent, unconnected sovereignties'.

In a *New York Herald Tribune* article of 5 February, Secretary of State Sumner Wells wrote that 'Europe desperately needs some effective form of political and economic federation'; and on 21 March 1947 a concurrent resolution was introduced into the Senate and the House of Representatives by Senator J.W. Fulbright and Hale Boggs, favouring 'the creation of a United States of Europe within the framework of the United Nations'. On 18 April an appeal for a union to end the threat of a third world war, signed by 81 prominent Americans and addressed to the citizens of the United States, appeared in the *New York Times*. It proclaimed that 'a United Europe would be a pillar of peace and a source of world-wide prosperity'; and added: 'It is up to us to assist the European peoples on this path towards union, peace and prosperity which our national interest demands they take.' Walter Lippmann explained in detail exactly how this should be done. In the *New York Herald Tribune* for 17 May he argued that American aid to Europe should be linked to, if not made conditional on, European unification. The American people would want to invest their money in a new, better, reorganised, united and viable Europe; moreover, no settlement of the German question was possible except in 'a framework of European unity organized by the European neighbours of Germany'.

The Marshall Plan

Behind the Marshall Plan thinking, which was adumbrated in these quotations, with its public emphasis on American charity and goodwill and the need for a European federation, there lay too the philosophy of the containment of Communism, as expounded in the Truman Doctrine of 12 March 1947, with its statement that 'it must be the policy of the United States to support free peoples who are resisting attempted subjugation by armed minorities or by outside pressures.' But there existed, too, an even more deep-seated fear than that of Communism: fear of an American depression. The suggestion that the Marshall Plan was a scheme to promote good business for America was openly and frequently made throughout 1947, and not only by the Russians. A columnist in *The Nation* pointed out in June 1947 that

> the Marshall Plan, put simply, is an attempt to re-establish the capacity of the world, starting with our best customers, to buy American goods. Our own economy will slump, our prosperity will disappear overnight, if the huge output of American factories, whose capacity to produce. . . increased fifty percent during the war, cannot find overflow markets outside the United States.

Molotov, Bidault and Bevin all seem to have thought the Marshall Plan was designed to prevent an American depression; so in September 1947, according to an opinion poll, did 57 per cent of Frenchmen.

All these ideas eventually came to fruition in the programme of so-called 'Marshall Aid', which was suggested by Secretary of State George C. Marshall at Harvard University on 5 June in a speech which really did little more than invite the Europeans to get together and draw up a list of their joint requirements for a new round of American aid. The desirability of the new round was underlined by deep-seated American disillusion and disappointment on at least three scores: the failure of Russia to live up to earlier, wartime, Rooseveltian expectations of peaceful cooperation; the failure of Britain to maintain her international power and responsibilities; and the failure of the Bretton Woods institutions to bring about multilateralism and economic recovery.

The Marshall 'offer' was made on 5 June 1947. The Marshall Plan, or European Recovery Program (ERP), was not made law until President Truman signed the Foreign Assistance Act on 3 April 1948; between these two dates the Americans conducted an intense public and congressional debate on the programme, and the Europeans formulated their response to it. In quantitative terms there was nothing new about Marshall Aid: it neither initiated, nor even increased, the flow of American aid to Europe. According to Paul Hoffmann, the total of US post-war aid before the start of Marshall Aid was some $12 billion; according to Harry B. Price, the historian of the Marshall Plan, the total, over the programme's four years, of loans and gifts, 'came to about 13.15 billion dollars'. Thus, in 1945-7, US aid was running at around $4 billion per annum, and from 1948-51, the 'Marshall' years, at little more than $3 billion. What *was* new about the Marshall offer was its intended Continental or all-European scope, for Russia and other East European Communist countries – lands west of Asia, explained Marshall on 12 June – were included. It represented a growing American realisation that post-war aid had failed to achieve European economic recovery largely because it had been doled out in uncoordinated bits and pieces, a British loan here, a Polish loan there, and in many different forms. The essence of the new plan was that the aid should be devoted to a joint European programme administered by the recipients working together in common. The Marshall offer may in part have represented a final American effort to avoid the further division of Europe into exclusive Eastern and Western blocs. However, it became increasingly clear that the Americans were this time determined that the programme envisaged would not become another UNRRA, namely escape their effective and continuing control: in the words of Under-Secretary of State William L. Clayton, 'The United States must run this show.' This determination somewhat undermined the sincerity of the offer so far as Eastern Europe was concerned.

If the whole of Europe (Spain always excepted) was to participate in the Marshall Plan, then clearly the all-European economic organisation newly established in Geneva in May 1947, the United Nations Economic Commission for Europe, would be the most appropriate body to administer it. Hopes were high in some American circles, in Scandinavia, even in Poland and Czechoslovakia, in June 1947, that this would be the case; on the other hand many Americans were convinced the Russians would reject the offer, and the Foreign Ministers of France and Britain, Georges Bidault and Ernest Bevin, were privately opposed to Russian participation. When they were joined in Paris by Vyacheslav Molotov and tripartite talks began on 27 June 1947, Russian insistence that the aid should be provided only to individual countries at their individual request clearly ruled out their participation in a general 'European' recovery programme. Accordingly Molotov withdrew in open dissent, the Soviet Union persuaded or bullied its Communist neighbours and satellites in the East into following his example, and in mid-July the Paris conference, rejecting the possibility of referring the entire matter to the ECE, set up a Committee of European Economic Cooperation (CEEC) to draft a report on the new programme, which was participated in by only 16 nations: Austria, Belgium, Britain, Denmark, France, Greece, Iceland, Ireland, Italy, Luxembourg, the Netherlands, Norway, Portugal, Sweden, Switzerland and Turkey.

Given this Russian rejection, how far was the Marshall Plan responsible for the Cold War? Certainly it did not originate it. It was in 1945, as we have seen, that the Russians began erecting their 'iron fence' around parts of East Europe, installing puppet governments there and refusing to collaborate with the West in all sorts of ways, including the future of Germany; and even before then they had stayed outside the International Monetary Fund and the World Bank. On the other hand the Americans had cancelled loans to Poland and Czechoslovakia in 1946, on the grounds that the governments were no longer friendly to the United States; refused one to Russia in 1945-46; and on 2 June 1947 withheld what remained of a $15 million loan to Hungary until the political situation there had been clarified.

Once Marshall Aid had been rejected by the Russians it became more and more an element, and an aggravating element, in the Cold War. In the first place, it stepped up the Cold War by serving as a pretext for the further hostility of the Russians. Zhdanov declared that the Truman Doctrine and the Marshall Plan were 'both an embodiment of the American design to enslave Europe', and, in retrospect and by comparison, he made Churchill's blunt speaking about the 'Iron Curtain' at Fulton, Missouri, on 5 March 1946, sound like 'the plaint of an apprehensive dove'. It may have also prompted Russian counter-measures, such as the riots and strikes organised by the Communists in France and Italy late in 1947, but it can scarcely be blamed for the Communist *coup* in Prague in February 1948, still less for the Russian withdrawal from the Allied

Control Council in Berlin on 20 March 1948 or the Berlin blockade of June 1948.

The Marshall Plan certainly had a divisive effect in Germany, where it significantly promoted the creation of a unified, separate West German state. In the American view, one of the principal objectives of Marshall Aid had been to ensure the economic revival of Germany which, in spite of earlier ideas, in Dulles's picturesque words, of 'trying to cover with manure the natural industrial basin of Europe', was now seen as essential to any general European recovery. Already Bevin and Marshall had privately agreed in April 1947, at the Moscow Council of Foreign Ministers, to reorganise the Bizone (the now amalgamated British and US zones of occupation in Germany) and make it economically self-sufficient by raising the West German level of industrial production. In spite of French protests, the Americans had their way, though in 1948 they did accept the French demand for the separation of the Ruhr from Germany under an international authority. The result was a massive injection of Marshall funds into West Germany which ensured her economic revival and her continued evolution as a separate unit.

So closely linked to the Marshall Plan as almost to be considered part of it was the American campaign against exports, especially of goods of so-called 'strategic' value, to the East. On 15 January 1948 an export-licensing system to come into force on 1 March was introduced for all goods being shipped to European countries, and in May 1948 a list of goods not subject to export control was published by the United States government. The Foreign Assistance Bill itself, which implemented the Marshall Aid programme, was amended before it became an Act to include a clause which denied Marshall Aid to any recipient state exporting 'strategic' goods to Eastern Europe. This embargo, which was broadly interpreted by the Americans from the start to include all kinds of civilian goods, including for example, rails for railway track, was later to be significantly extended. The only reason why a total embargo on all exports to Russia was not applied in 1947-8 was American dependence on the Soviet Union for supplies of platinum, chromium ore and, above all, manganese ore for her steel industry.

The Marshall Plan and European unity

In America the Marshall Plan was, in essence, a non-party affair, conceived and executed by a Democratic administration and a Republican Congress. Even so, not all Americans were behind it. The President of the National Economic Council, Merwin Hart, complained that Marshall Aid was 'un-American and unrealistic'; it would promote the socialisation of Europe and, in any case, Spain should be included. The US Maritime Commission objected to the gift of several hundred US ships to European countries, and the President of the National Steel Corporation threatened that

Marshall Aid would cause a depression in America. As the debate continued through the first half of 1948, a principal concern in the US became more and more apparent: the programme should if at all possible be accompanied by the creation of some kind of West European federation. But, in spite of the efforts of Senator Fulbright, John Foster Dulles and others, who proposed that the aid should be made conditional on cooperation and integration in Europe, this wish to promote European integration was inhibited by fear of seeming to interfere in other people's affairs. Even so, the following significant sentence, which was not in the administration's original draft Bill of December 1947, appeared in the final text of the Foreign Assistance Act: 'It is further declared to be the policy of the US that continuity of assistance provided by the US should at all times be dependent upon continuity of cooperation among countries participating in the program.' Later Acts in subsequent years were more strongly worded — the word 'unification' replaced 'cooperation' in the 1949 and 1950 laws — and no one in Europe was left in doubt about the hopes and intentions of their American benefactors.

Did the Marshall Plan actually achieve this desired effect of promoting economic integration in Western Europe? Between 12 July and 22 September 1947, when it produced its final report, the deliberations of the CEEC in Paris were closely supervised by Clayton and other US officials, who complained to little or no effect that too much emphasis was being placed on individual national sovereignties and that the ERP was looking far too much like a bundle of separate shopping-lists. When it came to integration, the CEEC report was judiciously vague, the signatories only going so far as to agree 'to cooperate with one another. . .in all possible steps to reduce the tariffs and other barriers to the expansion of trade both between themselves and with the rest of the world'; 'to remove progressively the obstacles to the free movement of persons within Europe'; and 'to organize together the means by which common resources can be developed in partnership'. As to the reduction of tariffs, a Customs Union Study Group was indeed set up in September 1947, but the British in particular were opposed, and, 'after a period of study', the Study Group, in the words of Miriam Camps, 'quietly transformed itself into a group for standardizing tariff nomenclatures' called the Customs Cooperation Council.

The OEEC

In the spring of 1948 the CEEC met again, transforming itself, after American insistence, into a permanent organ with the supervision of the European Recovery Programme or ERP jointly with the ECA or Economic Cooperation Administration of the US as its immediate task, to be called the Organization for European Economic Cooperation (OEEC), based in Paris. The OEEC Convention, signed in Paris on 16 April 1948, did not, however, mark any significant progress towards the goal of European unification or integration – beyond some rather vague promises, including one to 'continue the study of customs unions'. The structure of the institutions it set up, in spite of American, and French, efforts, had no supranational character. Decisions in the Council, on the insistence of Britain, supported by the Benelux and Scandinavian countries, were to be taken by unanimous vote. Thus the OEEC was a purely inter-governmental institution; a sort of continuous international conference or 'assembly of experts and of economic ambassadors from the various countries'.

How far did the OEEC come up to American expectations of European integration in the four-year period of Marshall Aid – namely between April 1948 and April 1952? The answer is, to a very limited extent, if at all. It did not even manage to produce the hoped-for joint European Recovery Programme. Instead it contrived nothing better than the present-ation of sixteen individual national plans, badly coordinated, the total exports of which exceeded imports by a substantial figure. Nor did the OEEC even succeed very effectively in the task which the Americans set it in May 1948, of allocating the aid between the different countries. The British in particular were bitterly opposed to such a method of distributing it; their attitude was identical to Molotov's, who had suggested that each country should negotiate its requirements separately in Washington. The OEEC had no proposals to make about European union, nor did it take any significant action towards customs unions or any other kind of integration; it was, however, partly successful in its efforts to liberalise trade and payments, as required by the Americans. In spite of stubborn British and other opposition, it established in September 1950 the European Payments Union, which was at least an important step towards the mutual convertibility of European currencies; it followed several earlier agreements on intra-European payments. Leaving the problem of lowering tariff barriers on one side for the GATT to tackle, the OEEC did also bring about a substantial freeing of trade from import quotas.

The Brussels Treaty Organization and NATO

It was not long before the ever-widening rift between Eastern and Western Europe – 1948 was the year of the Communist *coup* in Czechoslovakia and the blockade of Berlin – led to further consolidation, or bloc-building as the Swedes and other critics called it, in the West. The economic aid of the Marshall programme and the economic organisation of the OEEC were followed by a US programme of military aid to Western Europe and by the creation of an Atlantic security organisation, NATO. These further politico-military developments in 1948-9 involving North America originated in Western Europe in 1945-7.

Following various wartime proposals and discussions, especially between the Dutch, Belgians, French and British, several of Continental Europe's veteran statesmen declared their interest during 1945 in some kind of Western European union. The ex-Prime Minister of Belgium, Paul van Zeeland, the ex-Prime Ministers of France, Paul Reynaud and Léon Blum, and General de Gaulle all advocated such a union; the last two emphasising that France and Britain should form its nucleus. On 7 October 1945 the *New York Times* reported that Foreign Ministers Georges Bidault and Ernest Bevin, disillusioned by the failure of the Council of Foreign Ministers in London, held talks on the possible construction of a Western economic grouping around a Franco-British treaty. But these extremely tentative plans aroused hostility in Russia and in the West. A columnist in the *Red Star* argued that such a West European bloc would violate the Yalta and Potsdam agreements; and the Scandinavian foreign ministers, according to a *New York Times* correspondent on 12 December 1945, 'looked with distaste, fear and foreboding' on any such regional bloc. A year later these views were being repeated: the organ of the Russian military government in Berlin, *Tagliche Rundschau*, carried an article entitled 'Who needs a West European bloc?' on 8 December 1946; a week before, the Dutch government, in a review of foreign policy reported in the *Sunday Times* on 1 December 1946, claimed that 'the formation of blocs in Western Europe or anywhere else is not likely to compose ideological differences between "certain allies".' The process of bloc formation was in fact deferred until 1948, in spite of Churchill's 1946 proposal in his famous 'Iron Curtain' speech, for an Anglo-American defence alliance based on West European participation and the atom bomb, and in spite of the blatant creation of Stalin's East European empire from 1945 onwards.

The Franco-British Treaty of Dunkirk of 4 March 1947 created the potential nucleus for a wider alliance, but explicitly only in the context of containing the German menace, which was singled out for specific mention in the treaty. Security against Germany was certainly the principal goal of the treaty on the French side; for the British, on the other hand, it came to represent, rather, the start of a process of consolidation aimed against Russia. The treaty was by no means merely an old-fashioned political alliance: it was economically innovatory, for in Article 4 the High Contracting Parties promised 'by constant consultation on matters affecting their economic relations with each other to take all possible steps to promote the prosperity and economic security of both countries'. A standing Anglo-French Economic Committee was set up to implement this engagement.

Less than a year later, the Dunkirk Treaty signatories, inspired and led by Britain's foreign minister Ernest Bevin, began negotiations which, facilitated and accelerated by the February events in Prague, led to the signature in Brussels on 17 March 1948 of a fifty-year Treaty of Economic, Social and Cultural Collaboration and Collective Self-Defence between themselves and the three Benelux countries – Belgium, the Netherlands and Luxembourg. This Brussels Treaty, mainly as a result of French insistence, transformed the Franco-British treaty into a five-power alliance aimed not just at Germany – though the German menace was referred to in the preamble – but against any aggressor in Europe, and called for joint social security conventions, cultural exchanges, the coordination of economic policies, and the setting up of a standing organ called the Consultative Council. A month later, after some wrangling over protocol between France, which wanted Paris, and the Benelux countries, which did not want Paris, to be the seat of the new organisation, the Foreign Ministers of the Five resolved that the permanent Consultative Council, consisting of themselves, would meet at least every three months; that the ambassadors of Belgium, France, Luxembourg and Holland in London, together with a British diplomatic representative, would form 'the permanent organ of the council'; that a 'permanent military committee' would be established in London; and that periodical meetings of ministers or experts would be held as needed.

The Brussels Treaty Organization, also known as Western Union, which had been set up with American and Canadian encouragement, represented a new and significant development in European politics and collaboration between states. But it was regarded by many as incomplete. The Second Chamber of the Dutch Parliament, or Staten-Generaal, passed a resolution in April 1948 by 80 votes to 6 urging the government to do its best, building on the foundation of the Brussels Treaty Organization, to further 'the growth – within the United Nations – of a federal association of democratic states'. Others, emphasising the inadequate military strength of the new organisation, insisted that it must be transformed by the inclusion of America into an Atlantic Alliance. As a matter of fact, the Brussels Treaty Organization responded in 1948-9 in both these respects, namely by giving birth to a quasi-federal arrangement which took the form of the Council of Europe and which will find its place in the next chapter, and by helping to create the North Atlantic Treaty Organization, or NATO.

On the very day the Brussels Treaty was signed, President Truman informed Congress that

> This development deserves our full support. I am confident that the United States will, by appropriate means, extend to the free nations the support which the situation requires. I am sure that the determination of the free countries of Europe to protect themselves will be matched by an equal determination on our part to help them to do so.

In April the Canadian secretary of state for foreign affairs, Louis St Laurent, proposed in the Canadian House of Commons that the Brussels Treaty Organization should be transformed into an Atlantic defence system to include the United States and Canada; and on 11 June 1948 the Vandenberg Resolution, affirming that it was the policy of the United States to promote the 'progressive development of regional and other collective arrangements for individual and collective self-defence in accordance with the purposes, principles and provisions of the [United Nations] Charter', was passed by Senate by 64 votes to 4. From July 1948 onwards, as the Berlin blockade tightened, Canadian and United States representatives joined the Brussels Treaty military committee; seven-power negotiations had been initiated in Washington at ambassadorial level on 6 July. From September, US observers participated in the newly-established Western Union Defence Organization at Fontainebleau. The actual drafting of the treaty text of the new Atlantic organisation, which was undertaken by representatives of the seven powers, began in Washington on 10 December 1948; it was published in March 1949 a few days after the Brussels Treaty powers, Canada and the USA had invited Denmark, Iceland, Italy, Norway and Portugal to join the alliance, and finally signed on 4 April 1949 by these twelve powers, in spite of Soviet efforts to deter them.

The creation of NATO was accompanied by a programme of American aid legalised by the Mutual Defense Assistance Act of October 1949 (hurried through Congress by the explosion of the first Russian atom bomb), which provided about $1.5 billion worth of military aid to Western Europe. As with Marshall Aid, so with this NATO appropriation, the emphasis was on European integration; and, as with Marshall Aid, the results by no means came up to American expectations. It was only the outbreak of the Korean War in June 1950 which prompted some real progress in this direction: within a year an integrated European defence force had been created under the supreme command of General Dwight D. Eisenhower with headquarters near Paris.

Eastern Europe

The erection of an effective alliance system in the West really only got under way after the Russian refusal of Marshall's offer in July 1947. In the East, bloc-building as such took second place to direct expansion and exploitation on the part of Russia. This, however, could on occasion be masked behind a façade of international collaboration. The way Russia secured control of most of the Danube is a case in point. At Potsdam, Stalin turned down a proposal of Truman's for the internationalisation of inland waterways and, in particular, for the establishment of an international commission for the Danube and the acceptance of the principle of freedom of navigation on the river. In 1946 the Americans tried to use a fleet of some 800 Danubian barges, which General Mark W. Clark had captured from the Germans and which, constituting about a third of all Danube barges, had been requisitioned by them from their rightful owners in Czechoslovakia, Yugoslavia, Hungary and Bulgaria, to put pressure on the Russians, who eventually agreed to the holding of an international congress on Danube navigation in Belgrade in summer 1948 by the above-mentioned four riparian states plus Romania, Russia, the USA, Britain and France. The Belgrade conference was dominated by Andrei Y. Vyshinsky, and on all issues the Western powers were outvoted by Russia and the Balkan states; even Yugoslavia, in spite of Stalin's bitter attack on her at this time for 'deviation', voted with Russia. The conference rejected English as its official language, turned down a US proposal for free navigation, and refused to accept any links between the proposed Danube Commission and the United Nations. The Soviet formula for control by the riparian powers, most of which were both occupied by the Red Army and under Russian political hegemony, was accepted: 'I would say in general', declared Vyshinsky, 'that what is acceptable in the United States draft can be found in the Soviet draft and what is not in the Soviet draft cannot be accepted.' The 'Red Danube' became a reality, for the shipping on the Danube had already been largely transferred into Russian control by means of the joint shipping companies set up between July 1945 and March 1947 between Russia and Romania, Hungary and Yugoslavia respectively.

In spite of Russian intransigence over the Danube, it is arguable that, in general, Eastern Europe was not sealed off and transformed into an exclusive economic bloc until after 1948, when the United States contributed very largely to stifling East-West trade by the export controls already mentioned. On the other hand, bloc-building in Eastern Europe began, soon after the end of the war, to take the form of a framework of bilateral treaties linking the Soviet Union with her East European 'satellites' and linking the 'satellites' with each other. Although the wartime treaty of 12 December 1943 between Russia and Czechoslovakia could be regarded as the start of an East-bloc alliance system, at first, and even up to 1947, such bilateral treaties were widely used inside and outside Eastern Europe by the Russians and nearly all other European powers: in the preamble of the Treaty of Dunkirk, which was itself a bilateral treaty of this type, for example, Britain and France mention 'the Treaties of Alliance and Mutual Assistance which they have respectively concluded with the Union of Soviet Socialist Republics'. Up to and including 1946 some 22 political or commercial treaties of importance had been signed among the Eastern European countries; 62 more were signed in 1947 and 1948, and it was in these years that a specific East-bloc treaty network began to take shape. This treaty system was made up of numerous short-term commercial and longer-term cultural agreements between pairs of countries, and it was held together, as it were, by a series of bilateral (and therefore 'closed') political treaties, each for twenty years, of 'Friendship, Cooperation and Mutual Assistance'.

Some recent American historiography has tended to reject the notion that there was any such thing as a cut-and-dried 'Marshall Plan' in the summer of 1947. The so-called 'Molotov Plan', which is supposed to date from the same time and to have been conceived as a sort of riposte to the Marshall Plan, appears to have had even less basis in reality, except terminologically, merely as a (very misleading) name for the bilateral treaty web just mentioned.

The legend of the 'Molotov Plan' made its first public appearance in the *New York Times* for 9 July 1947 with the headline 'Vienna Reds tell of "Molotov Plan" '; and a leading article on 10 July was entitled 'The Molotov Plan'. Further articles and reports followed, but they were rebuffed by the *Manchester Guardian* on 14 August 1947, which dismissed the Molotov Plan as a myth, while *Soviet News* for 27 August carried an article called 'Lessons of the economic agreements in Central and Eastern Europe', which explained that these agreements merely represented the Russian approach to international cooperation — 'the development of political and economic relations between states with equal rights' — as outlined by Molotov in Paris two months earlier.

The spectre haunting Western Europe in the early autumn of 1947 of a gigantic Russian economic conspiracy designed to seal Eastern Europe off from the West and engineer its separate economic recovery, was given menacing political overtones, in the Anglo-American press especially, by reports of the establishment of the Cominform, the first of which appeared in the *New York Times* for 6 October. The true significance of this somewhat obscure event remains uncertain, but it may have had more to do with maintaining unity in the Communist camp than with opposing the Marshall Plan, though it now replaced the 'Molotov Plan', or was subsumed into it, in the Western press's rather distorted view of international relations at this time. The Cominform was regarded by many as a replacement for the Comintern or Third International, which Stalin had dissolved in 1943 in order to 'dispel the lie of the Hitlerites that Russia intended to Bolshevize other nations', and the *New York Times* of 6 October referred to it as 'a new Communist International'. In fact it was nothing of the sort; it was 'an Information Bureau consisting of representatives' of the Communist parties of Yugoslavia, Bulgaria, Romania, Hungary, Poland, the Soviet Union, France, Czechoslovakia and Italy, which was set up at Belgrade as a result of a conference at Wiliza Gora in Polish Silesia on 22-3 September 1947. It seems to have done little or nothing of any significance except to publish a rather vitriolic magazine called *For a lasting peace, for a people's democracy!* — a curiously cumbersome title given it by Stalin himself. It was dissolved in 1956.

Of almost equally dubious significance, in the early years of its existence, was Comecon or the Council for Mutual Economic Assistance (CMEA) which was established in Moscow on 8 January 1949 by an economic conference of representatives of Bulgaria, Hungary, Poland, Romania, Russia and Czechoslovakia. After meeting in April and August 1949, Comecon did not meet again until November 1950, after which date it seems to have more or less ceased to exist for several years. It apparently consisted, in 1949-50, of a secretariat in Moscow composed of one representative from each member state, and the Session of the Council itself, which comprised two delegates from each member. What exactly it did, or was designed to do, in 1949-50, is open to question, but it does seem to have been involved in organising economic sanctions against Yugoslavia and in coping with the commercial consequences of this boycott on the rest of Eastern Europe; it apparently also supervised and coordinated the bilateral web of trade agreements and other treaties in Eastern Europe; and it was in general undoubtedly designed to stimulate trade flows between Eastern European countries in order to compensate for the loss of trade with the West. For, even though in 1948 Britain, for example, was still taking nearly a quarter of Hungary's exports and was her 'best customer', and though at the end of 1948 she had signed a five-year trade agreement with Poland that made her Poland's 'second-best customer', none the less trade between East and West Europe was declining rapidly in the post-war years. In 1938 only 10 per cent of East European exports (Germany excluded) went to Russia; while 80 per cent went to the West. By 1950, well over half the exports of East European countries were going to East Europe or Russia. United States export controls, the Cold War in general, payments difficulties and Russian economic imperialism all contributed to this radical change. Comecon was also provided with funds which enabled it to render 'generous and disinterested aid' to Romania and other countries, and, according to an article in *Neues Deutschland* on 2 February 1951 celebrating its first two years of existence, Comecon had organised exchanges of personnel and information, and initiated various joint industrial projects including the building by the Czechoslovaks of a shoe factory in Poland with an annual output of two million pairs. In some sense, no doubt, Comecon was conceived of as a response, or counter-ploy, to the Marshall Plan. But it was neither a major instrument of industrialisation, nor was it an example of economic integration. The Eastern European countries were encouraged by the Russians to build up their heavy industries and to industrialise as separate national units. Economically, as well as politically and socially, each was to be a kind of miniature copy of the USSR and, in these early post-war years, there was no coordination of national plans, which were not even in step chronologically. Russian influence reigned supreme and Russian foreign trade, which had been almost non-existent before the war, was developed in monopolistic conditions. Moreover, if the increasingly monolithic character of the East bloc was eroded in 1948 by the defection of Yugoslavia, it was consolidated in the immediately following years by the creation of of a new Communist satellite, the German Democratic Republic, and by a series of purges in the People's Democracies.

A Divided Europe

Thus, as a result of the activities and confrontation of the superpowers in the immediate post-war years, integration of a sort began to take place separately in both Western and Eastern Europe. It certainly was not authentically 'European' integration, for in reality much of it was bloc-building, undertaken or encouraged primarily by the superpowers as a function of their opposing alliance systems. An important difference between the two areas was that, in the West, beginning with Benelux, integration took a variety of forms and was undertaken by various different groups of countries not always under American pressure; whereas in the East, on the other hand, almost all integration (the exceptions will be noticed in the next chapter), such as it was, took place under the direction of the Soviet Union. In spite of this bloc-building process, however, certain countries remained more or less outside the two opposing camps: notably Finland, Sweden, Austria, Switzerland and, after 1948, Yugoslavia; and, to a lesser extent and for a very different reason, Spain and Portugal.

5 THE STATE OF EUROPE AFTER THE WAR

The subject of the last chapter was the division of Europe into two hostile camps and the effects of the Cold War, and therefore of American and Russian policies, on European developments in the years 1945 to 1950. After this consideration of the external pressures shaping European history, we turn now to the internal or spontaneous moves towards integration that took place in the same years of 1945 to 1950. We have seen that the achievement of the superpowers, in terms of European integration, was extremely limited: OEEC was a purely intergovernmental organ; Comecon was, if anything, merely an instrument of Soviet power. What progress, then, did the Europeans themselves manage to make in these years towards that unity which had been talked about so frequently during the war?

The Effects of the War

The Second World War brought about remarkably few political changes in Europe. As regards the nation states, the incorporation of the Baltic republics into the Soviet Union and the eventual division of Germany into two were the most important ones. As regards political parties, apart from a remarkable upsurge of Communism, mainly in Eastern Europe but also in France and Italy, and the notable but short-lived Labour Party triumph in Britain, changes were small and few, and no really new parties of significance emerged anywhere, except perhaps the Mouvement Républicain Populaire in France. On the other hand, the economic transformations due to the war and its aftermath were of far-reaching significance. Prominent among these was Europe's overall balance of payments deficit of some $4 billion with the United States − the so-called 'dollar gap' − and the large-scale destruction directly caused by the war. In Germany almost one building in four had been razed to the ground; the European population was undernourished and much of it had been uprooted; nearly half the goods trucks had been destroyed or damaged, miles of railway track was wrecked and hundreds of road and rail bridges had been demolished; tunnels were blocked, ports were in ruins, coal mines and power stations were out of action. It is hardly surprising that the level of agricultural production in 1946 was a third below that of 1938 and that industrial production did not reach its 1938 level until 1947 or 1948. Even in 1949-50, consumption per head of basic foods was still below 1938 levels, except for bread, potatoes and milk. Trade patterns, too, were completely altered by the war. Eastern Europe could no longer provide food for the West, as it had done up to 1939, and the German market had disappeared;

naturally the volume of trade had everywhere shrunk to a trickle.

Motives for Integration

To many, a substantial measure of integration in Europe, if not outright unification, seemed either necessary or inevitable, especially in the economic sphere. Scarcely any European state emerged from the war without some loss of independence. Not one could hope any longer effectively to carry out on its own those two essential tasks of the independent nation state: the defence of its citizens and the proper management of its economy. Even victorious Britain had to go cap in hand to the United States for a loan; other countries, like Belgium, the Netherlands and Norway, had had their sovereignty stripped away by force of arms; still others, like Italy and, later, West Germany, became sovereign states again in name only. Against the possible creation of supranational institutions in Europe, national constitutions were written or rewritten with an appropriate clause accepting limitations on national sovereignty consequent on the setting up of international organs 'necessary to the organization and defence of peace' (France, 1946), or 'for assuring peace and justice among nations' (Italy, 1947), or 'which will bring about and secure a peaceful and lasting order in Europe' (German Federal Republic, 1949). In 1953 the Danes followed suit; the Norwegians left things late, but in 1962 they amended Article 93 of their constitution to allow them to join the Common Market.

The disastrous collapse of European world power and prestige also contributed to the widespread hopes for European unification after the war, for this seemed the only way of maintaining a European voice in world affairs. So did that same fear of Communism which had already been an important element in the pre-war Pan-European movement. More important, perhaps, especially in the early post-war years, was the need to prevent the outbreak of a new war between European powers; some sort of European federation seemed essential to ensure this. Then again, after 1948, and even more after 1950, a solution to the 'German problem' was essential; somehow a West German state had to be created, first for the economic well-being, then for the defence, of her neighbours, and to many the best solution was a restored Germany within the framework of a European federation. There was a French problem, too, for the French entertained 'Great Power' ambitions which might be satisfied within a European federation. Economic integration, especially the lowering of barriers to trade, seemed the only alternative to economic ruin; while technological advances, in the field of air transport for example, appeared to be bringing integration about willy-nilly. On top of all this was the steady American pressure towards European unification which accompanied the Marshall Plan. For all these reasons, in post-war Europe, integration or unification was in the air. 'Europe', a concept already popularised by the Resistance, now suddenly became fashionable.

'Europeans': Unionists and Federalists

Post-war 'Europeans' held every conceivable shade of political opinion except Communism, could be found in every country but predominantly in France, Italy, Germany, Belgium and the Netherlands, and varied in their approach from radical federalists, through the so-called 'functionalists', who believed in piecemeal, step-by-step integration or 'supranationalism', to the unionists, who advocated little more than close international collaboration among the European states. The influence of these 'Europeans' on public opinion was exercised in three ways: through the activities of a handful of private persons, through the press, and through various pressure groups or movements.

A number of prominent statesmen made speeches or other appeals for European union; two of them had been doing it for years; Winston Churchill ended a Swiss holiday in September 1946 in fine style. After a banquet in Bern he drove through the streets of Zürich standing in an open car giving his famous V sign while flowers were thrown at him 'in bunches and sprays'. In the great hall of Zürich University he gave a 25-minute broadcast, appealing to the academic youth of the world for 'some kind of United States of Europe'; but he annoyed the French by urging Franco-German *rapprochement* and collaboration. Field Marshall Jan Christiaan Smuts, the South African Prime Minister, addressed the Dutch and Belgian Parliaments in October 1946 on the same theme: if no all-European federation could be established, then regional unions should be created; in any event, a European Economic Council should be set up and Benelux could be extended.

The quaint figure of Count Richard Coudenhove-Kalergi reappeared on the European scene after the war, but he and his Pan-European movement had been out of touch with European developments and were now over-taken by the federalist and more radical enthusiasm of other groups. Having already, in 1946, returned to Europe and sent a questionnaire to over 4,000 European Members of Parliament seeking their views on a united Europe, he now turned his back on his original movement and founded the European Parliamentary Union at Gstaad in the Bernese Oberland, where he had bought a house, early in July 1947. A first meeting of what was originally somewhat ambitiously referred to as a 'Provisional European Parliament' but later took the more modest title of the 'European Parliamentary Congress' was held in Gstaad on 8 September. Some 114 MPs were present; the proceedings were marred by the withdrawal of the Swiss delegation and also of the British federalist and Labour MP, who was actually Australian, R.W.G. Mackay. His Conservative colleagues refused to allow him to make his proposed speech which, they claimed, 'besides being stuffed with inaccurate historical generalization, included the gratuitous assertion that there was no future, economic or political, for the British Empire'. A second congress of the European Parliamentary Union was held exactly a year later at Interlaken.

Another more or less individual effort towards European unity was made by Guglielmo Giannini, the phenomenal and most uncommon leader of the Common Man Party, who was accused by his political rivals of being both Fascist and Communist! He launched a new monthly magazine in January 1947, the first issue of which carried articles by Churchill, Truman, Chiang Kai-shek and Harold Laski. It was called *L'Europeo Qualunque – The Common European –* and one of its aims was the United States of Europe. Among the World Federalists, or *mondialistes,* who were very active at this time, a notable personality was Gary Davis, who renounced his American citizenship in September 1948 and applied to the United Nations for World Citizenship. He even opened a Registry of World Citizens which was said to have contained some 223,327 names by May 1949! The aim of his World Government Movement was the abolition of national states. By 1977 Mr Davis had been fined, and imprisoned 27 times for travelling in Switzerland and elsewhere on a 'World Passport' printed by himself. He had also sold some 25,000 World Passports for twenty dollars each, launched a World Referendum, and been recognised officially by six countries: Ecuador, Upper Volta, Mauritania, Zambia, Kuwait and the Yemen.

Besides Signor Giannini's magazine, many federalist or 'European' newspapers were founded in the late forties, though their hey-day was to come later. *L'action Fédéraliste Européene* appeared between 1946 and February 1948. *Fédération* survived from January 1947 until 1956; it was published in Paris monthly and edited by Max Richard. *France-Europe*, which succeeded *La République Moderne* in 1948, proclaimed itself to be 'the first French-language journal devoted to Continental unification'; the last issue appeared in 1963. *Le Bulletin Fédéraliste* started life in October 1948 as a supplement to *Fédération*; in 1954 it became *Le 20ᵉ Siècle Fédéraliste*. Besides these French periodicals there were the Italian *L'Unità Europea* (1943-9) and *Europa Federata* (1949-60).

Much more historically significant than the efforts of individuals and the influence of newspapers and magazines of somewhat limited circulation were the activities of the numerous 'European' groups, societies and movements which sprang up like mushrooms after rainfall from 1945 onwards, adding their number to the few such organs which already existed and have already been mentioned – the Swiss Europa-Union of 1934, Federal Union of London, 1938, and the Movimento Federalista Europeo, founded in Milan in 1943.

Pride of place, chronologically, among post-war federalist movements must go to France's La Fédération, founded in October 1944. Alexandre Marc, the philosopher-journalist and ex-Resistance fighter, joined it and, in 1947, it was thought to have some four or five thousand members. Close on its heels, on 29 January 1945, at The Hague, a group of Dutch Resistance leaders, together with the German Jew Hans Dieter Salinger, founded Europeesche Actie, Action Européenne, which was soon joined by Hendrik Brugmans. Also in 1945 a mass movement of revolutionary federalism was proposed by Umberto Campagnolo in his book *Repubblica federale europea*, published in Milan.

The following year, 1946, saw a remarkable surge of public opinion in favour of a united Europe; its impetus derived in large measure from the failure of the Paris peace conference in June. The federalists, mostly radical or socialist, many of them ex-members of the Resistance movement, gathered strength rapidly and held international congresses at Hertenstein in Switzerland in September and at Luxembourg in October; these were organised respectively by the Swiss Europa-Union and the British Federal Union. The former was in session at the very moment when Churchill made his famous speech at nearby Zürich. Naturally, Churchill stole the limelight, and his speech has been reprinted in numerous collections of texts on European unity. Yet students of this topic would do better to study the twelve-point 'Hertenstein Program', calling for a European federation to make war impossible, which would be a regional organisation under Article 52 of the UN Charter; its member states would renounce part of their economic, political and military sovereignty. Forty-one Swiss 'Europeans' assembled at Hertenstein; the next-largest national delegation was that from the Netherlands, thirteen strong, but only one of the 78 delegates came from Britain and one from Italy. The year ended with the creation in Paris on 15-16 December of the Union Européenne des Fédéralistes or Union of European Federalists (UEF) which united federalist movements in the Netherlands, England, Belgium, Italy, Luxembourg, Switzerland and France. Hendrik Brugmans became President and Alexandre Marc General Secretary of the Central Committee which was set up. The headquarters of the new organisation would be in Geneva, but the general secretariat was established provisionally in Paris.

While the more or less radical federalist movement, with its widely based membership, gathered strength, other more élitist and conservative groups were formed. In September 1946, three days after Churchill's Zürich speech, the International Committee for the Study of European Questions, comprising parliamentary and other delegates from Belgium, Britain, Denmark, France, the Netherlands and Norway, published a report recommending the Churchillian type of European union; already on 16 May 1946 Paul van Zeeland and Joseph Retinger had announced their intention of founding the Independent (later European) League for Economic Cooperation (ELEC) at Brussels; it aimed, among other things, at a customs union between the Benelux countries, Great Britain and France, and it later numbered Michel Debré and Harold Macmillan among its members. By the end of the year Churchill, with a small group of Conservative MPs, was planning to launch a United States of Europe Movement, and on 17 January 1947 *The Times* was able to announce the setting up of a provisional British committee to further the cause of a united Europe, with Churchill as chairman. A leading article made the somewhat cryptic point that 'one of the troubles about any form of European Union is that Great Britain can be neither excluded from it nor included in it'! On 16 July 1947 a Conseil Français pour l'Europe Unie was set up, largely by René Courtin, with Edouard Herriot as President and Paul Reynaud and Pierre Henri Teitgen among the Vice-Presidents; it was the French equivalent of Churchill's United Europe Committee. We have already mentioned the autumn 1947 foundation of Coudenhove-Kalergi's European Parliamentary Union.

This remarkable proliferation of 'European' organisations and pressure groups was accompanied, in 1947 especially, by repeated attempts at rationalisation and unification. On 22 February the Berlin (US Zone) paper *Der Tagesspiegel* produced a new year inventory of the winter's crop of European organisations in Germany: the Europa-Union based at Mönchen-Gladbach, the Deutsche Liga für Föderalistische Union Europas at Schwerte in the Ruhr, the Föderalistische Union at Opladen, the Pan-Europa-Union at Hamburg and the Europäische Gemeinschaft at Münster in Westphalia. But mergers between these and other groups proceeded apace and by 1948 the Europa-Union of Germany, not to be confused with the Swiss and Austrian organisations of the same name, with some 200 branches and the support of leading members of all political parties, had emerged supreme among German federalist movements, while in Europe at large the Union of European Federalists, establishing its headquarters at the Palais Wilson in Geneva, held successful international congresses at Amsterdam in April and, above all, at Montreux in Switzerland on 27-30 August 1947, where some 150 delegates gathered from 32 federalist organisations in ten countries.

The European Congress at The Hague

The post-war upsurge of federalist and 'European' enthusiasm culminated in the European Congress held in the thirteenth-century Ridderzaal or Hall of the Knights in The Hague on 7-11 May 1948. It was called into being and organised by the International Committee of the Movements for European Unity, created in Paris in December 1947 by the Union of European Federalists, Churchill's United Europe Movement, the French Council for United Europe, the European League for Economic Cooperation and Nouvelles Equipes Internationales – the last was an international union of members of Christian Democratic and centre parties which had been formed in June 1947. It was a Pole living in London, Joseph Retinger, who, as secretary of the International Committee, was mainly responsible for organising the Hague Congress under the aegis of the English unionists, Churchill, his son-in-law Duncan Sandys and their supporters.

The Hague Congress comprised 713 delegates, nearly half of them from England (140 delegates) and France (185); they represented thirteen different 'countries', which included Luxembourg (8 delegates), Liechtenstein (3) and the Saar (5). Present as observers only were delegates from the United States, Canada, the East European countries except Russia, and Spain. The Germans sent a strong delegation (51) led by Konrad Adenauer. The Congress was held in an atmosphere of extraordinary exuberance and enthusiasm and was widely acclaimed and reported by the international press. A *New York Times* article on 10 May was headed 'The declining years of the sovereign nation'. As a gathering of the great and famous — above all politicians and literary figures — it was probably a unique event in European history; some twenty ex-Prime Ministers were present, including Winston Churchill, Paul Reynaud and Paul van Zeeland, famous writers and academics such as the Spanish historian Salvador de Madariaga and the English philosopher Bertrand Russell, and, of course, leading federalists like Hendrik Brugmans, Alexandre Marc and Denis de Rougemont. There were a few notable absentees, in particular the British (and some other) socialists. The National Executive Committee of the Labour Party had officially discouraged members of the party from going to The Hague: it 'felt that the subject of European unity is much too important to be entrusted to unrepresentative interests' and that the proposed Congress 'can scarcely hope to make any practical contribution towards the furtherance of European unity and may, on the contrary, discredit the idea'.

Labour's dislike of the Hague Congress was of course partly explicable in terms of the role there of the Leader of the Opposition, Winston Churchill, who, according to the *Manchester Guardian* of 8 May, turned out in a frock coat for the opening ceremony, a garment not seen at Westminster since the last Liberal government, which went out of office in 1914! From start to finish the Congress was dominated by Churchill, Sandys and the unionists or moderates, who did their best to create a united front in favour of the mildest form of European union and against the federalists with their radical ideas on the need for some transference of national sovereignties to a federal or supranational authority. They tried to muzzle the Swiss federalist Denis de Rougemont both before the Congress, by making difficulties about the printing of his 'Cultural Report' because of its pronounced federalism, and also during the Congress, by persuading him to omit the phrase 'we desire a common defence' from his Message to Europeans, and even, it has been alleged, by switching off the electricity and, with it, the microphone and loudspeakers just before he was due to speak. These intellectual bullies meted out similar treatment to their rivals on the other side of the political spectrum. Coudenhove-Kalergi was not invited and had to write to Churchill and seek admission to the Congress; he was in the United States at the time. From New York he despatched a consignment of Pan-Europa flags — a red cross on a gold sun — to be flown alongside the new green 'E for Europe' flags; but when he arrived none of his flags were visible and Duncan Sandys told him they had been mislaid; they were only found after the Congress!

The moderates and unionists then carried the day. The Hague Congress ended by approving Denis de Rougemont's Message to Europeans, but this only demanded 'a united Europe, throughout whose area the free movement of persons, ideas and goods is restored'; a Charter of Human Rights; a Court of Justice; and 'a European Assembly where the live forces of all our nations shall be represented'. These vague words were somewhat elucidated in the resolutions of the three committees into which the Congress had divided between its plenary sessions: Political, Economic and Cultural. The Political Committee urged 'the convening, as a matter of real urgency, of a European Assembly chosen by the parliaments of the participating nations' (not, be it noted, by direct elections), and declared that 'the time has come when the European nations must transfer and merge some portion of their sovereign rights.' The phrase 'transfer and merge' had been substituted for the document's more strongly worded original reference to the 'joint exercise of national sovereignty'.

Besides all this hot air, the Congress did achieve some notable practical results, namely the establishment of a European Cultural Centre at Geneva directed by Denis de Rougemont; the creation of the College of Europe, mainly as a result of the efforts of Salvador de Madariaga and a Flemish monk who had also been at The Hague, Karel Verleye, at Bruges under the rectorship of Hendrik Brugmans; and the founding, in October 1948, of a broad-based international organisation for the promotion of European unity called the European Movement, under four Presidents of Honour: Léon Blum, Winston Churchill, Alcide de Gasperi and Paul Henri Spaak.

Origins of the Council of Europe

The tide of federalist public opinion which had begun to flow, as we have seen, during, and even before, the Second World War, seemed to flood in 1948. The international situation was at this time critical, but, because of the ever-widening East-West split, it could scarcely have been more favourable for moves toward European unification in the West. We saw in the previous chapter how the February 1948 Communist *coup* in Czechoslovakia helped to bring the five-power Brussels Treaty Organization into existence and how, in the second half of 1948, NATO was set up in the shadow of the Russian blockade of West Berlin. But the governmental initiatives that brought these organisations into being resulted mainly from external pressures, just as the OEEC had been set up in response to American demands, and they were limited in the main to defence. Surely the time had now come for the creation of a more spontaneous, a more wide-ranging and a more effective grouping of West European states; something along the lines of the 'Council of Europe' which Churchill had proposed back in 1943?

At The Hague, in the opening speech of the Congress, Churchill proposed the setting up of a European Assembly. The Congress endorsed this demand, and the newly formed European Movement, which was unofficially in being from the Hague Congress onwards, though it was not formally founded until the autumn following, took up the proposal. The monthly meeting, in July in Paris, of the International Committee of the Movements for European Unity unanimously agreed to urge Parliaments to pass resolutions in favour of the establishment of a European Assembly. At the end of the same month, a new coalition government was formed in France with a remarkably 'European' Cabinet which included Léon Blum, Henri Teitgen, Robert Schuman, who replaced Georges Bidault as Foreign Minister, Paul Reynaud and Paul Ramadier. The last-named, who had presided over the Political Committee as the Hague Congress, had been largely responsible for the drafting of a European Movement memorandum, which was sent to the five governments of the Brussels Treaty Organization on 18 August, urging them to take steps to set up the European Assembly. It is thus hardly surprising that, on the very same day, the French Council of Ministers announced that it would 'give this project its active support and. . .initiate all necessary action'.

As a matter of fact, the previous French government had already proposed, through its Foreign Minister Georges Bidault, at a meeting of the Consultative Council of the five Brussels Treaty powers at The Hague on 19 July 1948, that a federal European Parliament consisting of representatives of the national Parliaments should be set up, and that a customs and economic union should be established by the five which would be open to others to join. Moreover on 30 July the National Assembly's Foreign Affairs Commission had adopted by 21 votes to 6 (Communists) a resolution urging the French government to join with others in organising a European Union with a European Assembly.

None the less it was the French Council of Ministers' decision of 18 August which received the most publicity. The *Manchester Guardian*'s leader on 19 August was entitled 'Britain should say yes!'. The *News Chronicle* of 19 August declared enthusiastically that 18 August was 'a red-letter day in the annals of the movement for European unity!' In a perceptive leader on 20 August the *Corriere della Sera* described a cool, annoyed, even somewhat embarrassed London, and an exuberant Paris, basking in American favour and congratulating herself on taking the lead. *Le Monde* for 21 August proudly stated that 'everything points to the fact that 18 August will become one of the great dates in the history of Europe.'

All this was perhaps a little unfair on the Belgians, whose Prime Minister, Paul Henri Spaak, had already announced his support for the proposed European Assembly in the Senate on 29 July. Nor were the Italians slow to respond, though their memorandum of 24 August to the French government proposed taking the matter out of the hands of the Brussels powers and placing 'the definitive initiative of European Union into the hands of the sixteen states which are already collaborating in OEEC.'

While the 'Sforza Plan', as this Italian proposal was dubbed, was circulated to all member governments of the OEEC, the Brussels Treaty Organization continued its discussion of the proposed European Assembly, and in Paris on 26 October the five Foreign Ministers, comprising the Consultative Council of Western European Union, agreed on the appointment of a Study Commission to make recommendations about the Assembly and also about an alternative proposal, which the British put forward at this meeting, of a European Committee of Ministers. The British Labour government had from the start been consistently hostile to the proposed Assembly, and it sent an unimpressive delegation to the Study Commission. The only figure of even truly national status – he was a Cabinet Minister – on it was notorious for his public opposition to European union – Hugh Dalton. On the other hand, the French delegation was headed by Léon Blum, Edouard Herriot and Paul Reynaud. The Study Commission received further detailed suggestions in Paris on 9 December from the European Movement, which now urged that two new European institutions should be created: the Committee of Ministers proposed by Britain *and* the Parliamentary Assembly suggested originally by the French. The Study Commission, with the exception of the British delegation, who had received instructions from their government to reserve their position, adopted this plan in its January report. To the general surprise, the British eventually accepted these proposals which were incorporated in a statement issued in London on 29 January 1949 by the Foreign Ministers of the five Western Union powers: 'the Council agreed that there should be established a Council of Europe, consisting of a ministerial committee meeting in private and a consultative body meeting in public.'

After a conference of Foreign Ministers in London, at which the French and Italians vainly proposed the name 'European Union' for the new body, the Statute of the Council of Europe was signed there by ten countries on 5 May 1949. Apart from the British opposition, the most notable feature of the negotiations had been the role of the newly founded European Movement. As Belgian Prime Minister Paul Spaak put it, 'it is thanks to the Hague Congress and the subsequent campaign of the European Movement that the Council of Europe has been established.' Thus an

'unofficial' surge of opinion, elaborated and disseminated by effective discussion and publicity, brought about 'official' action by interested governments.

The Council of Europe

The radical fervour of the federalists was by no means reflected in the
European Movement's repeated representations to the governments, nor
in the Council of Europe itself, which was equipped with no effective
power whatsoever. The Committee of Ministers was a mere intergovernmental body consisting of the Foreign Ministers of the member states
each with a vote and a veto; the Consultative Assembly at Strasbourg was
a mere talking-shop of parliamentarians from different countries with no
powers except to make recommendations to the Committee of Ministers
which that body could and did ignore. Nevertheless, the Council of Europe
did represent a new type of grouping of states and it did represent an
effort of this group of states to work together in the common European
interest. The Statute said little specific about the aims and tasks of the
new organ, though its preamble was ideological enough, with its references
to a 'common heritage' of spiritual and moral values, 'individul freedom,
political liberty' and 'genuine democracy', to ensure that no Communist
state could join this group of 'like-minded countries'; that Spain and
Portugal would be excluded as undesirable dictatorships; and that the
consciences of sensitive neutrals like Austria and Switzerland would not
permit them to join. Thus was created yet another 'Western' group of
states, alongside the OEEC, Western Union and the newly created NATO,
comprising ten members: Belgium, Denmark, France, Ireland, Italy,
Luxembourg, the Netherlands, Norway, Sweden and Britain, to whom
Turkey, Greece and Iceland were shortly to be added.

The Council of Europe so exactly reflected the broad-based, conservative, unionist opinions of the European Movement as a whole, and in
particular those of Duncan Sandys, a heavyweight political operator who
dominated the Movement and succeeded to a large extent in imposing
his will on its upper, 'international' echelons at this time, that it had
virtually only two complaints to make of the Statute in its 9 May
memorandum, and these were in fact put right shortly afterwards. One
was that the Consultative Assembly should be empowered to draw up its
own agenda without having to have it approved by the Committee of
Ministers; the second was that the Germans should be invited to join. In
fact the newly created West German Federal Republic accepted the invitation to become an associated member without voting rights in the Committee of Ministers on 9 May 1950, the very day of the announcement
of the Schuman Plan; and she became a full member in March 1951.
However, English and French were then, and have remained, the sole
official languages of the Council of Europe.

The Consultative Assembly of the Council of Europe met in the Great Hall of Strasbourg University on 10 August 1949, two days after the first meeting of the Committee of Ministers had been held in the Hôtel de Ville there. Paul Henri Spaak became President of the Assembly and a series of lively debates took place during the ensuing weeks. Differences of opinion on the scope and functions of the Assembly were soon apparent; by and large the British and Scandinavians argued for inter-governmental collaboration of the traditional kind while the French and many others pleaded for common institutions. The French socialist André Philip and others wanted the immediate creation of 'a political authority of a supranational character'; the British Labour Party federalist, R.W.G. Mackay, introduced a motion calling for the creation of 'a European political authority with limited functions but real powers'. When the possible foundation of a Common Market was debated, the Labour Party delegates made their opposition to any supranational economic institutions abundantly clear. The session closed with the setting up of six Permanent Commissions and the despatch of a series of recommendations to the Committee of Ministers, several of which implied an extension of the Assembly's powers.

The Paris meeting of the Council of Europe's Committee of Ministers at the end of 1949 was overshadowed, as similar meetings were to be increasingly in subsequent years, by various other ministerial meetings held at that time and place, which normally involved the same people: in this case the Council meetings of OEEC and WEU. The Council of Europe meeting was held on 3 November and the ministers were confronted by an agenda with over fifty items on it, and only limited time to discuss them. They turned down or ignored virtually all of them, agreeing only 'not in fact to exercise their right to draw up the Assembly's agenda'. Paul Reynaud commented: 'The Council of Europe consists of two bodies, one of them *for* Europe; the other *against* it.' But the confrontation which thus developed inside the Council of Europe right from the start was not, in essence, one between governments and popular representatives, nor even between the Committee of Ministers and the Consultative Assembly, but rather between insular, aloof and still imperial Britain, supported by the Scandinavians, on the one hand, and her remaining Continental neighbours on the other.

A year after this first session, the Consultative Assembly's second session opened on 7 August 1950 in the (now former) Maison de l'Europe at Strasbourg, which had been hurriedly erected specially for it in the previous six months. In spite of some evident frustration and tension, the federalists were still hopeful that real progress might be made towards a united Europe. After all, could they not count on the support of the West German delegation, which had been more or less mandated by the famous resolution passed in the very first session of the new Bundestag on

26 July 1950, by the votes of all members except the four Communists, approving the setting up of 'a supranational federal authority' by means of a European federal pact? But the August debates, and those when the Assembly resumed in November for the second half of its second session, ended in a decisive defeat for the federalists and a victory for the proponents of the piecemeal, sector-by-sector 'functionalism' which is the subject of our next chapter. The European cause passed from inside the Maison de l'Europe to outside its doors, where on 23 November 1950 5,000 young people demonstrated in favour of a European government – as a small group already had done at Weissenburg on the Franco-German border in August. It passed, too, from the now fifteen member states of the Council of Europe to the six countries who had responded favourably to Schuman's declaration of 9 May 1950: the construction of the Europe of the Six had begun. It was on 21 September 1950 that Charles de Gaulle made his characteristically acute comment on the Consultative Assembly: 'It is clear that this Assembly will not make Europe. Its composition and the feeble means at its disposal will only permit it, as we have seen, to lose itself in sterile discussions.'

As a result of suggestions made originally in August 1949 by some of the Assembly's more experienced parliamentarians, among them Winston Churchill, at the end of August 1950 a selection of that institution's most important recommendations was sent direct to the national Parliaments, thus bypassing the Committee of Ministers. This somewhat desperate attempt by the Assembly to strengthen its hand was unsuccessful, though the results were interesting. After a seven-hour debate in the French National Assembly on 14 and 15 November, a resolution was passed by 353 votes to 184 urging the government to make all possible efforts to increase the political authority of the Strasbourg Assembly. A Dutch Second Chamber debate on 17 October ended with a unanimous resolution urging the government to accept the Assembly's recommendations, which was couched in similar terms to a Belgian Senate resolution of 10 October. The Italians, in a joint Chamber and Senate response in the first week of October, passed an elaborate rhetorical resolution by 268 votes to 132 urging the government to do its best to create genuine European federal institutions; and the debate in the Bundestag on 16 November was generally favourable to the Strasbourg Assembly's pretensions. But the House of Commons debate on 13 November showed that opinion in both major British parties regarded the Assembly as a 'clearing house for ideas', nothing more; it was no Parliament. As for the Scandinavians: their Parliaments never even took the trouble to debate the Assembly's resolutions!

So far in this chapter we have concentrated on Western Continental Europe and Britain; on the post-war situation, the thriving federalist and unionist opinion, and the eventual governmental initiatives which created the Council of Europe. We have traced the history of that Council far enough (up to 1950) to explain why it never succeeded in bringing about any significant degree of integration among its members. There were, however, other more or less spontaneous moves towards integration in the immediate post-war years – in Scandinavia, in the Low Countries, in Eastern Europe, and even in France and Italy – none of which can be ignored, though none can be regarded as outstandingly successful.

Nordic Cooperation and the Nordic Council

Among the Scandinavian countries, as we saw in Chapter 2, there was a long history of cooperation. Yet traditional antipathies persisted, and were even exacerbated by the Second World War, when the Swedes stood aside while Germany invaded and occupied Denmark and Norway, and allowed German troops to cross their territory, supplied Hitler with iron ore, and refused to intervene at the end of the war to stop the German devastation of north Norway. But the three countries still had much in common and, immediately after the end of hostilities, they resumed the ministerial meetings which had been held intermittently since the First World War. The three Prime Ministers met informally in Stockholm in July 1945, the Ministers for Social Affairs of the five Nordic lands conferred in Copenhagen at the end of August and agreed on the need for coordinated social legislation, a common labour market, economic cooperation, student exchanges and on the desirability of investigating the possible introduction of a common Nordic citizenship; and the Foreign Ministers of the three Scandinavian countries met on 5 January 1946.

While the Nordic governments talked, the leading airline executives of the Scandinavian countries acted. Meeting at 10 p.m. on 31 July 1946 in the shipowners' headquarters in Oslo for a final round of negotiations, they agreed at the end of a difficult all-night meeting to set up a joint Scandinavian Airlines System (SAS) in which capital and equipment, profits and losses, were all to be divided between the three countries in the proportions of 2/7 for Denmark, 2/7 for Norway, and 3/7 for Sweden. After the signature at 3 a.m. of the agreement setting up this constitution, the shipowners, industrialists, airline executives and government representatives of the three countries, overtaken with enthusiasm, marched singing through the streets of the Norwegian capital to the Grand Hotel, where they woke up the waiters at 4 a.m. and ordered champagne. Their jubilation was fully justified; these far-sighted men had created a remarkable, enduring and profitable institution which linked their three national airlines in a common endeavour. It was and remains one of the more notable examples in Europe of post-war international economic cooperation.

Another successful though modest example of international cooperation was the Nordic Council for Applied Research, or Nordforsk, which was set up in 1947 to arrange conferences, organise cooperative research efforts, and exchange information. But although by 1948 official Joint Nordic Committees were in existence in connection with the proposed Nordic labour market, the coordination of social policies, the development of joint legislation, the strengthening of cultural cooperation, the promotion of economic unity and possible collaboration in defence, it was not until 1953 that a real advance was made in Nordic collaboration with the setting up of the Nordic Council.

The creation of this institution had originally been proposed by the Danish Prime Minister Peter Munch in 1938, and it was the Danes who put the idea to the Stockholm meeting of Nordic Foreign Ministers in September 1948, again to no purpose. Finally, on 13 August 1951, Danish Prime Minister Hans Hedtoft, whose death in 1955 was a severe blow to the cause of Nordic collaboration, proposed the setting up of a Nordic Council at a meeting of the Nordic Inter-Parliamentary Union. This time the Foreign Ministers, meeting in March 1952 in Copenhagen, accepted the scheme, which had in the meantime been elaborated by a committee, and the first session of the Nordic Council opened in Copenhagen on 13 February 1953.

The Danes and Swedes as a whole were warm supporters of the Nordic Council — only the Communists voted against it in their national Parliaments; but in Norway a substantial opposition in the Storting was led by the veteran conservative statesman C. J. Hambro, who argued that the success of Nordic cooperation depended on private rather than governmental initiatives, that a new body would erode the position of the Nordic Inter-Parliamentary Union, and that it represented a threat to Norwegian national sovereignty. Another speaker suggested that Norway was quite well enough off with the sixty-odd international organs to which she already belonged! Nevertheless, on 25 June 1952 the Storting approved the Nordic Council by 74 votes to 39. The Finns hesitated because of their neutral status and special relationship to the Soviet Union, but joined in 1955.

The Nordic Council was in part inspired by the Council of Europe. The states which set up the two institutions made quite sure that neither could in any sense become a kind of super-parliament, by endowing them with extraordinarily limited powers. But, while the Council of Europe's Consultative Assembly tended to waste its energies in resounding debates on grandiose themes, the Nordic Council's deliberations were studiously diverted by the participating governments into trivial but practical matters of absolutely no importance: thus the first recommendation of the first session was that a Nordic parliamentary bulletin should be published. The Nordic Council, unlike the Council of Europe, has no statute and no fixed headquarters. Its 78 voting members are elected by the national Parliaments; the non-voting members are Cabinet Ministers appointed by the governments and they nearly always include the Prime Ministers. Thus the Nordic Council, like the Council of Europe, combines an inter-parliamentary and an intergovernmental element; but whereas in the Council of Europe the two formed two separate institutions, which frequently clashed, in the Nordic Council the two elements have been more or less harmoniously blended in the same assembly.

As against successes, namely the Scandinavian Airlines System and the Nordic Council, post-war collaboration in Norden suffered at least two considerable setbacks: neither the projected Scandinavian defence union of 1948-9 nor the much-discussed Scandinavian customs union of 1947 onwards were actually realised.

While the Communist *coup* in Prague of February 1948 considerably stimulated Western moves towards some kind of defensive union, which eventually led to the Brussels Treaty Organization and, a year later, NATO, in the Scandinavian countries it was the Russian pressure on Finland, culminating in the treaty between Russia and Finland on 6 April 1948, which was perhaps more important, causing the Norwegians to take up the question of military aid from the United States, and the Swedes to suggest the setting up of a Scandinavian defence pact. The Scandinavian Defence Committee came into being on 16 October 1948, but on 5-7 January 1949 the Prime, Foreign and Defence Ministers of the three Scandinavian countries, meeting at Karlstad in Sweden, failed to agree on a joint defence union and the negotiations broke down soon afterwards. Norway and Denmark joined NATO; Sweden continued in her now some-what isolated neutrality.

When in the late summer of 1947 the Committee of European Economic Cooperation began to discuss the problems connected with Marshall Aid, the Scandinavian countries, with the partial exception of Denmark, reacted very coolly to the proposal for a European customs union; for example on 10 November 1947 Norway and Sweden only sent observers to the Paris talks on this subject, though they did later join the European Customs Union Study Group as full members. Instead, the three Scandinavian countries, with Iceland, took up the possibility of forming a Scandinavian customs union, and a Joint Nordic Committee for Econ-omic Cooperation was set up in February 1948 charged with considering various forms of economic cooperation, including the establishment of a common external tariff and the reduction of trade barriers within Scandinavia. This so-called '1948 Committee' submitted a first report in 1950 which outlined some of the difficulties, many of which centred on Norway: her need to nurse and protect her war-damaged industry, the fact that her tariffs were higher than those of her neighbours, and that her raw-material and semi-manufactured exports to Denmark and Sweden were subject to much lower tariffs than her imports from those countries, which were mainly of manufactured goods. The implication was that

Norway was not industrialised enough to join a Scandinavian common market and would gain less from reduced customs duties than either Sweden or Denmark. Other objections were more widely based: the desire to conserve national sovereignties in full; agricultural protectionism in Norway and Sweden for reasons of national security; the small volume of intra-Scandinavian trade in any case (only 12 to 13 per cent of the total foreign trade of the three countries in peacetime), and the fact that Scandinavian tariffs were relatively low so that the benefits to be derived from lowering them were diminished. In spite of these difficulties, serious discussions continued, mainly along the lines of free-trade arrangements in certain sectors, and the Committee's second report, in accord with the developments in Western Continental Europe to be described in the next chapter, advocated integration in furniture, chemicals, paints and other specified branches of industry. Backed by a Nordic Council resolution of August 1954, which urged governments by 43 votes to 0 (but with 8 of the 16 Norwegians abstaining) to go ahead with 'as comprehensive a common Nordic market as possible', another committee took the matter up but still had not finished its work when it published a massive five-volume report in 1957! Remarkably, after all this, in 1958, the Nordic Council invited the governments to 'begin negotiations. . .on the forms of Nordic economic cooperation'.

Uniscan

At a time when these Nordic common market talks were already beginning to wear thin, at the end of 1949, Britain proposed some limited measures of financial and economic cooperation with the three Scandinavian countries. Twenty-eight experts from the four countries met in Stockholm on 15 December. The Scandinavians hesitated; it was unlikely that the Coal Board would offer them coal at the same price as it sold in Britain, still less allow Danish bacon to be sold in Britain at the same price as home-produced bacon. Nevertheless, in January 1950 'Uniscan' was set up. According to the Berlin paper *Der Tagesspiegel* this 'socialist bridge quartet' was designed to impress the Americans, who were at this time urging the creation of regional economic groupings in order to increase international collaboration and integration in Europe and enhance the benefits of Marshall Aid. Uniscan, which survived through the 1950s, was little more than an Anglo-Scandinavian Economic Committee of officials, which met once in a while to discuss Britain's fixing of minimum prices for buying wood-pulp and other contentious economic matters. As a matter of fact Uniscan did mildly promote tourism by easing exchange control regulations, and it did remove some restrictions on payments; but it was essentially insignificant.

Benelux

Just as the high hopes of many in the Nordic countries of substantial progress in Nordic cooperation in the years after the war were shattered by a series of setbacks, so in the Low Countries initial optimism about Benelux very soon proved unfounded. The planned and agreed customs union, which was supposed to come into force as soon as Belgium, the Netherlands and Luxembourg were liberated from German occupation, ran into unexpected and apparently irreducible difficulties. These caused repeated delays, reduced the planned moves towards full economic union into smaller and smaller steps, and frequently made it necessary to delay the start of the next tiny step forward.

What were the obstacles which, in the event, made the creation of Benelux such a slow and laborious process? Perhaps most important of all was the differential effect of the war, and especially its closing events, on the economies of Belgium and the Netherlands. Belgium was liberated from German occupation early on, in September 1944, and with relatively little material damage – perhaps 4 per cent of her capital wealth was lost. The Belgian Congo, moreover, had continued to prosper and earn foreign exchange for Belgium throughout the war, partly through uranium sales to the United States, and Belgium herself, in 1944-5, earned gold, dollars and sterling by becoming the Allies' main base for the prosecution of the war against Germany; Antwerp became Europe's major port.

On the other hand the Netherlands were liberated only right at the end of the war in May 1945, after the Germans had caused widespread destruction, partly through flooding; she lost around a third of her capital wealth while the Dutch East Indies, occupied by the Japanese during the war, involved her in substantial military expenditure soon afterwards. While Antwerp flourished, Rotterdam was ruined, and the obliteration of Germany destroyed the formerly dense and profitable transit traffic between Dutch ports and their Continental hinterland, causing widespread shortages and difficulties in Dutch industry, which had been heavily dependent on Germany for spare parts, machinery and so on, and removed one of the main markets for Dutch agricultural exports. All this had the effect of causing the Netherlands to suffer a chronic deficit on her balance of payments while Belgium enjoyed a surplus; inevitably Dutch imports from, and movements of capital to, Belgium (or, more accurately, throughout this discussion, the Belgium-Luxembourg Economic Union, or Belux) had to be restricted. The two economies drifted further and further apart: wealthy Belgium, with few controls and without rationing, experienced rising prices, wages and interest rates, and enjoyed plentiful consumer goods, including imports ranging from tinned pineapples to refrigerators, while the impoverished Netherlands imposed import and many other controls in order to keep prices and wages low. Removal of trade barriers between the two countries, as entailed by the planned customs and economic union, would have caused economic havoc by rapidly increasing the Dutch deficit with

Belgium and ruining the Belgian farmers by causing an influx of low-priced Dutch food into Belgium.

In spite of these and other difficulties, and albeit with delays, the Benelux governments were remarkably persistent. The three Councils mentioned in the 1944 Convention met from 1945-6 and one of them, renamed in 1946 the Council for Economic Union, began the systematic study of the problems involved in the harmonisation of domestic economic policies, now seen to be an essential prerequisite of the proposed customs union. A Board of Presidents, comprising the Chairmen of the three Benelux Councils, was set up, and a permanent secretariat was established in Brussels, as from 1 July 1946, with the Dutchman Edmond Jaspar as first Secretary-General. Besides setting up these institutions, the three governments took steps to implement the programme envisaged in the 1944 Convention, which was, first, the abolition of internal customs duties and the application of a joint external tariff on imports coming into Benelux from outside, that is, the establishment of a customs union and, in the second place, the unification of excise and other tax rates, the removal of quota restrictions on imports, and other arrangements necessary for a complete economic union. Meanwhile, since these measures could only be implemented slowly and one at a time, the three countries carried on their economic relations under the aegis of a series of old-fashioned one-year 'trade and payments' agreements (1945-8).

But progress was slow. Although a Benelux ministerial meeting held at The Hague resolved on 18 April 1946 that a common external tariff should be instituted on 1 November 1946 and internal tariffs abolished on 1 November 1947, at the end of October 1946 the Secretary-General issued a statement announcing the postponement of the common external tariff until 1947. Difficulties had emerged over the briefing of customs officers with the new regulations, over the fact that the Belgian customs duties were protectionist while the Dutch were mainly fiscal, over the fact that Belgian duties were specific while Dutch duties were *ad valorem,* and because the Dutch listed dutiable commodities under 850 sub-headings in alphabetical order, whereas the Belgians listed them under 3,600 classified sub-headings. On 2 May 1947 a Benelux ministerial meeting in Brussels, attended by the Ministers of Foreign Affairs, of Economic Affairs, of Agriculture, of Communications and of Finance, decided that the new common external tariff would operate from 1 September 1947. Meanwhile, in summer 1947, the Benelux powers sent a joint delegation to the GATT talks in Geneva and negotiated there as a single unit. Against this achievement, however, must be set the fact that in May 1947 more than half the Belgians had not heard of Benelux at all! None the less, Prime Minister Spaak claimed in the Belgian Lower House in July that the establishment of the Benelux common external·tariff was a great event in post-war European economic history. In the same month, however, the Belgian brewers declared their hope 'that Belgium would only commit itself to the economic union with prudence, wisdom, and taking its time (*longueur de temps*)'!

In the event, both the introduction of the common external tariff and the abolition of internal customs duties took place on 1 January 1948. This did not, however, mean freedom of trade between Belgium and the Netherlands: agricultural products had been dealt with in a special protocol of May 1947 which permitted Belgian protectionism against lower-cost Dutch products to continue. Moreover, because of the continuing Dutch deficit, quantitative and other restrictions on Dutch imports from Belgium continued; and the excise duties in the two countries differed so much that tax controls along the frontier had to remain in force. This explains why the joint Belgian-Dutch customs post at Roosendaal was still flourishing in April 1949, and why passengers still had to alight there and spend up to an hour on the platform!

In spite of the beneficial effects on the creation of Benelux of Marshall Aid and the European Payments Union, in spite of the further efforts of the governments to inaugurate full economic union in 1950 with a period of Pre-Union lasting a year, leading up to it, and in spite of conventions on social security and the partial unification of excise duties, Benelux was very much in the doldrums at the time when the ECSC was proposed and set up in 1950-2. It had also aroused opposition, especially in Belgium, where, according to one journalist, who labelled it 'Spaakistan', it had caused unemployment; he claimed that its annals were written in graffiti on the walls of the employment exchanges. It continued to make further progress, in small steps, towards economic union but, though it may well be legitimate to describe Benelux as 'Europe's pioneer post-war experiment in integration', it must be conceded that the experiment was, in the main, a failure.

Projected Regional Customs Unions

Benelux did at least constitute a customs union, though an incomplete one; other post-war customs unions got no further than the planning stage. Best-known of these was probably Francital (in English) or Francita (in French), a customs union between France and Italy originally discussed in November 1945 and proposed again by the 75-year-old Italian Foreign Minister, Carlo Sforza, at the CEEC conference in Paris on 15 July 1947, in an elegant French speech accompanied by the habitual adjustment of his aristocratic monocle. 'The concept was so much in the spirit of tomorrow's history', he afterwards commented, 'that even that cold assemblage of statesmen and economists applauded.'

With lightning speed and blinding optimism, the Joint Franco-Italian Commission for the Study of a Customs Union between France and Italy produced a detailed two-volume report between its appointment in September 1947 and the end of that year which concluded that

> the customs union between France and Italy not only does not present obstacles but would even. . .make it possible to find solutions to economic problems facing the two countries. . .and. . .would open larger possibilities and new perspectives for world trade.

The Americans were suitably impressed, and the political motives for this sudden gush of Franco-Italian goodwill were underlined when the Foreign Ministers of the two countries held a quite unnecessary and rather elaborate formal meeting in Turin in February 1948 to sign a protocol stating 'their formal desire to establish a Franco-Italian Customs Union', which Georges Bidault hailed as 'an important stage on the road of European organization'. The political dimension was also demonstrated in the April 1948 Italian elections: a Christian Democratic poster displayed a map of Europe with Italy and France coloured red and no frontier line between them! A year later, on 26 March 1949, another somewhat unnecessary signing ceremony took place, this time at the Quai d'Orsay, seat of the French Foreign Ministry in Paris, of the actual Franco-Italian Customs Union Treaty. Article 1 of this remarkable document stated a little too bluntly in the present tense that 'A customs union between France and Algeria on one side and Italy on the other is established'; Article 2 somewhat spoilt the effect by stating that a common external tariff would only be introduced a year after ratification; and another clause explained that the hoped-for economic union might take up to six years to realise. Within a few months this optimistic programme was modified by a protocol in which the two governments allowed the Council of the Customs Union to arrange for the gradual implementation of the customs union 'over as long a period as may be necessary'.

It was the French who were dragging their feet. Feeling in Paris was that the union was unnecessary in view of the more generalised efforts towards economic cooperation in OEEC; that, since the two economies were concurrent, major structural changes would be necessary for the union to work; that it was hopelessly unrealistic to suggest harmonising social and fiscal charges; and that Italian unemployment would, through the immigration of Italian workers into France, become a Franco-Italian problem. The proposed customs union rapidly faded into the background in 1950 and, at the Santa Margherita conference on the Italian Riviera in February 1951, between Schuman and Pleven for France and de Gasperi and Sforza for Italy, it was overshadowed by the Schuman Plan, the projected European army, the future of Germany and other matters. The lame duck was dead at last.

It is natural to think of Benelux and Francital as in some sense precursors of the Common Market: the same countries were involved, the same concept, of a customs union, was employed. Nor is it irrelevant, in the light of subsequent events, to mention the various schemes for a more extensive customs union, to involve France and Italy with Benelux, which went under the ridiculous names Fritalux, Finebel (naturally favoured by the Dutch) or Fibenel (a notice in a Belgian newspaper office said 'Always use Fibenel'). Within a few weeks of the end of the war a Franco-Benelux Council of Economic Cooperation met at the Quai d'Orsay in Paris; it had been set up by an agreement between France, Belgium, the Netherlands and Luxembourg signed the previous March, and it was supposed to meet monthly and to be supported by a permanent secretariat in Brussels. But Benelux was suspicious of French hegemonial intentions and France, somewhat cool towards Benelux, pursued economic and financial policies which soon made close cooperation between her and Benelux less and less feasible. Still, unofficial discussion of a possible Franco-Benelux economic union was continued into 1947; and indeed more talks took place in Rome in December 1949 on possible economic cooperation between representatives of France, Italy and the Benelux powers.

These various abortive regional customs unions in the West, although we have included them in a chapter dealing with more or less spontaneous, as opposed to directly American-inspired, developments in post-war Europe, were to some extent an indirect by-product of Marshall Aid and American pressure. In the East, by contrast, the comparable though less important plans and projects which emerged soon after the war were far removed from Russian initiative or even approval. They were indeed entirely spontaneous; and where they failed, they failed in the main because of Russian opposition.

Federal Schemes in Eastern Europe

The first of these schemes, originally mooted in March 1945, was for a union of Albania and Yugoslavia which was to take the form of Albania becoming one of the Yugoslavian federated socialist republics. The Western allies prevented this merger by recognising General Enver Hoxha's government, and a new scheme emerged at the end of 1946 for a customs union between the two countries. A thirty-year treaty was signed by Albania and Yugoslavia on 27 November 1946, which provided for the abolition of all internal customs duties within a month, and the setting up of a common external tariff which was to be equivalent to the Yugoslavian tariff. The Albanians promised to bring the *lek* into parity with the *dinar* within three months, and on 15 December 1946 a joint institution was set up to coordinate the national plans of the two countries. The speed with which this customs union was established and the radical nature of its provisions need occasion no surprise: Albania was a small country, Yugoslavia relatively large, and the union was more like Belux or the

Monaco-France union in character, than, say, Benelux. Albania had been forced to join a customs union with Italy in 1939; her union with Yugoslavia broke up in 1948 when that country quarrelled with Russia.

At the time of the original discussions for the union of Albania with Yugoslavia, the possibility of the inclusion of Bulgaria in this enlarged federal state was also considered; and it was reconsidered in the late summer of 1947 during talks at Bled between Tito and Georgi Dimitrov. It was at this time – on 2 August 1947 – that the two countries signed a treaty for economic cooperation which, one over-enthusiastic observer claimed, amounted to the abolition of the frontier between them. Any further moves towards union of whatever sort between Yugoslavia and Bulgaria were opposed by Stalin and brought to an end, in any case, by the open breach between Stalin and Tito which occurred in 1948. Much later, in 1952-5, Tito took steps to mitigate his isolation by signing a series of Balkan Pacts, in conjunction with Greece and Turkey, which provided for a permanent council of Foreign Ministers to meet twice a year, a permanent secretariat, and a Balkan Consultative Assembly. Unfortunately, rapidly deteriorating Greco-Turkish relations in 1955 prevented the establishment of these institutions.

Europe in 1950

In this and the preceding chapter we have considered moves toward integration in Europe between 1945 and 1950, dealing first with those directly inspired by America and Russia, and then, in this chapter, with those which had a more spontaneous and 'internal' character. The fact that they have been discussed in two separate chapters must not obscure the simultaneity of the more important of these moves: the Brussels Treaty Organization and the OEEC originated in March-April 1948; NATO and the Council of Europe in April-May 1949; and the same countries and even statesmen were involved in all these initiatives. By 1950 these and other efforts had resulted in a patchwork of partial unions, of incomplete, unsatisfactory or overlapping projects, brought into existence by more or less reluctant governments under pressure from the United States, or from European public opinion. 'Europe' had not come about; there was only West Europe or East Europe. Western European Union and Comecon each represented only a quarter of Europe; the Marshall Plan and the Council of Europe perhaps represented two-thirds of Europe. Efforts at more localised, regional unions had either failed completely or run aground and lost all forward momentum, usually for want of any kind of supranational organs. Nationalism and protectionism were rife: the Italians published a new high rate of customs duties in July 1950 just before the opening of the Torquay round of GATT negotiations for tariff reductions; the French, accused of mercantilism by the Germans, were dragging their feet throughout 1950 on agreed OEEC liberalisation measures. But it was the British attitudes which, above all, character-ised — and weakened — the motley assortment of moves towards integration which were made in these years. If no single European feder-ation had emerged, if no real progress had been made towards European union, this was very largely because of Britain's refusal to take the lead, though she was inescapably influential on the Continent since her role in the war. Now, in 1950, the efforts of create Europe with Britain drew to a close; they were superseded by the creation of Europe without Britain: the Europe of the Six, which will take up our attention through most of the next three chapters.

6 INTEGRATION BY SECTOR

Proposals for Sectoral Integration

Not quite a year after the Congress of The Hague, at a time when the finishing touches were being put to the Statute of the Council of Europe by a conference of Foreign Ministers in London, the newly established European Movement, in conjunction with ELEC, the European League for Economic Cooperation, organised a six-day European Economic Conference, which opened at Westminster on 20 April 1949. It was attended by some 200 delegates, who, as at The Hague the year before, split into various committees for detailed deliberations, then reassembled in plenary session to make their reports and have their recommendations approved by the Congress as a whole. All were agreed on the desirability of a European economic union, implying 'a full customs union, and indeed more than this; a full economic union, from which customs barriers, both tariffs and quotas, and all currency obstructions to economic efficiency would be eliminated'. The OEEC had made some kind of a start, but only United States support 'is today maintaining Europe from collapse'. Much more must now be done by the Europeans themselves, and the conference called for the free convertibility of the European currencies and, ultimately, a single European currency. But more important for the immediate future than these rather Utopian proposals were the recommendations of the Committee for Basic Industries which came up with a programme of what amounted to integration by sector, for which the French socialist and convinced 'European' André Philip was mainly responsible. It proposed that, in each of the four basic industries — coal, iron and steel, electricity and transport — three organisations should be set up: a 'European governmental body' to lay down 'general policies in the industry concerned'; a 'consultative body consisting of employers, employees and representatives of the public interest'; and 'one or more organizations of employers'. Moreover the Committee for Agriculture proposed the establishment of 'Commodity Councils' which would 'consider the steps to be taken to promote a European agricultural policy', frame measures for stabilising European markets, and administer 'international distribution schemes on behalf of a European authority'.

In so far as agriculture was concerned, these recommendations merely repeated earlier suggestions. Only a month before, in March 1949, Pierre Pflimlin had invited a German delegation to Paris to discuss the possibility of Franco-German agricultural collaboration and even some kind of 'European' agricultural policy. Insofar as coal, iron and steel were concerned, the Westminster Conference's recommendations were likewise far from novel. In May 1948 a French delegate at a meeting of the German section of the Union of European Federalists at Homburg argued that the Ruhr and the Lorraine ore fields should be linked in a common plan as a step towards a wider European federation. On 1 January 1949 the German Christian Democratic Union (CDU) leader Karl Arnold asked in a radio broadcast if, rather than international control of the Ruhr,

> one could not erect an association with an international legal status and a foundation of partnership? Into this association Germany would bring the Ruhr, France the ore resources of Lorraine, both of them the Saar, Belgium and Luxembourg their heavy industries.

Besides the voices of numerous other private individuals, among them André Philip and the British Tory MP Robert Boothby, which were raised in favour of the integration of European heavy industry in the years 1948-50, certain influential public bodies gave their support to the idea. In December 1949 the Committee for Economic Affairs of the Consultative Assembly of the Council of Europe recommended the creation of an intergovernmental European steel authority, and at the same time the Steel Committee of the United Nations Economic Commission for Europe, acting on a request for an investigation into the industry by André Philip, predicted over-production and surplus capacity in the steel industry unless plans were modified and some sort of international coordination achieved.

The Schuman Plan

The Schuman Plan of May 1950 thus contained nothing startlingly original. Its essence was enshrined in the words: 'The French government proposes that Franco-German coal and steel production should be placed under a common High Authority in an organization open to the participation of the other countries of Europe.' The text of the declaration went on to add: 'The pooling of coal and steel production will immediately provide for the creation of common bases for economic development as a first stage in the federation of Europe.' It was the manner in which this famous declaration was made, rather than its content, which gave it its novelty and effect. It did not emanate from the Quai d'Orsay, the French Foreign Office. The text was drafted in secret at the end of April by the head of the French post-war planning commission, Jean Monnet, and one or two of his closest associates. Foreign Minister Robert Schuman persuaded the French Council of Ministers to accept it after a somewhat perfunctory debate on 9 May. Two ministers had been won over in advance. René Pleven and René Mayer; the others apparently accepted it without appreciating the full implication of their decision and without any foreknowledge of the dramatic press conference in the gilded Salon de l'Horloge at the Quai d'Orsay, which Robert Schuman had arranged for 4 p.m. that very afternoon.

The principle architect of the Schuman Plan was Jean Monnet who, in the eyes of history, will probably always retain the place already given to him by his contemporaries, as the man more responsible than any other single person for the creation of the European Community. Born at Cognac in the Charente in 1888, he began life in his father's brandy business. Prevented by kidney trouble from serving in the First World War, he first proposed, and then served on, the Franco-British supply Commission before becoming, in 1919, at the age of 31, Deputy Secretary-General of the League of Nations. Already by this time Monnet had made contacts in Washington and London as well as Paris, and had become familiar with the working of the French, British and American administrations. He became a friend of John Foster Dulles; later his missions to the United States in 1938 and 1939 for the French government and his wartime service in Washington as a British civil servant on the British Supply Council deepened his American experience, and his circle of acquaintances in the United States grew to include John McCloy, Dean Acheson, George Ball, McGeorge Bundy, Walter Lippmann, James Reston and others. After years of varied services in the international field, Monnet at the end of 1945 submitted to de Gaulle an ambitious project for the modernisation of the post-war French economy. On 3 January 1946 a French national plan was instituted by government decree, and Monnet, moving into offices in the rue de Martignac, Paris, was charged as *commissaire au Plan* with drawing it up. Four years later, it was this same Jean Monnet, assisted by friends and colleagues from the Plan — notably Pierre Uri and Etienne Hirsch — who in the last days of April 1950, after a fortnight's strenuous walking in the Swiss Alps, was responsible for drafting the Schuman Declaration and for persuading Schuman and the French government to accept and propose it. His main motive in thus urging the construction of Europe was related closely to the international situation: he was above all anxious to halt the process of bloc-building, of the division of the world into East and West, and to control Germany.

Although the role of Robert Schuman was in some respects secondary, it was at the crucial moment decisive. He too will surely go down in history as one of the founders of the Europe of tomorrow. A Lorrainer born in Luxembourg in 1886, he was brought up as a German and served in the German armed forces, though not, because of ill health, in a military capacity, in the First World War. Educated at German universities, he only became 'a Frenchman in 1918 at the age of thirty-two', when he set up as a lawyer in Metz; but he still spoke French with a German accent. His long and distinguished career in the National Assembly began in 1919; from 27 July 1948 to 23 December 1952 he was Foreign Minister in eight successive

French governments, achieving a record of continuity in office only matched by those of Aristide Briand and Théophile Delaissé before him and Maurice Couve de Murville afterwards. A pious Catholic, Schuman did not share the bitter feelings towards Germany which inspired many of his compatriots in the post-war years; his personal inclination and his foreign policy coincided in the single-minded aim and hope of Franco-German reconciliation and the restoration of Germany within a European community of some kind. Moreover, he had taken his country into negotiations for customs unions with Benelux and with Italy, and even considered the possibility of one with both of these: Fritalux.

What exactly caused Jean Monnet and the French government to act when they did in the spring of 1950? In fact, their initiative came at a time when suggestions and plans for achieving European unity were becoming ever more numerous. In the early months of 1950 the Union of European Federalists organised a campaign to collect signatures for a petition urging the European governments 'to take all necessary measures to ensure that the democratic nations of Europe bind themselves irrevocably together by means of a Federal Pact', which would set up a democratically elected supranational political authority. We have seen how proposals for integration by sector were being made on all sides. Furthermore, existing institutions like the OEEC, the Council of Europe and Benelux had all caused widespread disappointment, and projects like Uniscan and Francital seemed to be getting nowhere. Yet economic cooperation and political solidarity were becoming more necessary than ever. Containment of the Communists had the highest priority among American foreign policy goals, and on 11 May 1950 the three Foreign Ministers of the United States, Britain and France – Dean Acheson, Ernest Bevin and Robert Schuman – were to confer in London on the problems of Western defence and the future of Germany. For some months, Schuman had been under pressure from Dean Acheson to make proposals for the future of West Germany in an integrated Europe. As to economic collaboration, serious attempts by Monnet and the planners had been made in 1948 and 1949 to secure cooperation, if not coordination, between the French and British economies, but these had been hindered by unilateral devaluations, first of the franc, then of the pound.

What really made the Schuman Plan or some similar move in the spring of 1950 almost inevitable, or at least essential for Western European peace and security, was the creation of the German Federal Republic in 1949 and, consequent upon it, the rapid emergence of the Franco-German problem in a new form. Unless urgent action were taken, it seemed that Franco-German relations could only deteriorate: hence Konrad Adenauer's repeated appeals early in 1950 for some kind of Franco-German economic union. On the French side suspicions and fears of Germany were still deep-seated. The Petersberg Protocol, signed on 22 November 1949 in the *de luxe* hotel of that name perched on one of the wooded Siebengebirge, or Seven Hills, above the Rhine opposite Bonn, and head-quarters of the newly instituted Allied High Commission, in which the Allies made major concessions to German independence, and agreed to stop dismantling a number of German industrial plants, was only approved in the French National Assembly by some seventy votes. But, while the French continued to feel unhappy about, and in some respects tried to resist and delay, the reconstitution of a more or less sovereign, indepen-dent and economically viable German state in the West, their allies, the Dutch and Belgians, the English and Americans, were determined on the removal of controls of all kinds and on the speediest possible recovery of the German economy. Moreover the Germans themselves, not unnaturally, were beginning to be increasingly vociferous and active in their own behalf. They resented continuing French attempts to control the Saar which culminated at this time in the Saar Conventions of 3 March 1950; they criticised the activities of the International Authority for the Ruhr (IAR) which the French had insisted on having set up on 28 December 1948; and especially now that on 9 May 1950 – the very date of the Schuman Declaration – they had been admitted to the Council of Europe, they were increasingly determined to be treated as near as possible as equals with the other member states of the international community.

It was thus imperative for the French, in the spring of 1950, to find some compromise between, on the one hand, the generally accepted policy of her allies, namely the economic and political reconstruction of Germany, and, on the other hand, their own desire to find some way of tying Germany's hands so that she could never again become a hostile threat to themselves, nor even industrially dominant over France. No wonder the French government protested when, on 8 May 1950, the day before the Schuman Declaration, the Allied Military Security Board, res-ponsible for the German level of industrial production, announced that German industry had already exceeded the limits laid down in the Petersberg Protocol the previous autumn. As to the Germans, they were likely to accept almost any viable alternative to the irksome restrictions and irritating activities of the Allied High Commission and the Inter-national Authority for the Ruhr: throughout 1950 the former was trying to restructure the German economy by breaking up big businesses like I.G. Farben, while the latter was allocating coal for export which the Germans maintained they needed at home. Thus both countries, for reasons which were largely political, were willing to embark on what was designed as the first step towards a federal Europe and a final solution to the Franco-German problem.

Why Only Six?

As an exercise, primarily, in Franco-German reconciliation, the Schuman

Plan is perhaps readily understandable. But why the Six? How was it that, almost within days of the original declaration, the Europe of the Six had emerged so decisively – at least in terms of governmental intentions of the time? Very largely, this was due to a handful of statesmen, all of them dedicated 'Europeans', who took the matter into their own hands. These men were in the right place at the right time. Robert Schuman's Europeanism was matched by that of the West German Chancellor Konrad Adenauer, who responded to the Schuman Plan at once on 9 May with all his heart; he had supported the linking of the German and French basic industries as long ago as 1923, when he was burgomaster of Cologne. In Italy, Count Carlo Sforza, the Foreign Secretary, himself a convinced European of long standing who has been mentioned more than once already in this book, conveyed Italy's acceptance of the plan on 10 May; and the adherence in principle of the governments of Luxembourg, Belgium and the Netherlands was thereafter never in serious doubt.

It was the omission of Britain which was the truly decisive event in the formation of the Six. Not that the French government slammed the door in Britain's face – Monnet and Schuman both went to London to try to talk the British round – but they certainly did force her hand. Conscious of the widely recognised fact that, thus far, the British had in the first place opposed every significant move toward European integration and then ensured that no supranational element was retained in any institutions actually set up, the French now insisted on Britain's prior acceptance of the principle of 'a new higher authority whose decisions will bind'. After all, the whole point of the Schuman Plan was to bring the newly reconstituted West German state under the wing of some superior authority. On 27 May the British government explained to the French that they could not accept a prior commitment to pool resources and set up an authority; the French retorted that all they wanted was agreement on principles and main objectives. Another historic declaration followed this Anglo-French altercation: on 3 June the Six issued their first communiqué, announcing their intention to go ahead with 'the pooling of the production of coal and steel and the institution of a new high authority'. Henceforth, the Europe of the Six was in existence; the history of the European Community began on 3 June 1950.

The reputation for hostile insularity toward European integration which the British had already earned was heightened in this same month of June 1950 by the publication of a Labour Party pamphlet written by Denis Healey entitled *European Unity*, which was widely read and discussed on the Continent. Its thirteen pages were thought to bristle with undiplomatic statements; for example that 'in every respect except distance' Britain was nearer to Australia than to Europe, and that any representative European supranational authority 'would have a permanent anti-socialist majority'. The general impression of British isolationism was by no means removed by Britain's subsequent association with the European Coal and Steel Community; indeed more than a decade was to elapse before any significant change of attitude occurred on either side. Europe was to be begun without Britain.

As to the Americans, they were so pleased with the Plan that the United States Congress enthusiastically voted to have the text of the Schuman Declaration printed in the *Congressional record*!

The Treaty of Paris

The negotiations between the Six which began on 20 June 1950 were brought to a successful conclusion, in spite of the fact that Monnet's original scheme was substantially modified, and in spite of considerable difficulties, in the remarkably short time of less than a year, on 18 April 1951, with the formal signing in Paris of the fifty-year Treaty establishing the European Coal and Steel Community by Foreign Ministers Adenauer, van Zeeland, Schuman, Sforza, Bech and Stikker, all of whom were practising Christians, incidentally, and all of them Catholics except the last. 'Printed in Louis XIV type with German ink on Dutch vellum', the treaty text was to be 'bound in Belgian parchment' with Luxembourg paste 'and adorned with a marker of Italian silk'. This success was due in large measure to the novel negotiating techniques employed. Basic principles had been agreed beforehand; all accepted that the objective was the political one of setting up a quasi-federal authority and the economic one of organising a common market. Talks were conducted in the main by delegations of expert civil servants meeting in secret to elaborate this common aim and without detailed governmental instructions; the Foreign Ministers conferred only from time to time.

The Korean War broke out on 25 June 1950, five days after the start of the Six's negotiations. The Americans now saw as essential the strengthening of the free world by the incorporation into it of a strong and viable West German state; and the German bargaining position in the Schuman Plan negotiations was thus transformed. Instead of having to accept the Plan in order to obtain what it wanted, the German government found itself in a position of being able to hold out against French demands — notably for the deconcentration and decartelisation of German heavy industry — because the restoration of German independence and power had suddenly become indispensable to the West. No wonder the negotiations ran into difficulties; and indeed they were only brought to a successful conclusion through American intervention. Two of Monnet's friends, John McCloy, the United States member of the Allied High Commission in Germany, and David Bruce, the American Ambassador in Paris, acted as intermediaries between the French and the Germans, and successfully imposed on the latter a compromise which allowed for a limitation on the size of individual steelworks and on the amount of coal output each could own; it also provided for the dismantling of the Ruhr coal sales organisation. In return for these concessions the Germans could welcome the end of all remaining Allied controls, including the International Authority for the Ruhr. As to the Saar, the significance of actual possession of that territory, then in dispute between France and Germany, was considerably lessened by the ECSC treaty, which ensured both countries access on equal terms to the products of its basic industries.

The one hundred articles of the Treaty of Paris provided for the establishment of a European Coal and Steel Community based on 'a common market, common objectives and common institutions'. The main executive institution was the nine-man High Authority. Its decisions were by simple majority vote, no more than two of its members might come from the same country, none was to be a national representative, and none of them was to be connected in any way with the coal and steel industries. The personnel of this collegiate agency proved remarkably stable. During the first five years of its existence there was only one change: the replacement of Jean Monnet, the first President, by René Mayer, in June 1955, as a result of Monnet's decision to leave the High Authority at the end of his first term of office in order to concentrate on forming his Action Committee. His resignation appears to have been occasioned by the defeat of EDC at the end of August 1954; some further moves seemed to him essential to support ECSC now that it was totally isolated and faced by a French government hostile to integration.

The High Authority consisted in the event of two Frenchmen, two Germans, two Belgians, one Italian, one Dutchman and one Luxembourgeois. The Benelux countries had seen to it that the supranational powers of the High Authority could be moderated, in certain important respects, by another, purely intergovernmental, institution, the Council, or Council of Ministers, consisting of one delegate from each of the member states, the assent of which to High Authority decisions was made necessary at certain important points. The other ECSC institutions were the Assembly, or Common Assembly, comprising 78 delegates (18 each from West Germany, France and Italy, 10 each from Belgium and the Netherlands and 4 from Luxembourg), which was to meet in Strasbourg at least annually, the Court of Justice, composed of seven judges, which had an authentic federal flavour, and a Consultative Committee of representatives of coal and steel producers, workers and consumers, to advise the High Authority.

So much for the institutions of the ECSC. What were its declared objectives and how were they to be achieved? It was to promote 'economic expansion, growth of employment and a rising standard of living' through the creation of a single common market to replace the six separate national markets insofar as coal and steel were concerned. In doing this it was to ensure the rational distribution of production at the

highest possible level, the lowest possible prices, expansion, modernisation and good working conditions. Certain nationalistic practices
considered incompatible with a common market were   :cribed by the
treaty: 'import and export duties', 'quantitative restrictions on the movement of products', discriminatory practices, subsidies. The High Authority
was empowered to make rules and recommendations for the maintenance
of normal competitive conditions, to remove restrictive practices and
cartels, to levy taxes, raise loans and provide funds, and – with the
consent of the Council – to allocate supplies during shortages and if
necessary to limit output to avoid over-production.

The six member states of the ECSC had each surrendered a small part
of their national sovereignty, though only in the admittedly limited
field of their coal and steel industries, for the common executive institution, the High Authority, as well as the Court of Justice, were to take
over some of the powers and prerogatives hitherto enjoyed only by the
member states. But there was no question of altering existing ownership
arrangements, many of the industries concerned remaining in private
hands while others, like the French coal industry, Charbonnages de
France, remained nationalised. The ECSC was essentially a pool, that is a
common market-sharing arrangement. It frowned on cartels and con-
centrations; unlike them, the purpose of which was to limit competition
and maintain prices, its aim was to ensure free competition and lower
prices.

Although the ECSC treaty had been signed in April 1951 it still had
to be ratified by the six national Parliaments of the member states before
it could come into force, and this process took almost exactly a year, from
June 1951 until 17 June 1952. During it intense debates were conducted
within each member state. In Luxembourg and the Netherlands opposition
to the ECSC was negligible; in Belgium there was concern for the future of
the outdated high-cost coalmines, and business interests campaigned
against ratification on the grounds that the High Authority had been given
excessive powers that would prove at best irritating, and were possibly
unconstitutional; even so, there was never any serious likelihood of
rejection. In Italy the ECSC was accepted largely for political reasons; it
was welcomed mainly as a first step towards a federal Europe. Potential
economic disadvantages were foreseen but for the most part had been
successfully warded off during the negotiations by an able team led by
Paolo Taviani: temporary exclusion of Italian steel from the common
market so that a protective tariff could provisionally remain; guaranteed
supplies of North African iron-ore and scrap on reasonable terms; and
inclusion in the treaty of provisions granting equal rights to immigrant
workers.

The ECSC was in the main a Franco-German affair, yet opposition to
it was more vocal and widespread in these two countries than elsewhere.

In Germany Kurt Schumacher, always suspicious of France and of Adenauer, took the SPD into firm opposition, partly on the grounds that the ECSC would not be viable without Britain and that Germany was not being treated as an equal in it. He claimed that, by accepting the Schuman Plan, Germany was subscribing to fifty years of foreign occupation, and he stigmatised it with the four Ks — Kapitalism, Klerikalism, Konservatism and Kartels. In France, where the Schuman Plan had originated, there was more opposition than in any other country; indeed France was the only one of the Six in which ratification was not a foregone conclusion. Already on 19 May 1950 de Gaulle had made the characteristically sarcastic comment at Metz: 'de Gaulle says we must create a new economy, and then we are handed this mish-mash about coal and steel in the name of some vague combine, without knowing where we are going.' In October 1950 a public opinion poll found that 65 per cent of Frenchmen favoured a United Europe, but 45 per cent had not heard of the Schuman Plan! French industry, led by steel, was against the Plan; other elements argued that the treaty gave too much to Germany. In the event, ratification of the treaty was opposed in the National Assembly both by Communists and Gaullists but was approved by 377 votes to 233; though only after the constitutionally and legally meaningless proviso had been made that there should be no French membership of the ECSC without construction of the Moselle Canal.

The ECSC

Right from the start of its history, which effectively began with the first meeting of the High Authority at No. 2, Place de Metz, Luxembourg, on 10 August 1952, and of the Assembly a month later, the ECSC found itself tackling difficulties, many of which were due to the nationalistic attitudes of the member states. Even the place of the headquarters became a matter for dispute, and the decision, which was provisional only, to establish the High Authority and the Court in Luxembourg, and the Assembly in Strasbourg, was hardly likely to inspire the Community at the start with any degree of strength and solidarity. It was only made after the Dutch had been persuaded to abandon their request that The Hague should be the seat of the Court by being granted an extra judge, seven instead of the original and more logical six; and after the Belgians had stoutly refused to offer Brussels on the grounds that the Flemings were against giving that city a monopoly in international institutions. As to the language problem: although the Benelux powers and Italy were prepared to accept French as the single official language, the Germans were not. The result was the seemingly clumsy expedient of four official languages, which did however have the advantage of providing an official text of Community law in the language of every Community citizen.

The formal establishment of a common market in coal, steel, iron and scrap was the first task facing the High Authority. Article 4 of the Treaty of Paris was uncompromising on this matter. It laid down that 'import and export duties, or charges having equivalent effect, and quantitative restrictions on the movements of products. . .are recognized as incompatible with the common market for coal and steel and shall accordingly be abolished and prohibited within the Community.' However, there were only four customs areas to be merged in the common market of the Six; and Benelux already had a low common external tariff and no internal tariffs. Moreover, there were no duties at all on coal, iron-ore and scrap except for a 15 per cent Italian duty on coke imports, and even steel import duties in France and Germany had been suspended before the opening of the common market. While there were thus few significant tariff barriers to remove, quantitative restrictions had for the most part already been abolished under the OEEC liberalisation programme. Thus the common market was formally established in 1953-4 more or less without difficulty and, though its introduction may have made little impact on the actual situation at the time, the treaty did ensure – and this was a truly notable achievement – that tariff and quota barriers to trade in the products of heavy industry would never again be imposed by the signatory states in its fifty-year lifetime.

However, the formal creation of a common market by legislating away tariffs and quotas is a very different matter from the patient removal of all discriminatory and distorting practices. Here the High Authority, though it scored some notable successes, soon ran into difficulties. It was only after a serious dispute that the Germans accepted a High Authority ruling which had the effect of permitting French steel to sell in Germany after paying a total turnover or transaction tax of only 13 to 14 per cent, while German steel exported to France carried a tax burden of 25 per cent. Though scarcely removing distortions, this settlement did at least boost the High Authority's prestige. An example of its success in removing distortions which could limit the efficacy of the common market was the abolition of the double-pricing system, namely the practice of selling a commodity at home for one price and abroad for another, higher price; though the Germans somewhat annoyed the French by achieving the necessary equalisation between their two prices for coal by raising the domestic price by 10 per cent and leaving the export price the same as before. The High Authority made very determined attempts to end discriminatory practices in transport rates, and by 1956 it had brought about the abolition of directly discriminatory rates, namely the charging of a higher rate for goods crossing an international frontier. It had also ended the system of breaking freight transport charges up into separate sections, one for each country of transit, which meant that international goods paid two or more so-called 'terminal' fees (the element intended to cover the cost of loading and unloading) and benefited much less from the 'tapering' of rates over long distances, because the total distance was divided into two or more parts. Moreover the international through rates, which the High Authority now substituted for these 'broken' rates, were extended by negotiation to include Switzerland and Austria. But against these successes must be set the fact that the High Authority completely failed to make any substantial progress towards the equalisation of the national freight rates themselves!

There were at least three large-scale organisations whose continued existence in an unmodified form would derogate in substantial ways from a true common market. The first, ATIC, was eventually liberalised more or less in accordance with the High Authority's requirements, but only in 1961 after repeated attempts and after the matter had gone before the Court and then been withdrawn to be settled by private negotiation with the High Authority. The Association Technique de l'Importation Charbonnière (ATIC) was a central organisation under direct French government control, solely responsible for all French coal imports. Its practices, which included a system of import licences issued by itself, and discrimination against purchases of foreign coal, mostly infringed the spirit if not the letter of the Treaty of Paris. With the centralised Ruhr coal sales organisation, Gemeinschaftsorganisation Ruhrkohle (Georg), the High Authority was less than successful. It managed to divide Georg up into what it thought were three separate units; none the less in many important respects they still pursued concerted policies and actions, though the High Authority did exercise somewhat more control over the divided organisation than it had done over the original Georg. The fact is that the Germans liked Georg, and the High Authority was only able to make him change his clothes. A far more serious — and permanent — breach in the ECSC common market was caused by the nationalised French coal industry, Charbonnages de France, against which the High Authority never dared lift a finger. It operated a scheme whereby profitable coalfields and pits subsidised those making losses and it relied on a permanent French government subsidy to keep it 'in the black', both of which activities were in direct infringement of the treaty provisions. Indeed it is nearly true to say that French coal was outside the ECSC common market altogether.

There were other successes besides the formation of a more or less complete common market. The first 'European' tax was levied in 1953. Non-members like Britain, Sweden, Norway, Switzerland, Denmark and Austria accredited Permanent Delegations to the High Authority in Luxembourg. Among the Common Assembly's 78 members, groupings according to political parties (Christian Democrats, Liberals, Socialists) soon became more important than national groupings, and this conferred a sort of supranationalism on the Assembly. On the other hand, that body had perhaps been over-enthusiastic in agreeing to hold several more than the single statutory annual session laid down by the treaty. A rather scathing article in the German weekly *Die Gegenwart* on 15 December 1956, entitled 'Before empty benches', pointed out that during a rather crucial debate on whether or not a serious coal shortage existed which might allow the introduction of controls under Article 59 of the treaty, only 22 of the 78 deputies were present. If they aren't interested, argued *Die Gegenwart,* how can one expect the public at large to be 'European-minded'? The Court of Justice enjoyed considerable success; the cases before it in the fifties were nearly all appeals – a number by national governments – against decisions of the High Authority, and nearly all of them were turned down. The really important thing was that the Court's authority was everywhere accepted.

The ECSC, though it still retains legal existence (with an address in Brussels), and though the Treaty of Paris is still in force, was important for a brief few years only, in the 1950s. Once the EEC and Euratom were brought into existence by the Treaty of Rome of 25 March 1957, the ECSC's Court of Justice and Common Assembly were merged into those shared by the three Communities; and the 'merger' treaty of 8 April 1965 established a single Council and a single Commission for all three Com-munities – ECSC, EEC and Euratom. Besides this loss of separate identity, the ECSC was badly disrupted by the coal crisis of 1959, which was due to over-production and falling demand; for the Council of Ministers repeatedly turned down the High Authority's proposals for reducing the utilisation of imported coal, maintaining or increasing consumption of coal as against oil, and so on. The three Benelux countries, with perhaps a certain show of 'European' solidarity, stood by the High Authority; but the most disastrous effects of the crisis were felt in Belgium, and this solidarity may have been that of neighbours. The three large members of the Community consulted their own interests in the most blatant manner, retreating into exclusivist economic nationalism of the worst kind. Without any effective consultation of the High Authority, the German government introduced measures of its own – including a cartel agreement between the suppliers of coal and oil designed to prevent any further substitution of oil for coal – which undoubtedly had a deleterious effect in the Netherlands and Belgium by increasing the pressure of oil sales there. The Italians, who alone among the Six actually benefited from the coal recession, since they imported 90 per cent of their consumption and could now obtain coal more cheaply, particularly from the United States, refused even to reduce their purchases from third countries to 80 per cent of the 1958 level. As to the French, they stood neither to gain nor lose from the High Authority's proposals; they apparently rejected them because they happened to be disillusioned with supra-nationalism at this time. Thus, in 1958-60, the ECSC was in utter disarray, incapable of coping with just the sort of crisis which a supranational authority *ought* to have been able to cope with.

More Integration by Sector?

At about the time when the Schuman Plan negotiations began and for some years afterwards, integration by sector, or the setting up of 'specialized authorities' to organise the integration of certain major industries or sectors of the economy, suddenly became popular. The reasons why not a single one of the many schemes proposed (apart from the Schuman Plan itself, and Euratom, which started only in 1958) came to fruition, are not difficult to ascertain. Above all, there was a feeling that the ECSC must first prove itself by actually working. It *did* work, as we have seen, but imperfectly; and many of its imperfections were due to the inadequacies of integration by sector — a single segment of a complex modern economy could not be treated in isolation. As early as 1952 Paolo Taviani argued that it would in many ways be easier and more advantageous all round to integrate entire economies rather than single sectors of economies. In particular, in the integration of any one sector, one or more partners or member states would stand to gain and the others to lose, leaving little scope for compromise — which would however be possible if several sectors were being integrated simultaneously. So the Italian government had serious reservations about sector integration; but it was in favour of a common labour market.

Another reason for the failure of these schemes was that, unlike the Schuman Plan, which was directly urged by one government on others, they were put up through one or both of those organisations which had already shown themselves more or less totally impotent when it came to new political initiatives — the OEEC and the Council of Europe. In other words, though this may not have been obvious at the time, the future now lay with the Six, and these schemes were not projects of the Six.

Why was it that, while the authors of these projects, including Dutch Foreign Minister Dirk Stikker, in his so-called 'Stikker Plan' of summer 1950, formulated their proposals in terms which implied that their schemes were designed to follow on from, or complement, the ECSC, yet the proposals themselves were not put to the Six? Evidently because the governments of the Six were not yet ready to build further on the still very incomplete ECSC foundations; at least they showed singularly little faith in that 'revolutionary attempt to pass from the international to the supranational', as Taviani described it in 1952. Stikker's personal enthusiasm for the Europe of the Six certainly lagged behind that of part of the Dutch public, and his plan of creating common markets or free trade in selected industries with the aid of a European Integration Fund, put before the OEEC Council, of which he was then President, on 14 June 1950, could almost have been construed as a wider-based alternative to the Schuman Plan, which of course at that time had only just been launched.

The first specific scheme of sector integration after 9 May 1950 related to transport, a field where cooperation clearly *had* to be on a wider basis than a mere six countries. It was proposed by the French economist and politician Edouard Bonnefous on 16 August 1950 in the Council of Europe's Consultative Assembly at Strasbourg. Later he presented a draft convention to the transport committee, which the Consultative Assembly had set up with himself as Chairman, to study his own proposals. The essence of the Bonnefous Plan was the establishment of a powerful supranational High Authority, the European Transport Authority, linked to the Council of Europe, which was to rationalise, coordinate and unify the European transport system. It would do the same job, only far better, as was being done rather inadequately by the Inland Transport Committee of the ECE at Geneva and, even less adequately, by the Inland Transport Committee of the OEEC in Paris. In the event, the Bonnefous Plan disappeared from history and instead, at the end of 1953, the sixteen-country Conference of European Ministers of Transport (CEMT) emerged under the aegis of the OEEC — yet another intergovernmental ministerial conference with no more than advisory powers over member states.

Some progress was however made at this time in the field of inter-state railway collaboration. On 2 March 1953 a European Convention was signed by ten West European national railways which created an international pool of trucks — Wagons Europ; and in 1955 an international limited company called Eurofima was established for the joint purchasing and renting of rolling stock. Actually it was not altogether international because a truly international company could not and still cannot legally exist in Europe. So the Société Européenne pour le Financement de Matériel Ferroviaire had to be domiciled in Switzerland where, however, it was excused from having to have a majority of Swiss nationals on its board, though it chose not to excuse itself from certain Swiss tax concessions.

It was likewise in August 1950 that the Council of Europe's Consultative Assembly passed on to the Committee of Ministers a recommendation for the setting up of a 'European organization' which would include Ministers of Agriculture, or governmental experts in agriculture, and representatives of the Consultative Assembly and of the various agricultural organisations, in order to study what institutions might be required to best 'organize production and agricultural markets'. There was at this time a Mansholt Plan (the original Mansholt Plan!), in which Sicco Mansholt, a Dutch farmer turned Minister of Agriculture, put forward an early version of his celebrated common market in agriculture: a supranational authority was to be set up which would lower 'internal' tariffs on foodstuffs, fix upper and lower price limits, and levy what was in effect a customs duty on imports to bring their cost up to the domestic cost of the same product. That is, free trade in agriculture within Western Europe to the advantage of efficient Dutch exporters, and protection of West European agriculture as a whole. Later on there was a very similar Charpentier Plan, accepted by the Consultative Assembly on 1 December 1951 (but opposed by the British), advocating the establishment of a High Authority, and other institutions with the aim of unifying Europe's agricultural markets. There was even an Eccles Plan, typically British, advocating instead a merely advisory body to make recommendations to the governments.

But it was the French government, spurred by its energetic Minister of Agriculture Pierre Pflimlin, which took the most serious initiative. After discussions in the French National Assembly and the Council of Ministers in June and November 1950 respectively, the Pflimlin Plan was submitted to the member states of the Council of Europe, and to Austria, Portugal and Switzerland, on 29 March 1951. This document opened with a statement recalling the Schuman Declaration of 9 May 1950 which, it claimed, 'expressed French loyalty to the constant aim (*idée*) of its foreign policy in the last twenty years: the realization of the political and economic unification of Europe'. It outlined a plan which included the main features of the others mentioned: the formation of common markets, product by product, to be supervised by institutions modelled on those of the ECSC; it even suggested that the Court of Justice and Common Assembly of the ECSC (which were not yet in being) could take over responsibility for these agricultural markets alongside coal and steel. However, a year elapsed before the French government had the satisfaction of seeing representatives of fifteen countries assembled in Paris under the presidency of Pierre Pflimlin (25-28 March 1952); but the plan for what had come to be called the 'Green Pool' was by that time considerably watered down − it had even lost its supranational authority − and little or nothing more was heard of it thereafter.

The Consultative Assembly had given its official blessing to 'specialized authorities' in November 1950 and the OEEC also favoured them. Other suggestions were made but mostly ignored. In 1952 the French government proposed a 'White Pool' or European Health Organization. A European Postal Union was proposed in December 1951, and in 1955 the indefatigable Bonnefous presented a detailed project to the Consultative Assembly for a European Organization for Posts and Telecommunications. Instead, the ministers met, but apart from the symbolic act of printing a European stamp in September 1956, the Conference of the Ministers of Posts and Communications of the Six, meeting twice a year from January 1956 on, achieved little. The twenty-nation Conference of European Postal and Telecommunications Administrations (CEPTA), which eventually emerged at Montreux in summer 1959, replaced it but did not meet annually in the 1960s.

It soon became evident that integration by sector was not the road to success but rather, perhaps, a blind alley; Spinelli referred to the *falsa via* of specialised authorities. Yet hopes were maintained for some years after 1950 because of the prolonged wrangle over the Pleven Plan for a European Defence Community (EDC), which represented a shift from the primarily economic integration we have so far discussed, towards political integration, but was still by sector.

The Pleven Plan

The Pleven Plan and the Schuman Plan were produced by the same people at the same time and in the same circumstances. Monnet's role was important, but it was the German Chancellor Konrad Adenauer who, it seems, first suggested the formation of a European army to solve the problem of German rearmament just as the ECSC had been proposed to solve the problem of German economic recovery. Used until very recently to managing without a foreign policy, Adenauer had learned to make the most of press coverage as an alternative. On 3 December 1949 the *Cleveland Plain Dealer*, a paper which he well knew was one of the handful regularly seen by President Truman, printed an interview of Adenauer with its European correspondent in which the Chancellor said 'The Allies disarmed Germany. They must insure her defense...Should they ask us to participate in insuring the security of Europe, I would not favour an independent *Wehrmacht* but rather a German contingent within a European fighting force.'

After the outbreak of the Korean War on 25 June 1950, most American and West European statesmen became convinced that West Germany would have to be rearmed, and that she would play an essential role in the defence of the West against any Russian attack. On 25 July the new American High Commissioner in Germany, John J. McCloy, taking up an earlier proposal of General Lucius Clay, suggested that Germany be asked to make a contribution to Europe's defence. But what the passionately anti-German French Defence Minister Jules Moch described as America's biggest post-war bomb was dropped on 12 September 1950 in New York: Dean Acheson formally proposed German rearmament in the shape of ten divisions, within NATO, to his Foreign Minister colleagues of France and Britain, Robert Schuman and Ernest Bevin. The Pleven Plan, drafted by Monnet and put to the French National Assembly on 24 October 1950 by Monnet's former assistant, now Prime Minister, René Pleven, was a French attempt to avoid total isolation from her allies on the subject of German rearmament by accepting this in a European context, namely German contingents in an integrated European army, still within the framework of NATO. Pleven claimed that his plan was 'directly inspired' by the proposal adopted by the Consultative Assembly of the Council of Europe in Strasbourg on 11 August calling for a 'common European army under the authority of a European Minister of Defence', which, on Winston Churchill's motion, had been passed by 89 votes to 5. This in its turn had been inspired by a debate in the same Assembly a few days earlier when André Philip had made an identical proposal. The French National Assembly approved the Plan in principle on 24 October 1950 — and approved it again, in principle, in February 1952.

Unlike the ECSC, the Pleven Plan was put forward in the firm hope that Britain would be one of the 'participating governments', and Britain's consistent refusal to join the proposed army was perhaps the single most important reason for the ultimate failure of the entire project. For most Frenchmen, in particular, British membership seemed essential. Hopes that this might be forthcoming after 25 October 1951, when Winston Churchill, the author of the 11 August 1950 motion in the Consultative Assembly, became once more Prime Minister of Britain, were dashed to the ground in Rome on 28 November 1951 when Foreign Secretary Anthony Eden categorically stated that his country would not join the EDC.

If the EDC was not killed by British opposition, it died of delay. The treaty itself was not finally signed until 27 May 1952; thereafter it was the French who stalled. Foreign Minister Robert Schuman, fearful that it might be defeated, kept the treaty in his briefcase for months, only submitting it to the National Assembly for examination by the committees and eventual ratification on 29 January 1953. Thereafter, throughout the French political crises of 1953-4, successive Prime Ministers were committed not to seek ratification from the National Assembly until British attitudes were clarified; and the French made repeated attempts in this period to force further modifications of the treaty on their partners, some of whom, like the Germans in March 1953, had already ratified it. On the other hand the Italians, mainly because of Communist obstruction, had still not succeeded in ratifying the treaty at the end of August 1954, when the French National Assembly's rejection of the prior motion finally killed it; but the Foreign Affairs Commission of the Italian Chamber of Deputies had approved the treaty on 31 July 1954 by 16 votes to 11 with 3 abstentions.

The EDC treaty specifically and perhaps somewhat rashly stated, right at the start, that the High Contracting Parties were setting up, 'by the present treaty. . .a European Defence Community, supranational in character, comprising common institutions, common armed forces and a common budget'. The Community was to 'work in close cooperation' with NATO, and its members were not allowed to maintain separate national armies in Europe outside their contribution to the 'European Defence Forces', which were to wear a 'common uniform' and to be integrated at the army corps level, that is to say, each combat unit would comprise men of a single nationality, but several of these would be combined together or 'integrated' to form an army corps. As to the Community's institutions: the nine-man Board of Commissioners or European Defence Commission was the equivalent of the High Authority; the Council of Ministers was modelled on that of the ECSC; and the Common Assembly and Court of Justice of the ECSC were to serve the EDC as well. Apart from Sforza, who had been replaced by de Gasperi, the same statesmen signed the EDC treaty in May 1952 who had signed the still not fully ratified ECSC treaty a year before.

The EDC treaty was totally different from the ECSC treaty in one important respect: it carried within itself a spark of federalism enshrined in Article 38, which may indeed have helped cause its downfall. It was the Italian federalists, who now at last had de Gasperi in their pocket, and who were well represented on the Italian EDC delegation, for its original leader P.E. Taviani had been replaced by the long-time federalist Ivan Matteo Lombardo, who in December 1951 had secured the insertion of Article 38 into the EDC treaty. It required the Common Assembly to study the possibility of setting up 'federal or confederal' institutions with 'a two-chamber system of representation', 'elected on a democratic basis', which would effectively combine the ECSC and EDC into an embryo European federal state or European political community. This was not a mere piece of gratuitous ideology; it seemed to many essential that the European army should have a European political authority to control it. Such was the general federalist enthusiasm at this time (the petition for a federal pact to inaugurate European union had been signed by over half a million Italians, including almost 250 MPs, when the campaign closed in autumn 1951) that the Common Assembly of the ECSC was asked to go ahead and draw up detailed proposals, acting as an Assembly *ad hoc,* even before the EDC treaty had been ratified. Naturally the federalists welcomed this move enthusiastically; for them the *ad hoc* Assembly was the long desired constituent assembly for which they had been campaigning in 1951 both in Italy and France. In the winter of 1952-3 they bombarded it with memoranda; and it produced the goods.

On 10 March 1953, at Strasbourg, the *'ad hoc* Assembly instructed to work out a draft treaty setting up a European Political Community' duly published a *Draft Treaty embodying the Statute of the European Community,* in 117 articles. The Community was to have a bi-cameral Parliament consisting of a Senate and a People's Chamber, a European Executive Council, a Council of National Ministers, a Court of Justice, and an advisory Economic and Social Council. Naturally this elaborate scheme, which was confederal rather than federal, scarcely supranational, and not at all radical, had to be shelved until such time as the EDC came into being; but shelved did not mean forgotten. Instead, the EPC was conspicuously round the neck of the embryo EDC and quite probably helped to strangle it.

What other reasons were there for the rejection of the EDC by its creator, France, on 30 August 1954? In Europe at large the EDC debate was prolonged and passionate; the federalists for the most part worked hard for ratification, while the Communists were everywhere violently hostile to the treaty. Every wall bore its message of *Vive!* or *A bas! la*

Ced. In France new words were coined: *Cédiste* and *Anti-cédiste*. It was certain important charges that occurred while this debate was in progress, namely between late 1950 and the summer of 1954, which brought about the eventual rejection of EDC. In French domestic politics, the 'European' political parties (Mouvement Républicain Populaire and part of the Socialists) lost votes and 'European' statesmen like Robert Schuman were forced out of office, while over a hundred Gaullist opponents of the EDC joined the National Assembly. Shifts in France's economic situation, especially *vis-à-vis* Germany, were as important as these political events. In 1950-1, when the ECSC treaty was negotiated and signed, France and Germany had seemed, economically, on a par, but in 1951-4 Germany forged ahead while France stood still. Industrial production and investment soared in Germany, which enjoyed an increasingly favourable balance of trade, enabling it to announce in July 1953 a 90 per cent liberalisation of its trade with OEEC countries. Meanwhile, the French deficit continued in spite of import restrictions; the French government even had to reverse its August 1951 announcement of a 76 per cent liberalisation of French trade with OEEC countries. This imbalance between the French and German economies made any further integration with Germany, even of defence, seem undesirable to most Frenchmen. Changes in the international situation also told heavily against EDC: Stalin's death in March 1953 was followed by some relaxation of tension, and the dangerous Korean War ended in stalemate in 1953. Russian tanks were no longer expected any day on the Rhine. However, Communist advances in south-east Asia continued, culminating on 8 May 1954, when the French Empire of Indo-China disappeared in the rubble of Dien Bien Phu, making any surrender of military sovereignty even less palatable in humiliated France.

Pierre Mendès-France apart, it was the 'men of the past' in France who threw out the EDC. Ranged against it were Marshal Juin and General de Gaulle and nearly all the French generals, E. Herriot, political patriarch of the Republic, Maurice Thorez, Communist veteran, as well as E. Daladier of Munich fame and the President of the French Republic, Vincent Auriol. In favour were men actually engaged in running France or directing French policies: Robert Schuman, René Pleven, P.H. Teitgen, Guy Mollet and René Mayer. Exceptionally, the veteran Paul Reynaud was in favour. As to French public opinion, it seems to have been in the dark. In May 1953 52 per cent of the French public were reported as not knowing whether or not the National Assembly had ratified the EDC treaty. One can forgive them, but perhaps not the 21 per cent who had never heard anything at all about the project!

The Aftermath of the Failure of the EDC

The EDC episode was in many ways a traumatic experience for Europe. Franco-German relations deteriorated seriously, especially in 1953-4, when the Germans, enjoying their new-found prosperity, were confronted by an outburst of the most vicious kind of nationalism from a France that seemed on the verge of political chaos and economic exhaustion. For the federalists, the defeat of EDC meant the defeat of their most cherished dreams for Europe's future. The movement represented by the Union of European Federalists (UEF) now entered a slow decline. Everywhere the 'Europeans' were shattered, disillusioned and disappointed. In the history of the relations of the United States and West Europe, the EDC episode was crucial. At first, the Americans were doubtful about EDC; was it workable, and did it represent a French scheme to exclude America to some extent from European affairs? Later, they took it up enthusiastically — too enthusiastically, thought some observers. It became part of the Eisenhower-Dulles policy of resistance to Communism after the inauguration of the Republican administration in America in January 1953; indeed it *was* American foreign policy as far as Europe was concerned. John Foster Dulles openly threatened an 'agonizing reappraisal' of US foreign policy in Europe if it was rejected; this pressure, which was indubitably resented, may have contributed to the failure of EDC, which in its turn caused a slackening of US pressure on Europe in the years that followed.

Although it has little to do with the subject of this chapter, the solution of the problems caused by the disappearance of EDC ought to be briefly mentioned. Britain now had no difficulty whatsoever in promising to keep her four divisions and her Tactical Air Force in Germany, 'and not to withdraw these forces against the wishes of the majority of the Brussels Treaty Powers', though she had found it quite impossible to give any such assurance during the EDC negotiations. But what was now being proposed by Foreign Secretary Anthony Eden was no longer a supranational authority but an intergovernmental one: a Brussels Treaty Organization reinforced by membership of Italy and Germany. Under pressure from Britain and America, the French now suddenly overcame their objections to German rearmament; they even agreed to German membership of NATO, which became effective on 5 May 1955. All this was agreed at a London conference in September-October 1954 held by the Six together with Britain, Canada and the United States, and at a four-power conference in Paris on 20-23 October 1954 between the United States, Britain, and France and the German Federal Republic.

Euratom

The architect of the ECSC and the EDC, Jean Monnet, had one more blueprint in his desk, for it was he, too, who was largely responsible for the creation of Euratom — the European Atomic Community. Mainly because of Monnet's pressure, the famous Messina Resolution of 2 June 1955, agreed by the Foreign Ministers of the Six, had stated the intention of 'creating a common organization to be entrusted with the responsibility and the means for ensuring the peaceful development of atomic energy', alongside the EEC itself. Later, the activities of Monnet in the autumn of 1955, after he had ceased being President of the High Authority of the ECSC, and the first official declaration (January 1956) of the Action Committee for the United States of Europe which he formed at that time, helped to ensure that such an organisation would be set up without delay and that it would be closely modelled on the ECSC.

Why atomic energy? It was a limited, clear-cut concept which meant something to most people; something more, thought Monnet, than the rather nebulous idea of an economic community. Furthermore, it might be that the proliferation of nuclear weapons could be halted if the new atomic community could be given control of all fissile materials, and if its members renounced individual nuclear armaments programmes. Nuclear research was a difficult and expensive field of activity in which European states would simply have to collaborate with each other to achieve anything worthwhile within their individual pockets. The 'three Wise Men' of Euratom, appointed at Monnet's instigation in 1956, had predicted that Europe's dependence on oil imported from the Middle East would increase rapidly and dangerously: the development of some alternative energy source was essential, and nuclear power seemed to fill the bill. The Suez crisis of 1956, when the Suez Canal Company was nationalised and the canal closed, clearly underlined this point. While five of the Six had so far embarked on little more than limited research projects in the field of nuclear power, and indeed could only hope actually to benefit from nuclear power by collaborating with each other, the sixth, France, might hope by joining such an atomic community to maintain her lead and indeed to dominate the scene to her own substantial benefit.

While the Six were thus planning what might have been a single powerful nuclear power programme controlled by a central supranational authority, discontented outsiders, who were fellow-members with the Six of the OEEC, set up a parallel or even rival, but merely intergovernmental, concern within that organisation: the European Nuclear Energy Agency (ENEA). Proposed on 18 July 1956, it actually came into existence on 1 February 1958 and has not been wholly unsuccessful. Thus an international company called Eurochemic was formed which built and operated a plant at Mol in Belgium for reprocessing nuclear fuel. The project went moderately well until the three leading participants, British Nuclear Fuels Ltd, the Commissariat à l'Energie Atomique, and Kernbrennstoff-Wiederaufbereitungs GmbH, together decided in 1971 to form a company of their own, United Reprocessors, thus giving precedence to their own national industrial needs.

Euratom, the treaty for which was signed alongside the EEC treaty at Rome on 25 March 1957, suffered fatal flaws from the start. Already in the case of the ECSC treaty, Monnet had had to accept a somewhat diluted version of his original 'supranational' scheme; diluted by the governments, which had insisted on reducing the supranational element to a minimum. Now, with Euratom, having, as Merlini and Panico pictures-quely put it, ordered a beefsteak, Monnet was served with a mere snack. The Council of Euratom was far too powerful; the requirement of Article 7 that 'community research and training programmes shall be determined by the Council, acting unanimously' proved to be a noose which slowly suffocated Euratom. Worse than this, however, was the fact that the member states neither forwent their right to pursue their own national programmes of nuclear armament (Germany apart: she had treaty oblig-ations to the contrary), nor did they for a moment consider abandoning their own separate programmes of research into the peaceful uses of atomic energy. Thus France embarked on a major military programme of nuclear research in 1955-6, though she promised a four-year interval before exploding her first bomb (cynical observers interpreted this as meaning that she could not explode one before then); and Italy set up a centre for the development of the military uses of nuclear energy in 1956-7. Nor did France have any intention of diminishing in any way her own very active programme of nuclear research for peaceful uses. The Commissariat à l'Energie Atomique, founded in 1945, had five research reactors as well as France's first two nuclear power stations at Marcoule (Gard) in operation by 1958, and this was just a beginning. In 1957 the National Assembly voted it £225 million for the five years 1957-61 — on 3 July, the opening day of the debate on the ratification of the Euratom treaty!

How far was Euratom able to carry out the somewhat limited tasks entrusted to it by the treaty: the encouragement of research, industrial development, and supervision of the supply of fissile materials? In the last it was moderately successful. Progress was made in the second, but President of the Commission Etienne Hirsch (a 'Monnet man' who had succeeded Monnet at the Plan) found himself unpopular with the French government because he insisted on making financial contributions out of community funds to four nuclear research centres which were installing American, rather than French, reactors. As to the promotion of research, in spite of lengthy Italian delays, four sections of the Euratom Joint Research Centre were eventually set up at Petten in the Netherlands, Geel in Belgium, Karlsruhe in Germany and Ispra in northern Italy, together employing over 2,000 persons. But the Germans developed a national establishment alongside the Community one at Karlsruhe, and the French refused to allow their centre at Genoble to be 'Europeanised'.

In the early 1960s Euratom began to be starved of funds, mainly because the needs of national programmes were given priority. When both France and Germany embarked on fast-breeder reactor programmes of their own, Euratom was further undermined. From 1967 onwards it survived on a provisional, annual budget only: most of its history so far is a history of failure, or of the victory of nationalism over integration. And this victory of nationalism has brought with it waste, duplicated effort, lack of coordination and, indeed, chaos. Thus in the very month, July 1974, that the Germans found it necessary to close down their heavy-water nuclear power station at Niederaichbach on the River Isar, the British decided to go in for heavy-water reactors — but they could find no partners among member states of the EEC!

Conclusion

Integration by sector, then, was little more than an episode, important chiefly because it saw the creation of the Europe of the Six. Neither the pioneering ECSC nor Euratom did much more than continue to exist after their first few years of activity. Both were soon overshadowed by their larger partner, the EEC, and it is to the origins and early years of this more robust institution that we turn in the next chapter.

Europe in 1955

In 1955 Gunnar Myrdal, Swedish politician and economist, who was Secretary of the United Nations Economic Commission for Europe from its inception in 1947 until 1957, and therefore in a position to know, included a rather pessimistic survey of the progress of integration in Europe in his book *An international economy*. The Scandinavians had created the Nordic Council in 1953 but had made no progress with their customs union. Benelux looked like a relative success; it had set up a more or less complete customs union for industrial goods, but the hoped-for Benelux Economic Union was still not attained. In September 1954 the tenth anniversary celebrations of Benelux were held in the Palais des Académies in Brussels and the Ridderzaal at The Hague: the speakers platitudinously and over-optimistically 'emphasized the great importance of Benelux cooperation and expressed their faith in the speedy realization of the Economic Union'. In May 1955 the Benelux ministerial committee decided in favour of the creation of an agricultural common market, but this would not be achieved for seven years, until 1962. During its slow and uncertain progress, in which defined goals were virtually never reached on time, Benelux had developed no supranational element whatsoever. It was an organisation for intergovernmental collaboration rather than a promoter of economic integration. Admittedly the OEEC in Paris had enjoyed some success in its trade liberalisation programme; none the less, there was still much to do. While some barriers to trade had been diminished, others had been set up. Even though the OEEC had banned export subsidies on industrial goods from 1 January 1956, there were other more sophisticated devices like credits and tax concessions which were widely used to promote exports. As to tariffs, the GATT conference at Torquay in 1950-1 failed to ease the rampant protectionism in West Europe, where, for example, in 1950 the mean Benelux external tariff on sixteen agricultural products was about 16 per cent, that of Italy on the same products was nearly 32 per cent, and that of France over 37 per cent! More important, in terms of successful integration, than any of the institutions so far mentioned, was the ECSC. But its success was due mainly to the fact that it covered a small part of the economy only and, even so, Belgian coal and Italian steel were still protected in 1955. As Myrdal saw it, a principal reason for the general failure of integration was the absence of any real unfreezing of capital and of any genuine international labour market. Mobility of labour and capital had simply not been achieved; the factors of production had by no means been internationalised.

Quite apart from the fact that the organisations so far set up had made

little progress towards European unity, the very existence of a number
of them side by side was itself divisive. Attempts to link them together
under a Council of Europe umbrella had not been successful. The most
elaborate of these attempts was the Eden Plan of 1952, originally worked
out in the Foreign Office as a response to the suggestion of Parliamentary
Under-Secretary of State Anthony Nutting that the British should 'find
some scheme which would enable us to play a leading role in Europe
without committing us to join the supranational club as full members'.
However, the various European organisations were not as separate as they
seemed to be, because the same statesmen were involved in nearly all of
them. Thus, for example, the members of the Council of Ministers of the
ECSC could also belong to the ministerial Council of the WEU, whose
members were likewise members of the NATO Council and, often, of the
Council of Europe's Committee of Ministers. Thus a relatively restricted
group of international statesmen tended to play a key role in all these
organisations. In 1949-50 the Belgian Socialist ex-Prime Minister Paul
Henri Spaak looked like becoming a sort of manager of the European
economy: elected President of the Consultative Assembly of the Council
of Europe at Strasbourg on 11 August 1949, he was already President of
the Council of the OEEC in Paris and moves were made in the winter of
1949-50, but blocked by the British, to give him substantially increased
powers there.

Franco-German Relations

The Western Europe of 1955 then, the Europe which saw the first beginnings of the Common Market, was a Europe in which moves towards unity
or integration had been made but had proved for the most part unfruitful;
it was a Europe which tended to be divided by these very moves: three-
power Benelux, seven-power Western European Union, the Six, alongside
the broader-based NATO, OEEC and the Council of Europe. More
seriously, it was a Europe increasingly divided by the time-honoured
Franco-German bugbear, for the creation of ECSC, allegedly initiating the
much-heralded reconciliation of France and Germany, had in fact achieved
nothing of the kind. Instead, Franco-German relations deteriorated rapidly
from about 1950 onwards; we have seen how they were exacerbated by
the debate over the EDC. But they took a turn for the better in the
autumn of 1954, soon after the French National Assembly's rejection of
the EDC. On 26 October 1954 a statement was issued announcing extensive economic cooperation and discussion of a long-term wheat agreement
between the two countries. A Franco-German cultural treaty was signed
at the same time.

An article in the weekly *Die Gegenwart* on 18 December 1954 complained that, if Franco-German trade remained buoyant, this was only
because German exports had overcome a series of French measures,
including the systematic reduction of import quotas in 1951-3, to hinder

them. It pointed out that French administrative obstructionism constituted a further barrier to German exports: it was almost impossible for a German to set up business of any kind in France; and French trade-mark regulations and the inadequacies of the Franco-German chamber of commerce in Paris were also criticised. However, the French had promised to put many of these things right. The article went on to elaborate other points of dispute: the French demand for an international Moselle Canal and German criticism of and counter-proposals to the French canal and barrages alongside the Rhine between Basel and Breisach. As to the promotion of French agricultural exports to Germany in return for imports of German manufactured goods into France, there were all sorts of difficulties. The French wanted five-year treaties covering exports of corn, meat, dairy products and sugar. The Germans were only prepared to sign for three years, would not touch milk, and were unwilling to sign a sugar agreement before 1956. Moreover, they were insisting on French measures of trade liberalisation to facilitate their industrial exports to France and on paying for French agricultural products at world prices and not, as the French proposed, at a higher price in return for the long-term assurance of provisions.

While these economic problems were far from solved at the beginning of 1955, widespread ill feeling was engendered in France by a decision of the Prime Ministers of the German *Länder* in February that the first foreign language in all West German high schools was to be English, and not French. According to the French, this was a direct infringement of the Franco-German cultural treaty signed the previous autumn, which called for the encouragement of the teaching of each other's language in schools; but Adenauer, who had signed the treaty, could point out that education was in the hands of the *Länder* and that the federal government was therefore powerless to intervene.

A giant leap forward in improving Franco-German relations was made on the eve of the creation of the Common Market: it concerned the Saar. This coal-rich German-speaking province, with its capital Saarbrücken situated half-way between Nancy and Mainz, had been returned to Germany after a plebiscite in 1935, occupied by the French in 1945, and organised by them in 1947 into a politically autonomous territory in economic union with France. The Germans resented this and gave some support to a compromise proposal of 1952-3 that the Saar should be 'Europeanized', that is administered as a 'European' territory under the European Political Community (EPC), and this was in part incorporated into the Franco-German agreement on the Saar of 23 October 1954. But, now that the EPC was no more, the Saar was to be administered by the Western European Union (WEU). The Saar problem was, however, still not solved, for the French regarded the 'Europeanisation' of the Saar as a permanent arrangement, while the Germans considered it only temporary. The final solution came on 23 October 1955 when an incredible 96.5 per cent of the Saar electorate voted in a referendum for or against a 'European Statute' for the Saar; the verdict was 423,655 against 'Europeanisation' and in favour of a return to Germany and only 201,898 in favour of 'Europeanisation'. A year later, in October 1956, the French government formally accepted the incorporation of the Saar into the Federal German Republic. The solution of the Saar problem brought with it – against the wishes of the Saarlanders, the Bundesbahn or German Federal Railways, and other elements in Germany – the setting up, as a result of an agreement of 27 October 1956 between France, Germany and Luxembourg, of the Société Internationale de la Moselle, which successfully constructed the 168 miles of the Moselle Canal (mostly in Germany) from Thionville to Koblenz between 1958 and 1964. This project constituted, in effect, a German compensation or *quid pro quo* to the French in return for French acceptance of the German annexation of Saarland.

The Messina Initiative

It is against this background of repeatedly unsuccessful attempts at integration in West Europe and continuing – though perhaps lessening – Franco-German disagreements that the origins of the European Economic Community should be considered. The original idea for the creation by the Six of a common market came from the Netherlands. It was the violin-playing ex-banker Dutch Foreign Minister Johan Willem Beyen who, on behalf of his government, circulated a memorandum to the Foreign Ministers of the other five on 11 December 1952 in which it was suggested that the wide-ranging political and military integration implicit in the EDC and EPC projects should be accompanied by large-scale economic integration. The Six should, in the coming years, create, step by step, a common market, the institutions administering which should make decisions by simple majority vote. The Dutch government, in fact, was in favour of a supranational common market. These proposals were reiterated in a letter of 14 February 1953 also addressed to the Foreign Ministers of the Netherlands' five partners, and they were entrusted to experts, for detailed elaboration, by the Foreign Ministers of the ECSC meeting in Rome on 24-25 February 1953 – that is, shelved for the time being while the future of EDC was in the balance.

Naturally, after the French National Assembly's rejection of EDC on 30 August 1954, the possibility of proposing some alternative scheme for further integration was raised. Jean Monnet and Paul Henri Spaak were agreed on a modest extension of the ECSC to cover transport and energy, including atomic energy; but Spaak got little response early in April 1955 from either Paris, Bonn or Rome. Adenauer preferred to wait, and Antoine Pinay, Foreign Minister in the new government of Edgar Faure, which also included Schuman and Teitgen, politely advised Spaak that Europe should be made step by step, not at a gallop. Bech and Beyen, however, were enthusiastic. Beyen, according to Spaak, was 'the true author of the relaunching (*relance*) which was to give birth to the Common Market'. On 4 April he sent Spaak a memorandum arguing against further integration by sector and for a 'supranational community' which would achieve generalised 'horizontal' integration by creating a customs union and, eventually, an economic union. These ideas, he suggested, should be put to the next meeting of the Foreign Ministers of the Six. They were, after being lucidly expounded in a memorandum based partly on Monnet's text and partly on Beyen's, which was sent from the governments of the three Benelux countries (not from Benelux itself) to their three colleagues in the ECSC on 20 May 1955.

The 'Benelux' memorandum urged further sector integration as well as the creation of a 'European economic community'. But other pressures were being brought to bear on the Foreign Ministers of the Six. A memorandum from the Italian government pointed out that integration by sector 'does not lead easily and rapidly toward general integration', and urged 'that the Common Market should not be limited to several sectors, no matter how vast and important, but should cover the whole of the economic and social life of the countries concerned, without neglecting the social and labour fields'. A last-minute German document proposed something less than a supranational authority, namely a 'consultative organ' responsible to the Council of Ministers of the ECSC to ensure 'close economic cooperation' – not integration. It represented the views of the Minister for Economic Affairs, the tubby, cigar-smoking Ludwig Erhard, architect of the German *Wirtschaftswunder* or economic miracle. Furthermore, a resolution of the Common Assembly of the ECSC on 14 May 1955 had called on the Foreign Ministers to see to the drafting of the treaties necessary 'for the achievement of the next steps in European integration'. Finally, the ministers were confronted when they actually arrived at Messina in Sicily on the evening of 1 June for their meeting, the first since the collapse of EDC, by a deputation of Italian federalists, urging them on in their work of creating Europe.

Who were these six Foreign Ministers, and who, besides Monnet, were the architects of the Common Market? Schuman was Minister of Justice in the Edgar Faure Cabinet, and it was Foreign Minister Antoine Pinay who represented France at Messina; after 2 February 1956, when the Socialist 'European' Guy Mollet became Prime Minister, the French Foreign Minister was Christian Pineau, but responsibility for the Common Market negotiations was entrusted throughout to the 34-year-old Secretary of State for Foreign Affairs, Mauric Faure, who had become a deputy at the age of 29. However, no single French statesman emerged at the time of the creation of the Common Market to capture the 'European' limelight as Schuman had done in 1950; rather it was top-level civil servants and technocrats who contributed most from the French side. Men like Louis Armand, head of the French State Railways, who became President of Euratom, Félix Gaillard, Monnet's principal private secretary at the Plan, who headed the French delegation to the Common Market negotiations, later becoming the youngest Prime Minister in the history of the Fourth Republic; Robert Marjolin, who had spent a year at Yale in 1931, headed the French delegation in Washington in 1943 and married an American, was appointed Secretary-General of the OEEC in 1948 at the age of 36 and held that influential post until 1955, and was now adviser on European Community affairs at the Quai d'Orsay; and the brilliant Pierre Uri, one of Monnet's team of initiators of the Schuman Plan, who had been in the French delegation which negotiated the ECSC treaty and indeed had been largely responsible for the actual drafting of that treaty. They were all Monnet men. They were France's contribution, in terms of personnel, to the creation of the Common Market or European Economic Community.

Konrad Adenauer, who combined in himself the offices of Chancellor and Foreign Minister of the German Federal Republic, was unable to go to Messina in person. He always had been a convinced 'European'; he even went so far, in March 1952, as to claim in a radio interview that 'The European national states have a past, but no future.' He sent the head of the German Foreign Office, Walter Hallstein, to the Council of Ministers. By profession a jurist, Hallstein had been in the United States in 1944-6 as a prisoner of war and in 1948 as a visiting professor. In 1950 he had led the German delegation to the ECSC negotiations. His contribution to the building of Europe was really made later, between 1958 and 1967, when he was the first President of the EEC Commission.

Also at Messina was Italian Foreign Minister Gaetano Martino; indeed it was he who acted as host. He had persuaded his colleagues to confer in his native town, where he was professor and rector of the university, partly in order to win himself prestige and support in the electoral campaign he was involved in at that time for the regional assembly; but the Foreign Ministers actually stayed at the Hotel Santo Domingo in Taormina, and drove to Messina each morning. In the chair was the veteran statesman and Prime Minister of Luxembourg, Joseph Bech, who combined the not very arduous duties of Minister of Foreign Affairs with the pleasant activity of Minister for Wine-growing or Viticulture. This jovial, bulky, shrewd statesman 'beamed. . .through a forest of snow-white moustaches'. He kept in close touch with his colleagues from the other two Benelux countries, J.W. Beyen of the Netherlands and Paul Henri Spaak, Foreign Minister of Belgium. These three, with fewer axes to grind than the others, were the driving force in the Messina deliberations; they were old friends and colleagues. 'Throughout the entire conference', Spaak later wrote, 'I kept in constant contact with Bech and Beyen. We always acted in complete agreement, each supporting the other, uniting our efforts in order to attain the objectives we had set ourselves. The result exceeded our expectations.' Together, in wartime London, this trio had dreamed up Benelux; now they pressed hard for, and eventually brought into existence, the

Common Market.

Besides the somewhat vague possibility of creating an extended common market, the Council of Ministers of the ECSC had only one concrete item of business on their agenda at Messina: the question of who was to be President of the High Authority. Jean Monnet had sent in his resignation the previous autumn, to become effective when his term of office expired on 20 February 1955, two years after the opening of the common market in coal. But the Council failed to appoint his successor and still had not done so, so that Monnet was still at his post. What is more, on 21 May 1955 he sent a somewhat ambiguous letter to the governments of the Six, made public three days later, in which he offered his services to them in the cause of any further developments they might engage in; nor did he rule out the possibility of his continuing after all in the office he had resigned from, namely that of the presidency of the High Authority. But the French government of Edgar Faure proposed the ex-Prime Minister of France René Mayer as Monnet's successor, and the Foreign Ministers of the Six accepted this. It was not a French move against Europe, for Mayer was a prestigious figure, a convinced European and a long-term friend and associate of Monnet. It was only some time after his two-year term of office as President of the High Authority came to a close in 1957 that the decline or eclipse of the ECSC set in.

The historian with the advantage of hindsight looks back to the now-famous Messina Resolution with its high-sounding phrases about 'a fresh advance towards the building of Europe' and about the Six's intention of establishing 'a European market, free from all customs duties and all quantitative restrictions' as the originating initiative in the creation of the Common Market. And he is right to do so. But at the time the resolution made no significant impact. Some thought that the Six had abandoned 'supranationality'; others, such as the German weekly *Die Gegenwart,* which carried an article on 18 June called *Europa provisorisch,* 'Provisional Europe', complained that the Council of Ministers had celebrated the fifth anniversary of the Schuman Plan by appointing just another committee to study various proposals – a time-honoured means of deferring decisions.

The Messina Resolution incorporated a substantial part of the 'Benelux' Memorandum. It began by stating that the six Ministers had resolved to pursue the following objectives: joint study of possible development plans for European transport; consideration of an 'overall policy' for conventional forms of energy; investigation of the possibility of setting up 'a common organization to be entrusted with the responsibility and the means for ensuring the peaceful development of atomic energy', creation of a common market, which would involve the removal of obstacles to trade and the harmonisation of economic policies; the establishment of a European Investment Fund; and the harmonisation of social regulations governing 'working hours, overtime rates. . .and the length and rates of pay for holidays'. Preparatory work to these ends was to be undertaken by a Committee of Government Representatives, to be chaired by a 'political personality', which was to report to the Foreign Ministers of the Six by 1 October 1955. The Committee would be assisted by experts from existing European organisations like the ECSC, OEEC, the Council of Europe, and even the Conference of European Ministers of Transport; and the government of the United Kingdom was specifically invited to take part in its deliberations. Even so, for many observers outside the Six, the Messina Resolution represented an inward-looking, somewhat exclusive, project.

The Making of the Treaty of Rome

The pessimists were soon proved wrong. The Intergovernmental Committee was far from becoming just another committee. It turned out to be dynamic and successful, for the simple reason that the 'political personality' appointed to chair it was none other than Belgian Foreign Minister Paul Henri Spaak. This burly, vivacious 56-year-old Socialist probably did more for the creation of Europe than any other statesman. Foreign Minister of Belgium, with short breaks, from 1936 to 1949, in 1954-7, and again in 1961-6, he was Prime Minister in 1938-9, 1946 and 1947-9. Apart from his activity in the European Movement, he had been, as we have seen, President of the OEEC Council in 1948-9 and first President of the Consultative Assembly of the Council of Europe – until he resigned in 1951 in protest at the inertia of the Committee of Ministers. From 1957 until 1961 he was Secretary-General of NATO.

Paul Henri Spaak cajoled, guided and inspired the Intergovernmental Committee into sifting its ideas and agreeing on certain fundamental goals. A preliminary report was produced in autumn 1955. Work continued. Sectoral integration in transport and energy, which had once looked so fruitful, was soon pushed into the background. How could the Six go ahead here without Austria and Switzerland? Instead, two quite distinct projects emerged to take pride of place: Beyen's Common Market and Monnet's Euratom. These were advocated in a report remarkable for its clarity and structure which was in fact drafted by Pierre Uri, the German committee member Hans von der Groeben, and the Belgian diplomat Albert Hupperts, although it was given the name of the 'Spaak Report'. It was submitted to the Foreign Ministers of the Six in time for it to be considered by them at their meeting in Venice on 29 May 1956. They approved it, and the Intergovernmental Committee was transformed into a treaty-making conference which continued to meet during the rest of 1956 and early 1957 in the same restored medieval manor house, the Château de Val Duchesse, on the outskirts of Brussels, in which the committee had met. At last, in February 1957, conferences in Paris, of experts first, then of Foreign Ministers, and finally of Prime Ministers, sorted out the remaining difficulties and the two treaties, one setting up the European Atomic Community, or Euratom, and the other the European Economic Community or Common Market, were signed in Rome on 25 March 1957. Ratification caused few problems; in every Parliament of the Six large majorities voted for the Treaties of Rome. On 1 January 1958 they came into force.

The extraordinary thing about the Treaty of Rome, which brought the Common Market into existence, was the speed with which it was negotiated. Clearly Spaak's drive and ability played a large part in this, but there were other reasons too. The negotiators (and many others) were anxious to have the treaty signed while régimes favourable to Europe were still in power in the two major countries of the Six, France and Germany. In Germany, Adenauer's European policy was now supported by the Social Democratic Party (SPD), thanks to its experience of the ECSC; but, on the other hand, Ludwig Erhard at the Ministry of Economic Affairs led or represented a substantial German opposition to the Europe of the Six, preferring a wider arrangement. Elections were due in autumn 1957 and it was generally hoped, both inside the Adenauer government and elsewhere, that the EEC treaty could be signed before then. In the increasingly unstable political situation of the French Fourth Republic there was a serious prospect that the Common Market would not be created at all unless this could be done while the pro-European Guy Mollet government remained in power. Thus the internal politics of both France and German favoured speedy negotiations.

The Franco-German *rapprochement* which took place on the eve of the treaty negotiations, and which culminated in Chancellor Adenauer's visit to Paris and meeting with French Prime Minister Guy Mollet in autumn 1956 during the negotiations, contributed decisively to their success. This *rapprochement* had been brought about largely by the French acceptance of the return of the Saar to Germany after the autumn 1955 referendum. The Federal German government also enjoyed close relations with Italy at this time, and Adenauer's visit to Rome in July 1956 to confer with Italian political leaders was not without its beneficial effect on the Common Market negotiations.

The successful conclusion of the Common Market and Euratom negotiations owed a great deal too to the unbounding enthusiasm and energy of Jean Monnet and to the political skill he deployed in creating and then making use of his Action Committee for the United States of Europe. This 'club of European majorities' comprised delegations from the principal political parties and trades unions of the Six which were favourable to Europe. Meeting for the first time in Paris on 16 January 1956, it issued a declaration calling for the immediate setting up of a European Atomic Community, which was submitted to every Parliament in the

Six and passed in each of them by an overwhelming majority. Further extremely effective pressure of the same kind was exercised by Monnet and his Action Committee at intervals during the months and years that followed.

Certain events outside Western Europe also acted powerfully to accelerate the Common Market negotiations. The nationalising of the Suez Canal Company by the ruler of Egypt, Colonel Gamal Abdel Nasser, on 20 July 1956, followed by the Anglo-French attack on the Canal at the end of October and its subsequent obstruction by Nasser, underlined the utter disarray among the Western powers, most of which condemned this Anglo-French aggression, and emphasised the need for unity. At the same time, it pointed to the perils of increasing European reliance on imports of oil from the Middle East and thus greatly encouraged Monnet and others to press for the creation of Euratom; for it was optimistically supposed at that time that nuclear power might soon provide a substantial proportion of Europe's energy needs. But, though the Suez affair certainly contributed to the setting up of Euratom, it also persuaded the French to step up their own national nuclear armaments programme, which impinged adversely, as the years went by, on efforts towards integration in the fields of nuclear power (Euratom) and of defence in general. On the other hand, the failure of the Suez venture also turned French political interests away from the world scene and towards Europe; towards further reconciliation with Germany and towards further moves in the building of the Europe of the Six. Some wit suggested that, should Europe one day become a reality, then in the Museum of 'Europeans' a place would have to be found for the bust of Colonel Nasser.

The Russians, too, made their contribution to the Common Market negotiations in making it clear to the West Germans in the autumn of 1955 that they would never permit German reunification on acceptable terms and thus persuading Adenauer to go all-out for European unification, and in suppressing the Hungarian uprising of October 1956 by force of arms — for this renewed Soviet threat prompted a renewed concern for unity in the West. A year later the process of parliamentary ratification of the treaties of Rome was facilitated by a further Russian move: the successful putting into orbit of the world's first artificial satellite, Sputnik I.

Ironically, an important stimulus towards the creation of the Common Market of the Six was provided by Britain. She alone was explicitly invited in the Messina Resolution to take part in the Common Market negotiations, perhaps because of her recent treaty of association (21 December 1954, not ratified until November 1955), with the ECSC; more likely because she was a member, with the Six, of the newly reconstituted Western European Union, which had started life on 5 May 1955. There was no question, on this occasion, of her having to accept supranational-ism as a prior condition of taking part in the talks; the Messina Resolution had said nothing of a supranational authority, of federalism, nor even of integration. Still, the British demonstrated their complete lack of interest by sending a mere Under-Secretary at the Board of Trade to the earlier post-Messina Committee meetings. He withdrew or was withdrawn in November 1955, when the British sent a note to the West German government announcing their opposition to the Common Market of the Six and inviting the Germans to support their plea for a wider European free-trade area based on the OEEC. Similar notes were sent to West Germany's five partners. The British made it clear that they considered the Common Market of the Six to be incompatible with their economic relations with the Commonwealth and against the interests of the OEEC. Privately, they seem to have been convinced at this time that it would never be created. If they ignored it, perhaps it would go away? Jens Otto Krag, then Danish Minister for Economic Affairs, recalled that the first British reaction he heard to the Messina meeting was from Chancellor of the Exchequer Harold Macmillan at a meeting of the OEEC Council at the end of 1955 or early in 1956. Macmillan raised a polite laugh round the table, shared even by Spaak, when he observed that he had learned of some archaeological excavations at Messina but hoped to hear no more about them.

On the other hand some, at least, of the Six were more enthusiastic about British participation in 1955-6 than they had been in 1950. Both Adenauer and the Italians proposed using the WEU as a bridge between Britain and the Six; Spaak wrote at length to Prime Minister Anthony Eden in February 1956 suggesting discussions in WEU and appealing for British sympathy and cooperation. But the British now launched what seemed to many to be a campaign to wreck the Common Market; and it was this campaign which did much to increase the solidarity and determination of the Six to press on with their own scheme. Just as she made use of the OEEC in 1955-6 to create a wider-based rival or alternative to Euratom in the form of the European Nuclear Energy Agency (ENEA), so, from June 1956 onwards, Britain repeatedly proposed, in the OEEC Council, the formation of a wide-based European free-trade area which would embrace (and, some feared, eclipse) the EEC. Spaak, and indeed most of the leaders of the Six, though by no means outrightly opposing this project, continued to give absolute priority to their own plans, and it was only during the final stages of ratification of the Treaty of Rome by the national Parliaments, after Germany, France and Italy had all ratified, that in October 1957 the so-called Maudling Committee was set up by the Council of the OEEC to negotiate the wider free-trade area advocated by the British and by a number of other OEEC countries, as well as by sub-stantial elements within the Six. A year later, on the eve of the first steps in the creation of the Common Market, which were due to take place on 1 January 1959, the French finally broke off the Maudling negotiations and the plan of linking the EEC into a European-wide free-trade area for industrial goods was abandoned and lost to view until it was revived in a modified form in 1973 after Britain had at last joined the EEC.

All these events then, aided by the personal enthusiasm and energy of many of those involved, conspired to accelerate and facilitate the Common Market negotiations. But speed and success were not their only remarkable feature; another was the way in which the French were able to pressure their colleagues into creating a common market and an atomic community very largely moulded to 'guarantee essential French economic interests', in the words of a National Assembly resolution of January 1957. Not that all the French demands were met in full; most were modified by some element of compromise before being written into the treaty. Prominent among them was the inclusion of the French overseas territories, mainly in Africa, as well as the Belgian Congo (now Zaire) as it then was, and some other territories, on the grounds that the social and economic development of the ex-colonial territories should henceforth be a European responsibility. Germany and France were to contribute the lion's share to the five-year $581 million Development Fund set up to achieve this, namely $200 million each. What this meant, in effect, was that Germany to a large extent, and Italy and Holland to a lesser extent, were obliged to provide very substantial financial assistance for the benefit of territories which were still in French control, though they themselves had been deprived of similar territories after the two world wars, in the case of Germany and Italy in part by France herself. As a matter of fact, the associated territories were nearly all granted independence in 1960 by the French and Belgian governments.

The French also insisted that the Five agree to align their social legislation with that of France, at least as regards the length of paid holidays and the principle of equal pay for men and women. Although this was an eminently reasonable suggestion, none the less the Five promised in effect to raise their costs of production, while French costs remained unaltered. France also persuaded her partners, since the franc was over-valued, to allow her to keep in being her system of export subsidies and special import taxes until she had achieved monetary equilibrium. They also agreed to various other 'safeguard' or 'escape' clauses which could be invoked in her favour.

These and other French stipulations reflected her critical situation at this time. She was in serious financial difficulties and her economy was in such a state of crisis that it seemed most unlikely that she could put aside her traditional protectionism, as required by the Common Market, and survive the chill winds of competition. Her government was also faced

by opposition from de Gaulle, Pierre Mendès-France and others, which contributed to the precarious domestic political situation, and with a serious
and ever-worsening crisis in Algeria.

The very reasons which obliged the French to make their demands
helped to persuade their partners to accept them. Adenauer was person-
ally determined that the Common Market should be brought into being
as a substantial part of the edifice of Franco-German reconciliation he
hoped to build; and the Italians, negotiating with a team of youthful but
enthusiastic experts who were given a remarkably free hand by their
government, maintained a constant pressure in favour of the Common
Market. The fact that the three major events in its formation, the meetings of ECSC Foreign Ministers at Messina and Venice, and the treaty-
signing in Rome, took place in Italy, serves to remind one of that
country's contribution to the *rilancio europeo*.

The French government, as well as France's partners, were determined
to do their utmost to see that the EEC treaty did not suffer the fate that
had overtaken the EDC. Aware that the 1956 National Assembly, with its
influx of Communists and Poujardists, was if anything less 'European'
than its 1954 predecessor, they did their best to remove every possible
objection to the treaty that French MPs might raise; the word supranational was avoided altogether. Great efforts were also made to secure
support for the treaty in governmental and ruling circles generally; indeed
it was said to have been 'floated' through on a 'sea of wine'. It was ratified
in the National Assembly by 342 votes to 239, on 9 July 1957, at the end
of a rather low-key five-day debate, before any of the Parliaments of the
other Five had done so except the Bundestag, where the treaty had been
accepted by a show of hands a few days previously.

The Treaty of Rome

The Treaty of Rome comprises 248 articles and certain additional texts,
namely four annexes, thirteen protocols, four conventions and nine
declarations. Article 240 states that it 'is concluded for an unlimited
period'; it is in fact irrevocable and has been found so in the German
courts. The European Economic Community is meant to be more than a
mere Common Market, that is a customs union and single market for
labour, goods, capital and services; it comprises also an elaborate institutional organisation, and it enshrines the principle that the economic
problems of any one member state are the problems of them all. It also
includes the ultimate political goal of bringing the Six together into some
kind of federation. Besides the territories of the member states, the treaty
applies also to Monaco and San Marino, for whose external relations
France and Italy respectively were responsible, and to the *Land* of Berlin,
namely West Berlin. It was in no way to affect the ECSC, Benelux or
Belux. It is open to any other European state to apply for membership,

and the Community is empowered to enter into an agreement 'creating an association' with any 'third country' — namely a non-member anywhere in the world. Nothing was laid down in the treaty about the languages to be used in the Community institutions nor as to the whereabouts of its headquarters or capital. While its institutions were to be set up as soon as possible after the treaty came into force on 1 January 1958, the first steps toward the creation of the Common Market would not be made until 1 January 1959.

Institutionally, the EEC was closely modelled on the ECSC, the main difference being that more power was given to the Council of Ministers and the governments which it represented, and less to the joint executive authority, whose name was changed in the EEC from High Authority to Commission. Two institutions, the Assembly — now called the European Parliament — and the Court of Justice, were to be shared by the three Communities (ECSC, EEC and Euratom). The new Assembly was to comprise 142 members nominated by the Parliaments of member states: 36 each from France, Germany and Italy, 14 each from Belgium and the Netherlands, and 6 from Luxembourg. Article 138, Clause 3, laid down that 'The Assembly shall draw up proposals for elections by direct universal suffrage in accordance with a uniform procedure in all member states.' But the Assembly, though it looked like a parliament and is now called one, was not a parliament: it had few powers worth the name. Admittedly it could, by a two-thirds majority vote of no confidence, compel the members of any one of the three executive bodies to resign *en bloc*; but this absurdly ponderous weapon has never been used. Otherwise, the Assembly's powers were limited to the right to give an opinion on decisions of the Commission and Council of Ministers, the right to debate the annual reports of the three executives, and the right to address oral or written questions to the Commission. It could not legislate.

The executive authority of the EEC was the nine-member Commission; but the word 'executive' here must not be taken to imply wide-ranging competence. The Commission's powers were more limited than those of the High Authority: questions of broad policy and indeed almost all important matters were to be referred to the Council of Ministers for decision, that is, to the governments. Its functions were set out in Article 155 of the Rome treaty: namely, to see that the other institutions of the Community and the member states implement and observe the treaty; to submit proposals to the Council for decision; and to enforce the rules laid down by the Council. No more than two of the nine members of the Commission were to be of the same nationality; they were to be appointed by 'common accord between the governments'; and to serve for four years, a term of office which was renewable.

Article 145 of the Rome treaty makes it quite clear that the destinies of the EEC were to be placed firmly in the hands of the governments of the member states: 'To ensure the attainment of the objectives laid down in this Treaty in accordance with the provisions of the Treaty, the Council shall: ensure coordination of the general economic policies of the Member States; have power to take decisions'. The Council was to consist of a minister from each government. According to the treaty, decisions of the Council were to be arrived at, 'save as otherwise provided', by a simple majority, that is with one vote for each member state. But in fact there are only six cases in the treaty, all of them involving internal or minor matters, where voting *is* by a simple majority. In many cases Council decisions were to be made by a 'qualified majority'. For these a system of weighted voting was laid down, France, Germany and Italy having four votes each, Belgium and the Netherlands two each and Luxembourg one. A decision could only be taken if twelve votes were cast in favour and, unless the motion had the support of the Commission, the twelve votes had to be cast by at least four member states. Thus a one-country veto was ruled out; nor could the 'Big Three' by themselves (without the support of the Commission) outvote their three smaller partners; nor again could any two of the 'Big Three' by themselves outvote the third. In still other cases, prescribed by the treaty, and these covered numerous and important matters, unanimous agreement was required for a decision of the Council.

The treaty provided for a shift in emphasis, as the years went by, from voting by unanimous decision to majority voting in the Council. During the first stage of treaty implementation, namely in 1959-61, qualified majority voting was applicable in twelve cases; it was extended to a further six during the second stage (1962-5). With the move to the third stage on 1 January 1966 most decisions were to be taken by majority vote, and in only a handful of cases was unanimity still required. Thus the Community was to become increasingly 'supranational'.

The general objectives of the EEC were set out in Article 2 of the treaty:

> by establishing a Common Market and progressively approximating the economic policies of Member States, to promote throughout the Community a harmonious development of economic activities, a continuous and balanced expansion, an increase in stability, an accelerated raising of the standard of living, and closer relations between the States belonging to it.

The Common Market, which meant in the first place the abolition of 'internal' duties and quotas on trade as well as any 'other measures having equivalent effect', and the establishment of a common 'external' customs tariff, was to be introduced step by step, four years at a time, over a 'transition period' of twelve, or at most fifteen, years. Transition from the first stage to the second was made conditional on the Council finding, unanimously, that the objectives laid down for the first stage had been achieved.

While the procedure and timetable for the introduction of the main elements of the Common Market were thus laid down in detail in the treaty, most of the rest of the programme was enjoined in principle only. Thus the introduction of a common commercial policy, implying that only the Community as a whole, and not its individual member states, could make commercial treaties or trading agreements with third countries, was clearly not envisaged until after the end of the transition period. Before then, member states were only required to 'coordinate their commercial relations with third countries so as to bring about, by the end of the transitional period, the conditions necessary for putting into effect a common policy in the field of external trade'. As regards the abolition, as between member states, of obstacles to the free movement of workers, employers, services and capital, this was to be achieved before the end of the transition period.

Apart from the statement that agriculture was to be included in the Common Market and that there was to be a common agricultural policy (CAP) which must be developed 'by degrees during the transition period' and brought 'into force not later than at the end of that period' (Article 40), there is little in the treaty to indicate what that common agricultural policy should be. Its objectives, however, were set out in Article 39: to increase productivity and the earnings of farmers and farm-workers, to stabilise markets, and to ensure supplies to consumers at 'reasonable prices'. Even less was said about the common transport policy which was to be formulated during the transition period, except that discrimination by carriers based on nationality was to be abolished before the end, that is, within eight years of the second stage.

It was the aim of the EEC to abolish and prevent all restrictions on or distortions of free and fair competition in its internal trade. Article 85 prohibited agreements between firms and other undertakings which might affect competition adversely, for example by fixing prices or limiting production; Article 86 prohibited such practices by any single firm with a dominant position in the market. Further articles prohibited dumping, that is the unloading on to the market of cheap surplus goods, and governmental aid in the form of export subsidies or indeed any state aid 'which distorts or threatens to distort competition by favouring certain undertakings or the production of certain goods'. The treaty also enjoined the coordination of member states' economic and monetary policies, the partial harmonisation of their fiscal and social policies, and any necessary harmonisation of laws. Finally, it set up three funds, the European Social Fund 'to improve employment opportunities for workers and to contribute to the raising of their standard of living'; the European Investment

Bank, 'to facilitate the economic expansion of the Community by opening up fresh resources' through a system of loans and guarantees; and the already-mentioned Development Fund for the associated overseas territories.

Such, then, in very broad outline, was the Treaty of Rome. In J.F. Deniau's words, it initiated 'a kind of cumulative European process'. Its signature put the Council of Europe, the OEEC and indeed every other move toward unity or integration so far made into the shade. For the next two decades the history of integration in Europe centres round the EEC; either this history directly concerns the further development of that organisation, and this must inevitably be the subject of our next chapter; or it relates to activities elsewhere which increasingly begin to look like mere responses and reactions to the EEC. These activities in Europe outside the Six will form the subject matter of Chapter 9. From whatever future vantage-point people may look back on the thirty or so years after the close of the Second World War in 1945, it seems unlikely that the most decisive date in the history of European integration will ever seem to be otherwise than 25 March 1957: the date of the signature of the Treaty of Rome.

The European Economic Community came into existence and developed at a time when the industrialised world was enjoying sustained economic growth and prosperity. But the transition, at the end of 1972, from the Community of the Six to that of the Nine took place during the onset of a serious – and global – economic crisis, the effects of which have dogged the steps of the Nine and hampered their activities ever since. Here we are concerned with the EEC of the Six during the thirteen prosperous years of its existence, from 1 January 1958 to 1 January 1973.

The World and Europe at the Time of the Six

The context of economic prosperity was probably the most important single influence on the EEC in these years, especially up to 1965. But the political context was important too. The sixties saw the end of so-called bipolarity in the world; that is, the solitary and angry confrontation of two great world powers, America and Russia, which perhaps reached its most critical stage at the time of the construction of the Berlin Wall in August 1961 and the Cuban missile crisis a year later. At this very time, the Sino-Soviet dispute presaged the rise of China to world power status: in 1964 and 1967 respectively she exploded her first atom and hydrogen bombs. Towards the end of this period America's economic strength was visibly sapped: in 1971 the almighty dollar was devalued and the United States experienced her first balance of payments deficit since 1893. On the other hand the Japanese economy went from strength to strength. Thus the earlier dominating position of both Russia and America was somewhat eroded. In this same period the international situation was transformed by the process of decolonisation and the emergence of the 'Third World'. What this meant, in effect, was that the links between the underdeveloped or less developed territories and their former European conquerors were broken. Instead, the newly independent countries tended to group together 'horizontally' in bodies like the Organization for African Unity (1963) and in the United Nations; but they were also involved in the forging of new links with the three great world powers, and with the Common Market. The entire economy of the world was modified in the course of this global political reorganisation.

Europe, although it was the scene of the most remarkable and far-reaching experiment in inter-state collaboration hitherto attempted, namely the creation of the EEC, was also increasingly divided in these years, for, to the old-established and perhaps still widening East-West rift was now added the division of the West into what looked like two rival trading blocks, the EEC and EFTA, though in fact the leader of EFTA, Britain, flirted repeatedly with the Six, notably in 1961-2 and again in 1967. None the less, economic integration among the Six had provoked the creation of an opposing Seven: Europe, as Benoit put it, was at Sixes and Sevens.

Important changes took place in the years 1958 to 1972 inside the member states of the Six. In France, General Charles de Gaulle achieved power on 26-27 May 1958 as an alternative to a military *coup*. The Fifth Republic was inaugurated at the end of the year with a fanfare of nationalistic sentiment and de Gaulle as the all-powerful president. From then until his resignation in 1969 the ageing general controlled France and dominated Europe, assisted by his able and dutiful minister Maurice Couve de Murville. In spite of an eccentric and somewhat unpredictable foreign policy, this was a period of unusual domestic political stability for France: during the Fourth Republic, between 1944 and 1958, 27 governments had succeeded one another. The inception of the Fifth Republic was accompanied by French attempts to assert herself as a world power, alongside America, Russia, Britain and China: in 1960 and 1968 she exploded her first atom and hydrogen bombs.

In the Federal German Republic, the aged Chancellor Adenauer remained in office until 1963, when he was succeeded by Ludwig Erhard, until 1966. Although Adenauer's and Erhard's Christian Democratic Union (CDU) remained the largest single party in the Bundestag, none the less, in the 'Grand Coalition' of 1966-9, the CDU formed a government jointly with their Social Democratic (SPD) opponents, with Willy Brandt, the ex-burgomaster of Berlin, as Foreign Minister and, as a result of a swing to the left in 1969, Willy Brandt became Chancellor (1969-72).

The 'opening to the left' was the dominant feature of Italian politics throughout the sixties: between 1963 and 1968 Aldo Moro, leader of the Christian Democrats, and the leader of the Socialists, Pietro Nenni, formed a series of centre-left coalitions. Italy's domestic political instability in the sixties was compensated for by extraordinary economic prosperity, which followed hard on the heels of the German 'economic miracle'.

Salient Events in the History of the Six

The Europe of the Six could not fail to be profoundly affected by these events and changes. The first thirteen years in the history of the EEC were chequered with vicissitudes: a succession of failures and inadequacies qualified by a number of sparkling successes. On 1 January 1959 the first step in the creation of the Common Market was taken: customs duties were reduced by 10 per cent and import quotas were increased by 20 per cent. France and Germany had dramatically demonstrated their commitment. The German government had already reduced their customs duties in anticipation of this event; the French, determined not to invoke the escape clauses they had insisted on inserting into the Treaty of Rome, had, at the end of 1958, not only devalued the franc, but also resolved to remove restrictions from 90 per cent of their trade. After this initial success in launching the EEC, which was followed by an acceleration of the timetable of tariff reductions as laid down in the Treaty of Rome, important possibilities for progress presented themselves in 1960-3, but the proposals then made for a political union and for an enlarged membership to include Britain came to nothing. In 1965 the Community experienced its first serious internal crisis when the French for a time boycotted meetings of the Council and other bodies; but in 1967 the so-called 'merger of the executives' was successfully carried out, and a single fourteen-member Commission assumed the functions of the three hitherto separate executive organs of the ECSC, Euratom and the EEC. In the following year the Community's customs union was triumphantly declared completed, eighteen months ahead of schedule. Thereafter, the attention of the Community was increasingly focused on its projected expansion, for the resignation of de Gaulle in 1969 had opened the way for the renewed membership applications of Britain, Denmark, Ireland and Norway. Such, in a few words, were some of the salient events in the thirteen-year history of the six-power EEC which is the subject of this chapter.

Nationalism and de Gaulle

If any single theme runs through this entire history it must by no means merely be defined as 'the headstrong nationalism of de Gaulle' hindering essential moves in the process of uniting Europe. Rather this theme is the constantly repeated confrontation, and even struggle, between the governments of the member states on the one hand and the Community they had given life to on the other. For, miraculously, out of the complex provisions of the Treaty of Rome a being of some kind had emerged; and it threatened, here and there, to tread roughshod over national interests. Over and over again, the nationalism of the governments clashed with the common interest represented by the Community and its Commission.

The French government of de Gaulle was, however, somewhat more nationalistic than any of the others. This is no place for a detailed analysis of de Gaulle's foreign policy. Repeatedly, in the pages that follow, we shall see how it affected, modified and often hindered the development of the Common Market. But de Gaulle's profound wish to rescue Europe from the all-embracing hegemony of America, which lay behind his support for the Fouchet Plan and his opposition to British entry into the EEC, was even more apparent in his attitude to NATO. Once his autumn 1958 proposal for a three-power directorate of this alliance by Britain, France and America had been rejected by his intended partners, he initiated the process of partial French abandonment of NATO: in 1959, refusal of French participation in NATO's integrated air defence system, which was a joint organisation for the detection, identification, interception and destruction of enemy aircraft; in 1959 and 1963, withdrawal of the French Mediterranean and Atlantic fleets from NATO command; in 1964, withdrawal of French officers from the inter-allied general staff and a barrage of criticism fired at NATO; in 1966, finally, withdrawal of all French troops and other personnel from NATO and the expulsion from French territory of all NATO bases and depots, including the NATO political headquarters, which was transferred to Brussels, the European military headquarters of Supreme Headquarters Allied Powers Europe (SHAPE) at Rocquencourt near Paris, which had to be moved to Casteau near Mons in Belgium, and the Paris-based NATO Defence College which was moved to Rome.

It is against this background of aggressive hostility towards NATO that one has to view de Gaulle's treatment of the EEC; his attack was spearheaded, in the case of both organisations, against 'integration'. On the other hand de Gaulle, in spite of his threats, was firmly committed to the Common Market and the common agricultural policy, and we must take Foreign Minister Couve de Murville at face value when he says, in his memoirs, that France intended to act as the driving force *(l'element moteur)* of the Community. Furthermore, de Gaulle was in most respects by no means a solitary figure; he was a mirror of his age: he was dreaming of a united Europe before Churchill's Zürich speech; his nationalism was emulated by others, indeed it expressed the nationalistic tendencies of his age; his suspicion and dislike of America was widely shared; and his fears of British indifference to 'Europe' were by no means ill-founded, as Harold Wilson's Labour government of 1974 was to demonstrate.

A Capital for the Six?

The first real problem confronting the Six at the start of their history was small but difficult. Where should its administrative seat and headquarters be? Now that two more Communities were being added to the existing ECSC, Jean Monnet and others urged in 1957 that there should be a single capital for all the institutions of the Six and that this capital should be especially built for the purpose in a 'European District' on the model of Washington, situated in a federal District of Columbia. No final decision had ever been made about the seat of the ECSC, most of whose institutions had in consequence been established provisionally in Luxembourg. With a display of nationalism not normally associated with the Grand Duchy, her Prime Minister, Joseph Bech, absolutely refused in 1957 to entertain the possibility of putting her diminutive capital city of 70,000 inhabitants at the disposal of the EEC, and equally resolutely insisted that, come what may, Luxembourg was utterly determined to hold on to the ECSC. In face of this, no agreement on a single seat for all the Community institutions was possible. When Coudenhove-Kalergi polled European MPs on this question, he found them divided: of 647 replies received, 216 favoured Brussels and 215, mainly French and Italian, favoured Paris. Strasbourg and Luxembourg were much less popular. Other governments besides Luxembourg consulted their own interests in this matter: the Dutch proposed The Hague and the Italians proposed Turin or Milan, apparently with the aim of reserving rights to some institution or other — the Court of Justice or the European Investment Bank — in the event of failure to agree on a single capital for all the institutions. Sadly then, when 1 January 1958 came round, there were no formalities or celebrations; there could be no official inauguration ceremony of the European Economic Community because it had no capital. Only on 2 July 1958 did the Six contrive an agreed statement which, while affirming the principle of a single capital for all the institutions, accepted that *for a provisional two years,* the ECSC should remain at Luxembourg, the two Commissions and some other offices should be established in Brussels, and that the Assembly or Parliament should meet mainly in Strasbourg. Such, broadly, is still the predicament of the EEC in 1978; those two years have become twenty. Further efforts were made in 1964-5, at the time of the fusion of the three executives, to agree on a single seat, but Belgium fought to retain what it already had in Brussels; France stood up for Strasbourg; and Luxembourg had to be compensated with some additional services when the High Authority's office there closed in July 1967. Will Article 216 of the Treaty of Rome, 'The seat of the institutions of the Community shall be determined by common accord of the governments of the Member States', ever be implemented by the establishment of a single headquarters?

The Fouchet Plan

In the first five years of its existence the EEC was confronted by two other problems, each of which constituted a challenge of some magnitude. Action was required, first, on the so-called Fouchet Plan for a political union, urged by France, and, second, on the possible enlargement of the Community. Partly because of the nationalistic attitudes of some member states or the absence among them of any real 'Community spirit', neither of these opportunities for development was grasped.

Ever since Charles de Gaulle founded the Rassemblement du Peuple Français party (RPF) in 1947, he and many of his followers, as well as others, had pronounced themselves in favour of a confederation or intergovernmental union of European states. Michel Debré had proposed schemes for a European political community or 'union of European states' in 1949-50, and again in 1953: the former to make good the deficiencies of the Council of Europe; the latter as a counter-proposal to the European Political Community (EPC), planned at that time. Foreign

Affairs Minister Antoine Pinay expounded such a plan to Konrad Adenauer in the spring of 1955. A political union, which would take the form of a Conseil Confédéral Européen, meeting, say, regularly every two months, with a permanent secretariat in Paris, would act as a sort of coordinating organisation for sector integration. Respecting to the full the sovereignty of the national states, it would, hopefully, be joined by Britain and other non-members of the Six.

It was thus only natural that, once de Gaulle was installed as President of the Fifth Republic, he should try to modify the character of the EEC in a confederal direction, or to impose over it, as it were, an umbrella of political union. Nor should it be forgotten that Jean Monnet — at least for a time — and many other 'Europeans' supported this idea.

On a visit to Rome in June 1959, de Gaulle put the idea of a permanent secretariat to back up regular Foreign Ministers' meetings to the Italian President Giovanni Gronchi, and German agreement to such a scheme was obtained without difficulty. Although others of France's partners were opposed to the permanent secretariat, the six Foreign Ministers agreed on 23 November 1959 in Strasbourg to regular three-monthly discussions of international and other political problems, and three such meetings actually took place in January-July 1960, though at irregular intervals; thereafter a series of bilateral conferences was held by the heads of governments, in which the British participated. These culminated in the Macmillan-de Gaulle discussions at Rambouillet on 29 January and the Adenauer-de Gaulle conference in Paris on 3 February 1961. Political consultations became the order of the day and on 10 February and 18 July 1961 the first 'summit' conferences were held by the Six in Paris and Bonn respectively. At Bonn the heads of government of the Six agreed to a modified version of the plan for a political union which de Gaulle had been publicly urging in 1960. A committee under the chairmanship of Christian Fouchet, French ambassador to Denmark, set to work, and on 2 November 1961 produced a draft treaty for 'a union of States, hereafter called "the Union" ', which had in fact been submitted by the French delegation. This Union was to have two principal institutions. A Council, consisting of heads of state or government or of Foreign Ministers, was to meet regularly and come to unanimous decisions; and a permanent European Political Commission was to be set up in Paris consisting of 'senior officials of the Foreign Affairs department of each Member State'.

The original Fouchet Plan for a European Political Union, a second French version of it, and a counter-proposal of the five, were all discussed by the committee during the winter of 1961-2, by the Foreign Ministers on 20 March and 17 April, and by de Gaulle, who saw Adenauer at Baden-Baden on 15 February and the Italians at Turin on 4 April 1962. But all to no purpose; the negotiations came to a virtual deadlock on

17 April, and were never resumed. They broke down because the Dutch and others were against the proposed union unless British participation was assured; because the Germans and Italians feared that such a union might derogate from NATO and the EEC by arrogating to itself defence and economic matters properly belonging to those organisations; because the French, directly inspired by de Gaulle himself, pushed their partners too hard; and because the British intervened in the debate in a way which irritated the French, if not some of their partners also, and convinced de Gaulle that they *would* join the new organisation. De Gaulle's preference for unilateral action, or bilateral negotiations, caused resentment among some of France's partners; but Adenauer, who seems to have been captivated or even mesmerised by de Gaulle, partly because his growing suspicions of British and American policies coincided with de Gaulle's fears, was quite prepared to do bilateral deals with him behind the back or over the heads of his smaller partners. They in their turn were totally unable to present a joint 'Benelux' viewpoint. Luxembourg usually followed the French lead; the Belgians were in favour of a six-power political union, while the Dutch were not. Dutch intransigence, indeed, contributed substantially to the impasse of 17 April. The political union project collapsed very largely because of the nationalistic attitudes of the member states of the EEC in general, and of France in particular.

The Franco-German Treaty

The allegedly superfluous and, in 'European' circles, deservedly unpopular Franco-German Treaty of 22 January 1963 really represents a surviving fragment of the political union. A sort of bilateral version of the Fouchet Plan, it provided for institutionalised cooperation, especially in foreign policy, defence, and education and culture, but it was effective only in the last of these. Perhaps it helped to cause the curious increase in the annual rate of Franco-German marriages from 996 in 1962 to 1,064 in 1963 and 1,527 in 1966. Nevertheless, the socialist parties of the Six condemned it for endangering 'the trust between the partners of the European Community'; creating the possibility of prior understandings between the two governments on matters of Community concern; and being 'inspired by the outworn concept of the absolute sovereignty of states'. 'In no way', they declared, 'does this treaty represent a contribution to the realization of the United States of Europe.' All its aims, they argued, 'could have been achieved more effectively in the framework and with the methods of the wider European Community'. Italian Prime Minister Amintore Fanfani said much the same, maintaining that it was 'harmful to the Common Market, harmful to the progress of European unity, and harmful to the internal equilibrium of NATO'. So much for de Gaulle's dictum: 'As for me, I say that Europe must be built on the foundation of an accord between Frenchmen and Germans.'

Enlargement?

In 1957 the Six accounted for nearly one quarter of world trade, yet in the early years of the EEC little attention was paid to external relations. The Treaty of Rome, Article 237 of which stated that 'Any European state may apply to become a member of the Community,' made it at least implicitly clear that the EEC's policy should be to expand itself to include the whole of Western Europe, if not Western and Eastern Europe. Besides making provision for new European members, the treaty also allowed for the conclusion by the Community with third countries of 'agreements establishing an association involving reciprocal rights and obligations, common action and special procedures'. Opportunities for expansion in Europe, either by creating links of some kind with other states or by welcoming them as new members, were there from the start. Not that it would necessarily be fair to regard the proposed link-up of the Six with the other member states of the OEEC to form the British-inspired wider European free-trade area as such an opportunity. On the contrary, for many this kind of enlargement was looked on with suspicion and dislike; de Gaulle brought the Maudling Committee negotiations to an abrupt close in November 1958.

But possibilities for more effective enlargement soon presented themselves. In October 1958 Israel made the first of a series of approaches to the EEC. On 8 June 1959 the Greek government requested association with the EEC under Article 238 of the Treaty of Rome and by 1 August of the same year a similar request had been received from Turkey. Although these last applications were enthusiastically accepted, the EEC was dilatory and hesitant and the negotiations long drawn out, partly because of disagreements among the Six, partly because they never had had any effective agreed policy about possible expansion. By the time the Treaty of Athens was signed on 9 July 1961, establishing an Association between the EEC and Greece, and promising her full membership within twenty-two years, a regular queue of candidates was lining up. Ireland had announced her intention of applying on 4 July 1961 and did so on 31 July; Denmark's Foreign Minister, J.O. Krag, had stated on 11 May that his country would apply if Britain did, and it did so the day after Britain's formal application was sent in on 9 August; and the Norwegian Prime Minister announced on 28 February 1962 that Norway would be applying.

These applications for membership provoked a similar response to those for association: an immediate and enthusiastic acceptance by the Commission, except for some reservations in the case of Ireland, whose economy was thought weak and who, incidentally, was a member neither of NATO nor of EFTA, then long delays while the Council, a prey to disagreements among the Six, dragged out proceedings. The membership applications were accompanied by applications for association on the part of those EFTA countries whose neutrality would not allow them full membership of the EEC. The Austrian government announced its intention of seeking some kind of participation in the EEC on 1 August 1961; they and the Swedish and Swiss governments submitted formal applications under Article 238 in December 1961. This wholesale flight of all the members of the newly constituted (3 May 1960) EFTA save Portugal into the arms of the EEC was followed on 9 February 1962 by an application for association from Spain, and by overtures from Portugal on 28 May and from Malta in June 1962.

Here then, in 1962, was an excellent opportunity for the EEC to expand. Everybody outside the East European Communist countries was looking towards it. But because of her economic power and political influence, the waiting-room for potential members was dominated by Britain: their applications depended entirely on hers. Although the Irish had been careful to apply separately from and in advance of Britain, membership of the EEC was economically unthinkable for them without British Membership. For Norway, the political pull of Britain was then of overriding importance; while Denmark, with 90 per cent of her agricultural exports — which then represented about three-quarters of her total exports — going in about equal proportions to Britain and the EEC (mostly West Germany), could not conceivably stay out if Britain went in, nor could she possibly afford to go in without Britain. The waiting-room for association applications, apart from Austria, was dominated indirectly by the British application for membership, for the Swedes would not have dreamed of participating in the EEC unless their Scandinavian neighbours were members of it; nor would the Swiss have associated themselves with anything less than a substantially enlarged EEC. Quite apart from all this, the EEC could not undertake to negotiate with several different countries at once. Inevitably, then, the decision was to negotiate first and foremost with Britain.

It had been agreed that the negotiations would be undertaken, not by a Community organ, but by ministers of the Six, acting as representatives of their respective governments. But the EEC had first to launch its common agricultural policy and negotiate a second association agreement with the overseas African territories, for the first, attached to the Rome treaty, expired at the end of 1962. The Community was also, as we have seen, involved at this very time in the so-called Fouchet Plan discussions for a political union. Thus, really serious negotiations with Britain did not get under way until April-May 1962. Between then and the holiday break in August the Commonwealth was at the centre of discussion; after the autumn resumption the negotiations centred on British agriculture. The talks were held on the seventh floor of the Belgian Foreign Ministry building in Brussels, lent for the occasion by Spaak.

Why had Britain changed her mind so completely about the Common Market in the seven years between 1955 and 1961? In view of the obstinate way in which her economy continued to lose ground in relation to those of the Six, was it simply a case of 'If you can't beat 'em, join 'em'? Or had the disastrous deflation of British national pride caused by the failure of the attack on the Suez Canal in 1956 and the forced abandonment of the Blue Streak rocket in 1957 caused her to value less highly her much-prized national sovereignty? More important, perhaps, was the realisation that, owing to changes in world economic structure, the system of imperial preferences, which had been set up in 1932, was of very much diminished importance in 1960. Indeed, Britain was becoming rapidly less important to the Commonwealth in terms of trade: in 1913, 41 per cent of Commonwealth exports went to Britain; in 1956 the figure had fallen to 27 per cent. Moreover, in 1962, for the first time, Britain exported more to Western Europe than she did to the Commonwealth. Other reasons for the swing in British policy towards Europe in 1960-1 under the Conservative government of Harold Macmillan were fear that Britain's 'special relationship' with the United States might otherwise be undermined by increasing US connections with the EEC, the attraction for Britain of the French moves towards a political union of states in 1959-60, and the fact that the Dutch, and to a lesser degree the Belgians, were enthusiastic supporters of British entry.

The negotiations for British entry were broken off because on 14 January 1963 General de Gaulle said 'No!'. In exercising this veto, he was acting entirely within the bounds of the Treaty of Rome. But why did he say no? Was he perhaps justified in fearing that Britain was not fully committed to a European future? After all, Hugh Gaitskell and the Labour opposition in Britain were opposed to British entry, and the Tory government itself had conducted the negotiations with considerable obstinacy, and shown little political enthusiasm for joining the Common Market. In the first phase, the jovial, dynamic 45-year-old Edward Heath, Lord Privy Seal, who led the British delegation, doggedly stuck to the technicalities of trade preference for the Commonwealth, holding out stubbornly for apparently trivial points – limited protection for desiccated coconut and Canadian railway sleepers or nil tariffs on cricket bats, polo sticks and Australian kangaroo meat. Later, during the second phase, the British negotiating positions on agriculture were equally rigid: weeks were devoted to discussing ways and means of subsidising bacon and eggs, the British being unwilling to abandon their system of deficiency payments overnight. On the other hand, the British could and did accuse the French and particularly the chief French negotiator, Maurice Couve de Murville, of repeatedly raising superfluous objections merely to spin out the proceedings.

But de Gaulle's veto was based on firmer and more self-interested foundations. He regarded Britain as a rival for Continental leadership whose entry into the EEC might deprive France of her potential hegemony there.

He feared, too, that Britain would act as a kind of American 'Trojan Horse', in the sense that her entry, bringing with it closer ties between the EEC and the United States, would serve to increase the 'Atlantic' element in, or American dominance of, Europe. As France's Foreign Minister Maurice Couve de Murville put it, 'our aim is to determine whether the Europe we are creating is a truly European Europe.' That the general had a point here seemed to have been amply demonstrated a few weeks before, at Nassau in the Bahamas in mid-December 1962, when Macmillan accepted Polaris missiles from the United States in lieu of the cancelled Anglo-American Skybolt, thus, in de Gaulle's eyes at least, capitulating to the United States by abandoning Britain's 'independent' nuclear weaponry. Finally, the general was intent on safeguarding French agricultural interests: the common agricultural policy, so dear to his heart, which had been formulated with great difficulty, seemed directly threatened by British entry.

The French veto had two immediate effects: it annoyed France's five partners, and it brought to an end the immediate aspirations to join or be associated with the EEC of all the other applicant countries save perhaps Austria. In spite of de Gaulle's appeal to Danish Prime Minister J. O. Krag, in Paris a few days before his 14 January 1963 press conference, Denmark abandoned her application as soon as it became clear, at the end of January, that the negotiations for British entry had broken down; Ireland, Norway, Sweden and Switzerland all followed suit. There was to be no significant enlargement of the Community for a decade.

The 1965 crisis

By blackballing Britain de Gaulle unquestionably aroused hostility and even anger among his partners, but his efforts to undermine the supra-national elements in the EEC by no means always met with opposition. There were Gaullists elsewhere within the Six, especially in Germany where their views were articulated by the founder and leader of the Bavarian Christian Social Union (CSU), Franz Josef Strauss, and, in spite of the failure of the Fouchet Plan, the French succeeded in persuading their partners to accept a series of measures which combined to transform the EEC into more of a union of states or an intergovernmental organisation and less of a community. Much the most important of these was France's successful reversal of the principle, enshrined in the Treaty of Rome, of the step-wise shift in the procedure of the Council of Ministers from unanimous to majority voting. To achieve this she virtually had to blackmail her partners, both by threatening to leave the EEC and by actually boycotting its most important organs in the second half of 1965. Nevertheless, they not only agreed, in January 1966, at Luxembourg, to the retention of unanimous voting in practice though still not recognising its continuing existence in theory, but some of them, notably

Italy and the Netherlands, subsequently exercised the right of veto thus permitted them.

The Luxembourg agreements of 29 January 1966, which ended the French 'empty chair' boycott of Community institutions and thus brought the crisis to a close, also included certain distinct though informal limit- ations on the powers of the Commission which, under the able and forceful leadership of its President Walter Hallstein, had been mainly responsible for provoking the 1965 crisis in the first place. For on 24 March 1965 he had outlined, not as would have been the normal practice in the first place to the Council of Ministers, but to the European Parliament or EEC Assembly in Strasbourg, a series of far-reaching proposals for increasing the budgeting powers of the Parliament. In Paris, reaction was immediate. A French minister is said to have declared that

> Hallstein is having a fit of megalomania. For a long time he has been acting as if he were the government of Europe. He has been negotiating with foreign states without bothering to consult the Council of Ministers. He almost annexed Afghanistan. Now he claims the right to impose his decision on the Council.

The alleged ambitions of Hallstein and the Commission, to arrogate further powers to themselves in the name of a supranational Europe, were successfully resisted by the French government, which again took its partners along with it. As a result of French opposition, it was the Belgian Jean Rey who became President of the enlarged Commission which took office on 1 July 1967 after the merger of the three executives, and not Hallstein.

Constitutional Changes

One of the limitations on the power of the Commission agreed to at Luxembourg on 29 January 1966 amounted only to the formal recognition of accepted practice, namely that the Commission's right to initiate proposals should be exercised in future only in collaboration with the Committee of Permanent Representatives (COREPER) in Brussels. The main task of this committee, which consisted of the diplomatic representatives or ambassadors of the member states accredited to the Community, was to prepare for, and assist with, the meetings of the Council of Ministers. COREPER's activities increased in importance, and its discussions tended to take on the character of negotiations, espec- ially after its existence was formalised by the 1965 treaty merging the three executives and as the balance of power within the Community swung in favour of the Council and the governments and away from the Commission. This swing had become evident in the early sixties, even before the 1965 crisis. Thus, in general, the Council had delegated executive powers to the Commission in more or less technical matters only, reserving economic and political affairs to itself. Moreover, the Council insisted, when it came to implementing the common agricultural policy, that the Commission act only in consultation with an intergovernmental 'Management Committee' of national officials, one committee for each group of products. Another example of what could be called the increasing Gaullism of the Community was the re-emergence of the intergovernmental political cooperation which the Fouchet Plan was intended to institutionalise in the form of 'summit' conferences, or meetings of heads of state or government, which began with those we have already mentioned in Paris and Bonn on 10-11 February and 18 July 1961 respectively. They were now followed by others in May 1967, December 1969 and October 1972, the last two of which drew up detailed, timetabled programmes for future activities, of a kind which the Treaty of Rome had clearly intended to be the responsibility of the Commission.

Other constitutional changes within the Community, which had been provided for in the treaty or subsequently proposed, either came to nothing or were only partly implemented. After a series of proposals dating back to 1959, it was agreed early in 1964 that the three executives should be merged into a single enlarged fourteen-man Commission on 1 January 1965, and, on French insistence, that the remaining institutions and rules of the Communities should be merged some time later. The 1965 crisis, as well as the opposition of Luxembourg, delayed implementation of the first part of this plan, which was however successfully accomplished in 1967. As to the fusion of the Communities as a whole, which would necessitate an entirely new treaty, this has still not been achieved and seems in any case unnecessary. The 1965 crisis likewise delayed the transition from a system of Community expenses financed from contributions by the member states to a system whereby the necessary funds would be found from the Community's 'own resources', namely the common agricultural policy's levies on imported foodstuffs and the common external tariff on industrial goods. It was only in 1970 that the Council finally agreed on the gradual introduction of a régime of 'own resources' over a period of seven years starting on 1 January 1971. This decision represented, of course, a shift in attitude towards extending the competence of the Community, namely the Commission, which would be responsible for administering, and the Parliament, which would have to approve, the new budget, at the expense of the member states. This particular door, like others, was opened only after the departure of de Gaulle in 1969.

The further evolution of the Assembly or Parliament of the EEC was another internal, constitutional change which was delayed by the nationalism of the sixties and, more particularly, of de Gaulle. Indeed the French even refused to use the name 'European Parliament' which the Assembly adopted for itself in 1962, and instead insisted upon calling it the 'European Assembly'. As to the transition envisaged in the Treaty of Rome from an Assembly whose members were appointed by the national Parliaments to a more authentically federal one whose members were directly elected by universal suffrage, the European Parliamentary Assembly as it then was lost no time in working out appropriate proposals. As early as 22 October 1958 a working party on direct elections was set up under the chairmanship of the Belgian senator F. Dehousse, and on 17 May 1960 the Assembly passed a resolution embodying a 'Draft Convention of the election of the European Parliamentary Assembly by direct universal suffrage.' Submitted to the Council on 20 June, it was not so much as discussed by that body, which indeed contrived to ignore it completely for a period of years. It was only after the Parliament threatened in March 1969 to take the Council to the Community's Court of Justice, if it did not consider the project at once, that the Council reacted by issuing a communiqué on 12 May 1969 stating that it had invited the Permanent Representatives (COREPER) to consider the matter! The public may have been gratified to learn on reading the statement issued in December 1969 after the summit conference of the Six that 'the problem of the method of direct elections is still being studied by the Council of Ministers.' Others beside the Parliament had been losing their patience with the Council's long delay: in 1968 the Movimento Federalista Europeo (MFE), the Italian Association of the Council of European Municipalities (CCE) and the Italian National Council of the European Movement collected the 50,000 signatures to submit a draft law to the Italian Parliament providing for the unilateral direct election of the Italian delegates to the European Parliament. On 14 May 1970 a similar draft bill was before the Belgian Parliament, and in 1972 the Bundestag approved a Bill for the direct election, from 1973 on, of the German delegates at Strasbourg. Now at long last it seems that the much-deferred direct elections will take place not, as agreed in 1974, in 1978, but, because of British procrastination, only in 1979.

Failures and Successes of the Six

Throughout the sixties, then, nationalism, or disagreements among the governments of the Six, call it what you wish, hampered the development of the European Economic Community as that development was envisaged by the creators of the Treaty of Rome: no enlargement; no political union; no shift of power from governments to community, rather the reverse. Only after the departure of de Gaulle from the political scene was the way opened for some, but certainly not for all, of these and other developments. But although the summit meeting at The Hague in December 1969 pointed the way forward, little could be done to reform and develop the Community until the problem of enlargement was settled.

Thus the years 1970-2 were taken up with negotiating, once again, the accession to the Community of Britain, Denmark, Norway and Ireland, and it was not until after the successful creation of the Community of Nine (Norway having opted out), in itself a major achievement of the Six, that new progress in other fields could be made. It was only then that 'own resources' and 'direct elections' could be planned and brought about; only then that the other glaring omissions of the Six in implementing the Treaty of Rome in the 1960s, notably in the fields of transport, energy, social, regional and monetary policies, could begin to be made good. But these matters will concern us in the last chapter. We must turn now to chronicle the successes achieved by the Community of the Six, for successes there certainly were, to offset the failures and lost opportunities so far mentioned.

Not only did the European Community of the Six make a significant impact on world history: it also reshaped Europe. It set up the modern world's first effective industrial common market between states and it created the common agricultural policy; together these modified the economic structure of the entire world. It evolved an embryo foreign policy which enabled it to begin to act in world affairs as a single unit. And, finally, it established a body of European or Community law which perhaps constituted its most remarkable, but least publicised, innovation. Each of these successes in some way or other bit into national sovereignties, and each of them promoted reactions outside the Six. Yet none of them was in any sense complete; they represented the merest beginnings only. The Common Market was still vitiated by countless non-tariff restrictions on trade; the CAP was circumvented in all sorts of ways and periodically disregarded by member states; and the Community's foreign economic or trade policy was often hesitant, sometimes ineffective, and at other times wholly non-existent. None the less, in thirteen years the political landscape of Europe had been transformed: it was no longer merely a system of nation states.

The Common Market for Industrial Goods

> July 1, 1968, will go down as a milestone in the history of Europe. On that day the first and major stage on the road to economic unification of the European continent will be complete. The customs union which is one of the first aims of the Treaty of Rome will have been brought into being.

With these words the Commission proudly but perhaps somewhat hyperbolically announced the successful establishment, eighteen months ahead of the treaty schedule, of a single external customs duty for the Six and the abolition of all duties between member states. Quotas had already been abolished. Nevertheless, the date 1 July 1968 can only be allowed, at best, a symbolic importance, as marking the completion of the industrial Common Market of the Six. In fact the Commission has still, in 1978, ten years later, by no means finished its long-drawn out fight to remove non-tariff, so-called 'technical' obstacles to trade between member states of the EEC, which can be caused by varying safety regulations, different national standards for numerous articles, differential taxation, export subventions, and a hundred and one other devices and procedures. As to the factors of production, their integration had by no means kept pace with that of goods. Admittedly, as from 29 July 1968, the complete freedom of movement of workers was achieved; but this did not apply to members of professions, nor will it ever, under the present treaty, apply to state employees, and a truly unified labour market for the Six had still not been achieved in 1972. As to the free movement of capital between member states of the Six, this seemed in 1972 even further from attainment than it had been in 1962 — the Council simply ignored the Commission's 1964 proposals for further liberalisation in this sphere.

The Agricultural Common Market

Alongside the common market for industrial goods, the Six aimed, by the application of the common agricultural policy, to create an agricultural common market, and this aim had in large measure been achieved by 1 July 1968. Why was it that agriculture came to be included in the Treaty of Rome and why was so much importance attached to the CAP in the 1960s? The sheer size of the agricultural sector, which in 1958 still employed about one-fifth of the total work force of the Six, meant that their projected economic, and indeed political, unification could not possibly be achieved without it. Moreover it was an essential part of the Franco-German deal which was one of the basic elements of the EEC and had helped to make it possible: the French needed access to the German market for their farm products which were partly in surplus while the Germans were only 65 per cent self-sufficient in food, and the Germans wanted to break into the protected French market for their manufactured goods. But perhaps the overriding reason for creating a European farm policy was the fact that agriculture was everywhere beset with complex problems that seemed only solvable at a European level.

These problems were historic. Throughout the nineteenth and twentieth centuries, as industrialisation proceeded, workers were drawn away from what was the only more or less hereditary economic activity, namely farming, into the expanding industrial and service sectors. As the proportion of agricultural workers in the total work-force declined, so the proportion of the gross national product deriving from agriculture likewise declined; and while national income increased, the proportion of it spent on food decreased — the rich spend proportionately less of their income on food than the poor. At the same time, technological advance in the shape of fertilisers and tractors and other machinery greatly enhanced agricultural productivity. But, although efficient farmers with large farms could become more and more productive and more and more wealthy, others, especially those with small farms, could not – and two-thirds of the farms in the EEC were smaller than 10 hectares (about 25 acres). Thus agricultural earnings differed, from one farm to another, as well as from one region to another, by factors of four or even five. What is more, agricultural earnings, taken as a whole, were falling increasingly behind those of other workers. Only a European farm policy, it was thought by many, would be capable of coping with these difficulties.

The CAP

What exactly is the CAP and how does it work? When the EEC was created, every European country had its own agricultural policy based on a variety of measures to maintain or support prices of foodstuffs internally, and to protect home producers against cheaper imports from outside. Adoption by the Common Market of the quite different British system, whereby prices were kept low, imports of cheap foods encouraged, and the farmers subvented directly by a system of government grants or 'deficiency pay-ments', was out of the question because of the absence of political pressure from Continental consumers, who were used to paying high prices, and because of the enormous cost in taxes. Not unnaturally, therefore, the Common Market decided on a joint price support system which would replace existing national policies.

The genius behind the creation of the CAP, and indeed the man very largely responsible for implementing it over more than a decade, was the Dutch Socialist Sicco L. Mansholt, who was 50 years old when he became Vice-President of the EEC Commission, with special responsibilities for agriculture, in January 1958. Before then he had been a tea-planter in Indonesia, a farmer in the Wieringermeer Polder, a Resistance fighter, and Minister of Agriculture in 1945-8 and 1951-6. He was an enthus-iastic sailor, and a keen skater: a debate on agriculture in the Dutch Parliament once had to be broken off because the Minister of Agriculture was taking part in the Eleven Towns Tour, a famous skating occasion demanding a round trip on ice through eleven Frisian towns. Mansholt remained at his post in the Commission throughout the thirteen-year history of the Six, finishing as President when he retired at the end of 1972. He was responsible for putting forward the Commission's original CAP proposals in 1960 and for the revised 'Mansholt Plan' of 1968 with its emphasis on reducing the total acreage of farmland, increasing the size of farms, persuading farmers to leave the land, and, if possible, reducing the cost of the CAP.

The mainspring of the common agricultural market was the fixing by the Community of prices of foodstuffs throughout the Six at a relatively high level and the total abolition within the Community of all duties, subsidies and quotas. This common price was supported or maintained against imports from outside the Community by a Community levy of varying amount which was applied to imported foods to raise their price to the threshold price fixed by the Community. The common price was supported internally by a system of Community intervention buying, for the Commission, acting through national agencies, was empowered to intervene on the market and purchase surplus farm produce if supply exceeded demand and the price dropped. Later, if prices rose, this produce could be released back on to the market; more likely, it would be sold abroad at a loss borne by the Community, or given in the form of food aid. The expenditure incurred in support buying, cold storage of surplus produce and export refunds to allow exporters to sell at the lower price on world markets, as well as part of the costs of various measures of farm reform to increase agricultural efficiency, was met by the 'Farm Fund' or European Agricultural Guidance and Guarantee Fund.

Throughout its history so far, but especially in the sixties, the CAP has met with a barrage of criticism and even hostility, much of it unfounded. French and German farmers demonstrated against it repeatedly in the sixties, but this agricultural unrest had begun in France in the mid-fifties before the CAP was introduced, and it was concentrated in the peripheral regions of small farms: tractors were driven through towns, public benches thrown into rivers, enormous omelettes made in the streets, fruit spread on the roads. Meetings of the agricultural ministers of the Six to fix prices were often accompanied by demonstrating farmers, who sometimes brought their cattle with them, on occasions even into the building. On 17 October 1962 the streets of Göttingen were blocked by 8,000 peasants. Speakers standing on tractors draped in black cloth accused the 'Common Market professors' of being the 'gravediggers of the German peasantry'. The Italian and Belgian farmers demonstrated in their turn: on 6 July 1968 Rome was disrupted by 30,000 rural demonstrators demanding the total abolition of the CAP.

The underlying reason for these demonstrations was the profound difficulty of fitting a primitive agriculture of independent peasant landholders into a modern industrial society. Not wholly dissimilar in character to the attitude of these farmers was the criticism levelled at the CAP by old fashioned nationalists who resented the undeniable supranationalism of the Commission's price-fixing activities. On 25 September 1962 the London *Daily Telegraph* conjured up the vision, horrifying to its patriotic British readers, of 'a Dutchman', S. Mansholt, with complete dictatorial powers, controlling prices by means of a radio telephone link between his private yacht and Brussels! On 2 October a report in the same paper from 'Château Mansholt' described how the European Wine Management Committee, or 'Professor Mansholt's wine committee', was insisting on details of the size of grapes and of stocks, and how it would decide whether the emphasis would be placed on Burgundy or Moselle! On 1 March 1966 the *Daily Telegraph* pointed out that not the national capitals, but 'Brussels will have control over the cost of bread, of the Sunday joint'; and suggested that 'the Brussels common agricultural institutions' might soon 'move much further towards being a federal-type European Ministry of Agriculture, run by Dr Mansholt'!

Perhaps the most popular criticism of the CAP was occasioned by the surpluses it was supposed to have created. But were they a product of the CAP? Any price support system might produce them: in 1958 the Swedish government was already wrestling with the now familiar problem of a butter surplus. Should they increase the margarine tax, reduce the price of butter and risk losing the farm vote, or sell at a loss to Britain? In the event they bartered 2,000 tons of butter with the Russians in return for manganese, chromium, asbestos and coal. EEC surpluses in dairy products first emerged as a serious problem in 1963, when it became clear that the Council of Ministers would not, or perhaps could not, bring themselves to fix the common price low enough. On 13 November 1963 *Le Monde* complained that EEC surplus butter could not be placed on the London market because it was already amply supplied by New Zealand at dumping prices. The problem was serious: France's numerous cows could easily provide far more milk than they were producing at present; after all, Dutch cows produced twice as much! Later, eggs, beef, wine and other products had to be 'taken off the market', but the annual French and Italian fruit gluts could hardly be blamed on the CAP. If the CAP did aggravate the problem of surpluses, this was simply because, year after year, the Council of Ministers insisted on fixing the common price too high.

Outside Europe an outcry was raised against the CAP on account of its alleged protectionism. At the agricultural conference held at Stresa on Lake Maggiore in northern Italy in July 1958 to initiate the CAP, a Danish memorandum arrived which mentioned a rumour that France was urging that the EEC should become self-sufficient in food, and threatened retaliatory measures against the Six's industrial products if they tried to reduce their imports of Danish dairy products. In November 1963 United States Secretary of State for Agriculture Orville L. Freeman complained that the CAP's farm price supports and protective levies on imports could not fail to encourage producers and would certainly have an 'adverse impact' on world trade. The so-called 'Chicken War' of 1963, when United States broiler exports were alleged to have been halved by the Common Market import levies, which was arbitrated by GATT in America's favour to the tune of £9 million worth of compensatory duties, did not improve the image of the EEC in world trading circles. Nor did the report in the *Neue Zurcher Zeitung* of 21 February 1965 help matters. Under the curiously mixed-language headline 'Poulet-Dumping der EWG', the Swiss paper reported that the Commission was dumping frozen chickens on the East European market at a price less than half that of the production cost! The EEC's protectionism became increasingly apparent during the sixties; at the end of the decade EEC price levels of basic foodstuffs were twice or even four times (in the case of sugar and butter) as high as those of the world market, which were, however, artificially low because of dumping. As to self-sufficiency, the Six produced 85 per cent of their own cereals in 1956-60 and 91 per cent in 1969-70, but in all other foods together they were 94 per cent self-sufficient in 1969-70, whereas in 1956-60 the figure had been 95 per cent. Yet even though the EEC had to import less than 10 per cent of its food, it remained the world's most important single importer of farm produce, absorbing in 1969 not much less than a quarter of the world's agricultural exports. Throughout the 1960s its agricultural imports from the rest of the world increased, but not nearly so fast as intra-Community trade in farm produce.

Among the CAP's most vociferous critics, outside France, were those who maintained that the CAP was a French device to promote French agriculture and the French economy at the expense of her neighbours. It certainly was France which benefited most in budgetary terms from the operations of the CAP. Thus, according to the *Financial Times* of 11 December 1964, France had received $45.5 million from the 'common' Agricultural Fund in 1962-4, Germany had paid in $18 million, and their four partners were also in deficit with the Fund, though for smaller amounts. What had happened, in effect, was that the five had accepted the French contention that French agricultural surpluses were a European problem and a European responsibility and should therefore be paid for by Europe. But the CAP was by no means forced through by the French alone; especially in the crucial meeting at the end of 1961, Dutch support for it was of decisive importance, and its high prices were imposed at German insistence.

Some other criticisms of the CAP have been less than fair. The spectacular frauds associated with it can hardly be blamed on it. The *Financial Times* on 24 February 1970 described how Belgian customs officials checking a lorry on the quayside at Zeebrugge found 15 tons of old railway track under a layer of beef. The owners were not smuggling scrap metal into Britain — they were exporting non-existent beef out of the Community in order to claim the Community export rebate of $300 a ton! Nor should the CAP be blamed for the dislocation, after 1969, of the agricultural common market as a result of the revaluation of the German mark and the devaluation of the franc.

The most profound criticism of the CAP of the Six was that it had failed to achieve some of its aims and that it had no indisputable success to its credit. The *New York Times* announced on 21 January 1970 that the European cow, which had been producing 711 gallons of milk annually when the CAP started six years ago, was now (1969) producing 740 gallons. But was this increased agricultural productivity really due to the CAP? And was the undeniable increase in intra-Community agricultural trade also due to the CAP? Certainly it had not succeeded in maintaining reasonably low prices, for these had risen well above the world level; nor in reducing the wage differential between agricultural and industrial workers. In West Germany, for instance, agricultural workers earned 27 per cent less than the average of all other workers in 1959-60, and 34 per cent less in 1966-7.

Perhaps it was the actual, laborious step-by-step negotiation of the CAP through the sixties, punctuated by French threats to demolish the Common Market altogether if the CAP did not go through, and accompanied by the famous 'marathon' all-night sessions of the Council of Ministers, which was the most notable thing about it. One of the longest of these sessions was the first and most important; it lasted from 12 December 1961 until 17 January 1962, was reputed to have taken up 180 hours of discussion, used 800,000 sheets of paper, and caused two agricultural experts to be taken to hospital with heart attacks. Well might the *New York Times* claim, as it did on 17 December 1961, that 'agreeing upon a common farm policy. . .is not much less difficult than launching a man into orbit in space.' The CAP was indeed, in itself, a remarkable and unqiue achievement.

The Economic Performance of the Common Market

In the nine years 1958-66 the gross national product of the EEC increased by 51 per cent, that of the United States by 46 per cent, and that of Britain by a mere 31 per cent. As for industrial production, in the ten years 1957-67, this rose by 71 per cent in the EEC, 73 per cent in the United States and only 35 per cent in Britain. Trade growth was remarkable, too: in 1958-64, while world trade as a whole increased by 50 per cent, intra-Community trade grew by 168 per cent; and in the same period EEC trade as a whole grew faster than United States trade. Put in another way, it could be said, crudely, that Community industrial production grew by 5 per cent per annum, external trade by 10 per cent and intra-Community trade by 20 per cent per annum. How far this astonishing economic performance can be attributed to the Common Market remains open to question; some of the trade growth may have been due to it, and it may have contributed importantly to the rise in standards of living. Leaving this debate for the time being in the hands of the economists, the historian is bound to conclude provisionally that the Common Market of the Six, taking the rough with the smooth, was an economic success. Certainly it was thought so at the time.

The Common Market's Voice in the World

In its common external tariff the EEC possessed an external policy instrument which the ECSC had lacked. But did the Community of the Six have a foreign policy? It certainly appeared to behave as an international entity and to develop external relations just like other powers. State after state accredited ambassadors to the Commission in Brussels until, by 1969, more than 76 countries had diplomatic relations with the EEC. On the other hand the Council for a long time refused to allow the Commission systematically to accredit ambassadors of its own to third countries. Eighteen mainly French ex-colonial African territories were associated with the EEC supposedly as equals in the two five-year Yaoundé Conventions of 1963 and 1969 and a further three — Kenya, Uganda and Tanzania — signed the Arusha Convention in 1968. As we have seen, the EEC also undertook elaborate negotiations with applicants for membership like Britain — whose 1961 bid under Conservative Prime Minister Harold Macmillan was repeated by the Labour government of Harold Wilson in 1967, and again rebuffed by France — and applicants for association like Greece and Turkey.

But these various contacts and connections did not of course amount to a single joint foreign policy of the Six. In spite of efforts at collaboration between the Foreign Ministers in 1960, and the attempts to institutionalise that collaboration from 1970 on along the lines of the Davignon Report, which we shall discuss in Chapter 11, there was only consultation, no effective coordination, still less unification, of foreign policy at this level. In any event the conduct of external relations had been almost from the start taken out of the hands of the Commission and exercised by the Council, where national disagreements made a joint Community approach exceedingly difficult. In the General Assembly of the United Nations the five Member States of the EEC who were members of that organisation (West Germany did not join until 1973) just as often voted separately as they spoke with a single voice, and they voted different ways just as often after 1958 as before. The same discord was apparent in foreign commercial policy. In 1969, just as the Commission had contrived, in readiness for the introduction of the new Community commercial policy, to see that all existing bilateral agreements with East European states had run out, the French signed a bilateral economic agreement with the Russians for the period 1970-4, as well as other agreements with Bulgaria, Hungary, Poland, Romania and Czechoslovakia. Moreover, this unilateral French move, which seemed so evidently in breach of the 'Community spirit', if not of Community regulations, was at once imitated by France's partners. Italy even contrived an agreement with Albania as well. In these circumstances the Commission had to defer its proposed replacement of bilateral by Community treaties for a further three years.

None the less, in spite of these delays and inadequacies, the EEC did very successfully make its voice heard in world affairs in the multilateral negotiations for tariff reductions organised under the auspices of GATT. In the so-called 'Dillon Round' of these negotiations, named after United States Under-Secretary of State Douglas C. Dillon, which took place in 1961-2, the Community found itself acting as one of the world's greatest trading powers in direct confrontation with the United States. The tariff reductions which emerged from the Dillon Round were never designed to be other than limited; the far more extensive bargaining of the Kennedy Round negotiations resulted in average tariff cuts of about 35 per cent by some fifty countries. These talks took place at Geneva over a four-year period, ending with the signature of the final act on 30 June 1967 by 48 of GATT's 72 members. Again, the negotiations largely took the form of a confrontation between the United States and the EEC, which spoke throughout with a single voice. They were conducted on the EEC side with a relatively free hand on behalf of the Community, especially towards the end, by the Commission in the person of Jean Rey, who had been Belgian Minister for Economic Affairs in 1954-8 before becoming the Commissioner responsible for external relations and subsequently Commission President. The Kennedy Round negotiations constituted the first truly successful example of EEC participation as a single unit in world affairs; in 1978 it still remains the most spectacular so far.

Common Market Law

The only true innovation and the only unqualified achievement of the Europe of the Six was the creation of a new and authentically supranational legal system. As the European Court of Justice in Luxembourg put it, 'the Community constitutes a new legal order in international law, on behalf of which the states have, albeit to a limited extent, restricted their sovereign rights, and whose subjects are not only the Member States but individuals as well.' In fact, the principle of the priority of Community law over national laws has been repeatedly affirmed by the Court of Justice of the EEC and accepted by the courts of the member states. For example on 18 October 1967 the German Federal Constitutional Court admitted, in Edward Wall's words, that 'the sovereign rights of the Communities. . .constituted a new sovereign power, autonomous and independent, so that their acts were directly applicable without approval or ratification by Member States; the Member States had no power to abrogate Community Acts.' And the Belgian Cour de Cassation conceded on 27 May 1971 that 'The treaties which created Community law have established a new legal order for the benefit of which the Member States have limited the exercise of their sovereign powers in the spheres dominated by these treaties.' Moreover, these spheres were widespread and ever-increasing: agriculture, customs duties, movement of labour, services and capital, restrictive practices, monopolies, and so on; indeed much of the economic and social life of the member states was likely to be affected.

Community law is, of course, applied in the main by the courts of member states. The Court of Justice itself was not overloaded with work. It registered around or rather less than a hundred cases a year in the sixties. In 1970, of the 80 such cases, 48 were appeals, two by the Commission against member states which were alleged to have levied taxes equivalent to customs duties; one by the Commission against the Council which was accused of infringing the Treaty of Rome by negotiating agreements with non-member countries when this should have been done by the Commission; one by a member state, nine by firms or private individuals, and 35 by officials. The other 32 cases were requests from national courts for a 'preliminary interpretation' under Article 177 of the Treaty of Rome, which gives the Court of Justice power to make

> preliminary rulings concerning (a) the interpretation of this Treaty; (b) the validity and interpretation of acts of the institutions of the Community; (c) the interpretation of the statutes of bodies established by an act of the Council, where those statutes so provide.

In the same year, 1970, the Court handed down 63 rulings, in three of which it held that the Italian government was in breach of Community rules: it had failed to make the required survey of vineyards, it had imposed higher customs duties on zinc and lead than those allowed by a Community decision, and it had levied a tax or duty of half a per cent on imported foods.

The tentacles of Community law not only stretched out over national sovereignties, but also extended outside the frontiers of the Six. In 1969 the Commission fined ten of Europe's giant chemical companies for concerting together to fix prices of aniline dyestuffs in violation of Article 85, Clause 1, of the Treaty of Rome, which 'prohibited as incompatible with the common market: all agreements between undertakings' which had the effect of fixing purchase or selling prices. On appeal, the Court of Justice upheld these fines. Among the firms fined were Britain's Imperial Chemical Industries (ICI) and the Swiss firms Ciba-Geigy and Sandoz. Although the fines totalled some half million dollars, they were likened to shooting peanuts at a herd of elephants. Still, the elephants were scared off!

The Achievement of the Six

The EEC of the Six, then, experienced successes and failures, but the general impression, the dominant theme, of these thirteen years, especially of those between the 1965 crisis and the departure of de Gaulle in 1969, is one of retarded progress. On the whole, the interest of member states prevailed over that of the Community, which, as it grew, was transformed into something less of a real Community, and rather more of an inter-governmental organ. Decisions were increasingly arrived at not by consulting or discovering the common good but by a process of the 'synchronisation' of concessions set against compensations. Nevertheless, the European Economic Community was successfully created. 'A new giant is arising in the world's economy,' as the *New York Herald Tribune* put it on 16 January 1961. And, after its creation and consolidation, the foundations were effectively laid, in spite of difficulties, for its expansion from a Community of Six to one of Nine. But the history of the enlarged Community, from 1973 onwards, is the subject of the concluding chapter of this work.

EUROPE BEYOND THE SIX, 1950-70

In the previous chapter we saw that, in spite of some outstanding achievements, the Europe of the Six, that is, the EEC, was often divided against itself. Although we discerned integration here and there, disarray obtruded at every point. But when we turn from the EEC to the populace at large, and to the rest of the European continent, we find disarray even more to the forefront and, in spite of scattered examples of cooperation between states, little that goes further than this; little or nothing that merits the name of integration. The West continues to suffer from a multiplicity of organisations all aiming at promoting unity but yet operating as more or less separate entities: some or all of the member states of the Six belonged to Benelux, the OEEC (OECD), the Council of Europe and NATO. From 1960 onwards, EFTA was ranged against the Common Market of the Six, to which EEC members did not belong. We shall glance briefly, in this chapter, at the − mostly somewhat unimpressive − developments in these organisations in the fifties and sixties. Then, turning away from the West, we shall look north to consider the progress towards unity made by the Nordic countries in this period, and finally east to the Communist People's Democracies. But this examination of developments outside the narrow confines of the EEC must begin with some discussion of the forces of public opinion in the West.

Public Opinion in the West

At any rate within the Six, public opinion seems to have been consistently in favour of European unification throughout the 1950s and 1960s. In France, apart from a drop in the second half of 1954 after the collapse of EDC, over 60 per cent of those questioned consistently favoured moves towards European unification. Between 1957 and 1962 support for a European federation grew from 37 to 40 per cent in France, from 46 to 54 per cent in West Germany, and from 40 to 44 per cent in Italy. As to the Common Market itself, the comparable figures in 1957 and 1962 were: France, support up from 60 to 76 per cent; West Germany, up from 73 to 85 per cent, and in Italy, up from 73 to 76 per cent. On the other hand, the formation of the Community does not seem to have had much effect on Europeans' feelings about their neighbours, except as regards Franco-German relations. In the fifties these were none too good. A 1956 UNESCO poll found, perhaps predictably, that the Germans, Belgians and Dutch thought the French were lazy, sloppy or dirty, boastful, arrogant and chauvinistic; while the French, Belgians and Dutch thought the Germans were authoritarian, militaristic, cruel, brutal and hard. But as early as 1962 Gallup's International Survey could find no more evidence of a Franco-German problem; fear, distrust and rivalry on the French side had disappeared. On the other hand, a 1970 poll mentioned by R.T. Shepherd in his book on 'European' public opinion recorded that, while 86 per cent of Germans had confidence in the French and 48 per cent of Frenchmen had confidence in the Germans, both had greater confidence in the English, the Americans and the Swiss! We may perhaps disregard the author's comment that 'This indicates the existence of an Atlantic-European pluralistic-security-community'; it certainly shows that many people in the two leading members of the Six had developed little EEC solidarity. That nationalism was still a force in these countries at the end of the period under review is shown by the fact that, in 1970, while there were majorities in each of the Six for a single European currency, there were large majorities everywhere for the retention of national flags, and only one country, Luxembourg, favoured fielding a European Olympic Games team instead of national ones!

Pressure Groups

'European' public opinion was based on self-interest rather than intellectual or ideological considerations. Fear of Russia and Communism was important, but also a firm belief that economic growth, expanding trade and industrial modernisation were all to some extent products of the Common Market. This 'European' opinion was led and encouraged by various organisations and pressure groups, many of which dated from before 1950. Most widespread of these was the European Movement, founded in 1948, which was organised into a number of national councils. It held international congresses and was broadly based enough to number among its members both unionists, functionalists and out-and-out federalists. However, it experienced a 'swing to the left' in the years after 1951, when P.H. Spaak was elected its President after his resignation from the presidency of the Consultative Assembly of the Council of Europe in Strasbourg. He formed an Action Committee of the national councils of the European Movement of the six member states of the ECSC to support that organisation and the EDC. The June 1957 'European Congress' of the European Movement in Rome, presided over by Robert Schuman, created quite a stir. It comprised nearly a thousand delegates in all, a quarter of them from France (including Valéry Giscard d'Estaing), but a mere sixteen from Britain. The Congress accepted F. Dehousse's proposal for a European political authority and asserted its belief, in its final resolution, that 'Europe forms an indivisible historical and cultural entity of which the Europe of the Six constitutes the advance guard on the institutional level'. But not everyone greeted this Congress with enthusiasm. The Italian weekly *Mondo Economico* was scathing in the extreme. An article entitled *Modi (eloquenti) di non fare l'Europa* – '(Eloquent) methods of not making Europe' – claimed that 'When President Gronchi had finished pronouncing his eloquent appeal for European unity, one could conclude that the solemn international congress of the European Movement had nothing more to say.' Five years later, in June 1962, the European Movement held a congress at Munich specially to promote the idea of a 'European Political Community'. This brought together, besides the various national councils of the European Movement, some dozen affiliated organisations. However, these activities did nothing to prevent the influence of the Movement from declining from the high peak it had achieved in 1948, when it had made an important contribution to the founding of the Council of Europe.

Founded in 1946, the Union of European Federalists (UEF) was an international federation of federalist movements. The success of its congress at Montreux in Switzerland in autumn 1947 was somewhat overshadowed by the Hague Congress of May 1948, out of which the European Movement emerged. But the UEF came into its own again in 1950, when it launched and conducted for several years a popular campaign for a European federal pact. Known in West Germany as the *Feldzug der Völker*, or 'people's campaign', it was organised there by the Europa-Union and backed by a Bundestag resolution and federal funds. By the time of the UEF congress in Venice in April 1953, a petition had been signed by 1,647,395 people in the German Federal Republic, and over half a million Italians had signed a similar petition for a federal pact by the time it was approved by the Chamber of Deputies in November 1950. But the UEF was in no position to follow up these successes. In 1952 its principal French member organisation, La Fédération, seceded from it, and in 1955-6 it was torn apart by internal wrangling. While Altiero Spinelli and his – mainly Italian – followers, convinced after the failure of EDC in August 1954 that there was no future in the Europe of the Six, raised the standard of revolutionary opposition to the national states, the Dutch, German (Europa-Union) and French (La Fédération) federalists joined at The Hague on 21 July 1956 to form the Action Centre of European Federalists (AEF), coming out in firm support of the Common Market then under negotiation.

Spinelli's plan of action, which was supported by radical French federalists like Guy Héraud and Alexandre Marc and in general by his own Movimento Federalista Europeo (MFE), was certainly novel and radical, if not quite revolutionary in the traditional sense. The man who had formerly helped to persuade the governments of the Six to accept Article 38 of the EDC treaty, which provided for the creation of a European Political Community (EPC), now made a direct appeal to the people of Europe. From autumn 1957 onwards, popular elections of delegates to a series of Congresses of the European People, with the aim of setting up a European constituent assembly, were organised by Spinelli and his associates.

The first Congresso del Popolo Europeo was held at Turin on 6-8 December 1957. Some 240 delegates from eight European cities – Antwerp, Düsseldorf, Maastricht, Lyons, Strasbourg, Geneva, Milan and Turin, directly elected by 75,000 voters, solemnly resolved that 'The constitution of the United States of Europe cannot be achieved merely by the national governments and parliaments. It can only be the creation of a constituent authority emanating from the European people.' Spinelli launched a monthly paper called *Popolo Europeo* in support of the European People's Congress movement; the first issue was published in January 1958 in Turin in four languages. By the time the fourth session of the Congress was held in 1960 at Ostend the electorate numbered nearly half a million. But the movement lost momentum in the early 1960s; it was absorbed into the Movimento Federalista Europeo (MFE) and its paper finally ceased publication in 1964. The MFE too, losing all political influence in Italy from about 1963 onwards, fell upon evil days. By 1967 the Italian federalists were said to be 'prisoners of the fantasies of the past, continuing to speak a language which had become incomprehensible to most' of their fellow-countrymen.

Other less influential pressure groups continued to work for European unity in one form or another, through the 1950s and 1960s, but made little impact on public opinion. The European League for Economic Cooperation (ELEC) could still muster a hundred or so delegates in January 1953 for a conference which pleaded for the convertibility of currencies and the removal of all restrictions on imports. Richard Coudenhove-Kalergi's European Parliamentary Union did not survive into the fifties; instead, he reorganised the Pan-Europa Union, which still exists, in spite of its founder's death in 1972, but has little real influence outside Austria. In the sixties he and his movement, always right-wing, became openly Gaullist. An exchange of correspondence took place between Colombey-les-deux-Eglises and Gstaad which displayed a certain mutual rapture on either side. De Gaulle received Coudenhove several times while he was president; in 1965 Coudenhove even resigned from being one of the *présidents d'honneur* of the European Movement because it had become too anti-Gaullist for his tastes. Finally, in 1970 he sent an open letter to Brandt, Colombo, Heath and Pompidou, urging them to execute de Gaulle's 'European testament' by developing political cooperation through 'Great Power' initiatives. He appealed to Britain and Italy to join the Franco-German treaty, set up a political general secretariat, and organise a foreign policy in common. Although his motives were a response to the time-honoured Communist spectre – he wanted a more effective counterweight to the Warsaw Pact – which was not widely shared in 1970, nevertheless, as we shall see in the last chapter, some of the ideas Coudenhove put forward in his open letter were indeed taken up by the leaders of the Six and then the Nine.

We have already underlined the vital role in the history of European unity played by the Resistance movement, whose ideas had once been in the van of European federalism. Now in the 1950s, its dying embers leaped momentarily into flames: in 1952 the Union des Résistants pour une Europe Unie (URPE) was founded in Brussels. By 1955 the organisation included national sections in Belgium, France, Italy, Luxembourg and the Netherlands and it survived into the sixties: on 5 May 1965 at Strasbourg 300 ex-Resistance fighters from thirteen countries, including over fifty ex-Ministers and MPs, made a stirring appeal for more progress towards a united Europe.

More influential than the URPE was another organisation, the Conseil des Communes d'Europe (CCE), or Council of European Municipalities, which owes its influence partly to the fact that its membership has never been confined to the territories of the Six. It was founded at a conference in Geneva on 28-30 January 1951 attended by some sixty burgomasters and town councillors from Denmark, France, West Germany, Italy, Luxembourg, the Netherlands and Switzerland. The inspiration of, and initiative for, this federation of local authorities or communes came from Edouard Herriot, himself long-time mayor of Lyons, and the Swiss academic Adolf Gasser, who had advocated the post-war reconstruction of Europe in terms of a federation of independent communes instead of the system of national states in his book *L'autonomie communale et la reconstruction de l'Europe,* published in 1946 (a French version of his *Die Gemeindefreiheit Rettung Europas* of 1943). A powerful stimulus came from Italy, where Umberto Serafini soon devoted his energies to building up the Italian section of the CCE – the Associazione Italiana per il Consiglio dei Comuni d'Europa. Serafini was a disciple of Adriano Olivetti, a publisher who had translated the English federalists into Italian and whose remarkable book *L'ordine politico delle comunità*, originally published in Switzerland in 1944, made its author one of the most profound and influential political theorists of post-war Europe.

The French, German and Italian sections of the CCE publicised their activities in their respective monthly papers – *Communes d'Europe, Der Europäische Gemeindetag* and *Comuni d'Europa.* Enthusiasm ran high. An editorial in *Comuni d'Europa* of 15 January 1953 proclaimed:

> 1953 must be the year in which the European federation is constituted. Either the governments will do this or it will be launched by the communes and local communities, in spite of the governments and in the name of the people.

Needless to say, the communes and local communities did not bring about a European federation, but they did hold a series of assemblies or 'States

General of Europe', to use their own phrase, and they did much to encourage town twinning (see Chapter 10 below). The membership of the CCE continued to increase. By 1958 some 37,000 communes (there are about 66,000 communes in France, West Germany and Italy) in nine countries, including Austria and Britain, belonged to it. In July 1970 it even held its States General in London. Throughout the sixties it remained one of Western Europe's most popular and effective pressure-groups, supporting moves of every kind toward European unification, both within and outside the Six.

Intergovernmental Organisations

The historian of European integration would rightly be accused of negligence if, in his account of the 1950s and 1960s, he entirely omitted to mention the activities of those firmly established organs Benelux, the ECE at Geneva, OEEC, the Council of Europe, NATO and the WEU. But the briefest mention only must suffice, for they were for the most part passive, more or less inert or ineffective, or even in overt decline. They remained part of history but they had long since ceased to make it.

Benelux, surprisingly perhaps, continued in existence in spite of the EEC, which might have been expected to swallow it up. The Treaty of Rome was indeed in many ways more far-reaching, more supranational for example; but its Article 233 specifically allowed for 'the existence or completion of regional unions between Belgium and Luxembourg, or between Belgium, Luxembourg and the Netherlands, to the extent that the objectives of these regional unions are not attained by application of this Treaty'. Less than three months after the signature of the Treaty of Rome, the Benelux Council of Ministers agreed in June 1957 in substance to a new fifty-year Treaty of Economic Union, which was signed in February 1958 and came into force on 1 January 1960. Thereafter Benelux struggled on through the sixties with its three-man Council of Ministers, its 48-strong Inter-parliamentary Consultative Council meeting annually from 1957 on, and its committees and other institutions, trying hard to secure the free movement of workers, to abolish barriers to intra-Benelux trade, to implement fully the 1950 excise duties convention and complete it with a further convention which was still not ratified in 1978, to create an agricultural common market of its own, and in general to construct a more or less complete economic union. It did not fall far behind, nor did it forge far ahead of, the EEC. It avoided forming a 'directorate' within that organisation, but sometimes acted as a stimulus to it and, sometimes, emulated it. Thus in 1965 its member states signed a treaty setting up a Benelux Court of Justice; characteristically, this did not come into force until 1 January 1974. In Benelux, everything is in slow motion.

The United Nations Economic Commission for Europe, with its secretariat based in Geneva, remained throughout the fifties and sixties, and still remains, the only all-European regional organisation for economic cooperation. The Commission, whose working languages are English, French and Russian, meets once a year and comes to decisions by unanimous vote. Some thirty countries belonged to it by 1970. One of its main tasks was the promotion of East-West trade, but it has also been concerned with economic projections and planning, scientific and technological cooperation and environmental improvement. Among its many publications was the annual *Economic survey of Europe.*

In Paris, the seventeen-nation OEEC continued its activities in the 1950s, working through its Council, which met two or three times a year at ministerial level, but virtually every week at the level of the member states' permanent representatives. By 1959, however, two of the OEEC's principal objectives had been reached: the European currencies had become generally convertible at the end of 1958, when the European Payments Union (EPU) had been replaced by the European Monetary Agreement; and more than 90 per cent of intra-OEEC trade had been successfully liberalised. At the very same time, namely the end of 1958, the breakdown of the Maudling negotiations for a wide industrial free-trade area to embrace the whole of the OEEC effectively brought to an end that organisation's role, which had never been of much importance, in the promotion of European economic integration. Partly for these reasons, in 1959-61, on mainly American but partly Jean Monnet's initiative, the OEEC was transformed from a European economic organisation into a club of developed Western nations with the prime objective of solving the economic problems of the less developed countries, chiefly by coordinating and increasing aid to them. The re-named Organization for Economic Cooperation and Development (OECD) continued to be responsible for the European Nuclear Energy Agency but it was no longer a purely European body: the United States and Canada, which had been associate members of the OEEC, became full members of the OECD, and Japan joined in 1964. By 1965 the budget of OECD amounted to about 82 million French francs, and its staff numbered some 1,200 civil servants.

Neither NATO nor WEU contributed significantly to European integration in the 1950s and 1960s. Seven-power WEU scarcely formed a significant political entity; its *raison d'être* was to allow Germany to contribute to Western defence; it also formed a useful link between Britain and the EEC. Its Council was identical in membership to that of the Six, with a British Minister in addition. For example, the WEU Council communiqué of 18 March 1957 was issued in London by Spaak, Pineau, Hallstein, Bech, Luns and Martino — the very same people who signed the Treaty of Rome a week later — and British Foreign Minister Selwyn Lloyd. As to the WEU Assembly, all its members also represented their countries in the Consultative Assembly of the Council of Europe at Strasbourg.

Defence was one of the special responsibilities of the WEU yet, up to 1964 in the course of nine sessions, the vast majority of the Assembly's forty or so recommendations on defence matters were ignored by the WEU member governments.

Western European Union existed within the framework of NATO, which itself was in serious difficulties in the late fifties and sixties. We have already seen how France was withdrawn from NATO by de Gaulle, who forced it to move its headquarters from Paris to Brussels. NATO has remained a largely intergovernmental organ but it does comprise certain 'supranational' elements, namely the integrated staffs at the different NATO headquarters, some air defence units on constant alert, the standing Naval Force Atlantic of destroyers set up in 1967, and the standing Naval Force Channel of minesweepers, both of ships from different NATO countries. NATO's central institutions are closely similar to those of WEU: the North Atlantic Council meets twice a year at ministerial level and weekly at the level of permanent representatives; the 'North Atlantic Assembly', which holds an annual plenary session, is not, however, formally part of NATO. In spite of the lengthening list of so-called 'NATO projects', such as the Jaguar tactical and training aircraft and the Tornado multi-role combat aircraft, NATO has in fact achieved very little in terms of the standardisation and joint production of defence equipment. The responsibility for equipping defence forces has remained firmly national, and joint production and procurement has been limited to a few projects only, none of them shared by more than a handful of NATO partners. Thus the Jaguar, agreed in 1965, is an Anglo-French project, and the Tornado, agreed in 1968, which went into production in 1976, is manufactured by West Germany, Italy and Britain; their governments plan to share 807 of these aircraft between them. NATO did, however, set up a 'common infrastructure', mainly of pipelines (10,000 kilometres) and airfields (over 200), which is financed collectively by member governments (though France opted out of much of it in 1966), but this infrastructure is administered piecemeal by the member governments on whose territories it is situated. On the whole, NATO has utterly failed to develop into a single effectively integrated defence force. Each member of the alliance maintains its own independent military establishment which, in the case of three members – the United States, France and Britain – includes a national nuclear force. Since 1968 the Eurogroup, consisting of twice-yearly meetings of defence ministers, has emerged within NATO and has tried to rationalise and standardise equipment procurement and harmonise defence policies. One would be able to take its efforts more seriously if Iceland, Portugal and, above all, France, were members.

In many ways the European Free Trade Association (EFTA) was a sort of club of countries that had been, as it were, left out of the EEC, yet still hoped to be associated with it in some way. Its first Secretary-General,

Sir Frank Figgures, pointed out in 1966 that the EFTA powers were all agreed that their organisation was a bridge towards an eventual settlement with the European Economic Community. The puzzling thing about EFTA is why it was created and who initiated it? Asked the former question, Frank Figgures replied blandly that he had no idea; *he* certainly had not recommended it! It did not emerge from the Anglo-Scandinavian Economic Committee, or Uniscan, the meetings of British and Scandinavian ministers or officials which had been taking place two or three times a year through the fifties. It seems to have been discussed at a luncheon given in Paris by Paymaster-General Reginald Maudling for the three Scandinavian Ministers of Commerce — Gunnar Lange, Arne Skaug and Jens Otto Krag — immediately after the breakdown of the Maudling negotiations in November 1958. But the idea had been put to Maudling in June 1958 by the then Director of the Commercial Division of the Swiss federal Department of Economic Affairs, Hans Haffner. In any event, since the British were the dominant power among the 'outer Seven', they preferred to leave it to the Swedes or Swiss to play the role of initiators, at any rate in public. So it was that a first, secret meeting of officials without government instructions took place on 1-2 December 1958 in Geneva on Haffner's invitation, to discuss the possibility of a smaller seven-power free-trade area; a second meeting was held in February 1959 in Oslo, and negotiations between the Seven formally began at Saltsjöbaden near Stockholm on 1 June, after a great deal of activity by the Swedish official Hubert de Besche. A draft plan for EFTA was drawn up there in just under a fortnight: 'This was no negotiation! We all agreed', Figgures is reported to have said. The Convention of Stockholm establishing the European Free Trade Association was signed on 4 January and EFTA came into existence on 3 May 1960, largely through the efforts of a handful of civil servants.

EFTA was a much more modest affair than the EEC. Its treaty, which was in fact only a Convention, contained a mere 44 articles and 7 appendices; its institutions were limited to a Council meeting at ministerial level 2 or 3 times a year and weekly in Geneva at the level of permanent representatives, and a small secretariat of about seventy persons also in Geneva; the population of its member states totalled only around a hundred million, over half of them in Britain, as opposed to the Common Market's 180 million; and its immediate aims, successfully accomplished by 1966, were limited to the abolition of tariffs and quotas on most industrial goods. Moreover, EFTA, unlike the Common Market, enjoyed no internal balance as between its members; Britain by far outweighed her partners in every important respect. Yet Britain had little or no real interest in EFTA. While, by 1967, all EFTA members save Britain had increased their exports to fellow members by well over 100 per cent, Britain had increased hers by only 94 per cent. Seemingly mesmerised by the EEC, she had, in 1961 and again in 1967, applied for membership of that organisation, on the second occasion evidently ignoring her obligations under the so-called 'London Declaration' of 28 June 1961 to coordinate the negotiations with her EFTA partners. Nor was her standing in that Association improved by the action in October 1964 of her new Labour government, in slapping a 15 per cent import duty on industrial goods.

In spite of these shortcomings, EFTA forms part of the history of integration in post-war Europe. It did seem to have a favourable trade effect, it did create a partial Nordic common market which the Nordic countries had been unable to set up on their own, it did bring Finland some way further out of her isolation when she joined as an associate member in 1961. For the smaller members especially, it did provide some economic compensation for their exclusion from the Common Market of the Six and, more important, it did give them a sense of solidarity and indeed of participation in the movement towards European unification. Nor should it be forgotten that EFTA did link together groups of states that had for centuries been closely associated, namely Portugal and Britain, Britain and the Scandinavian countries, the Nordic countries themselves and, of course, Austria and Switzerland, with the latter's diminutive customs union partner Liechtenstein. Thus it was not an entirely haphazhard or artificial association of states.

The only one of the EFTA Seven to persevere without interruption through the sixties in her approach to the EEC was Austria. Because of her neutrality, which was laid down in a law of 26 October 1955, the promulgation of which coincided with the withdrawal of the last occupation forces, she could not consider full membership. But Germany was her traditional trading partner and over half her exports went to the EEC, so she applied for associate membership. After long delays, the Council of Ministers offered in March 1965 to begin negotiations for a trade agreement, but these were subsequently broken off by Italy, then at loggerheads with Austria over the South Tyrol, which had been ceded to Italy in 1919 though it had wanted to remain in Austria. It was only in 1969 that Italy withdrew her opposition to further negotiations with Austria, and she was eventually able, along with her EFTA partners, to sign a free-trade agreement for industrial goods with the EEC, to come into force on 1 January 1973. But, as a reward for her persistence, Austria obtained concessions from the EEC three months before the treaty dateline.

In discussing the EEC and EFTA, only two West European countries have not been taken into consideration, and these may, for the sake of completeness, be mentioned here. They are Ireland and Spain. Although not a member of EFTA, Ireland became indirectly associated with it in 1965 when the Anglo-Irish Free Trade Area was set up, which abolished quotas and the remaining duties on imports of one partner from the other. Spain's relationship with the EEC in the sixties was not unlike Austria's. Having joined OEEC in 1959, it was only natural that she should apply for association with the EEC in 1962. But, though France and the Federal German Republic supported her application, Belgium and the Netherlands opposed it on ideological grounds, and Italy regarded her as an undesirable commercial rival. So Council and Commission dragged their heels. Spain lowered her sights, and eventually, in 1967, negotiations began for a trade agreement which was finally signed in 1970; it was blatantly unfavourable to Spain.

One other Western organisation, outside the Six, remains to be considered – the Council of Europe which, with its eighteen members, its azure flag with a circle of twelve gold stars or mullets, its splendid newly rebuilt (1977) Palais de l'Europe at Strasbourg, its pioneering early history, and its proud celebration of 'Europe Day' on its own anniversary, 5 May, is supposed to form a framework and centre for European integration in the West. But, even though its Consultative Assembly (renamed Parliamentary Assembly in 1974) receives and debates the annual reports of the OECD, the European Parliament, the EEC Commission, EFTA and others, the Council of Europe never has been in a position to take the lead in European integration. Its flimsy intergovernmental structure has never provided it with any political muscle; from 1958 onwards it was in any event increasingly overshadowed by the EEC which, diverting away from the Council of Europe the attentions and energies of six of its members, had originated spontaneously in 1955-7 with scarcely more than a whisper of encouragement from the Consultative Assembly.

By the early 1970s the EEC employed some 10,000 persons (fewer, though, than the Wandsworth Borough Council) compared to the Council of Europe's mere 700, and the Council of Europe's budget was well under 1 per cent of that of the EEC. What did the Council of Europe achieve in the 1950s and 1960s? It expanded only very slowly, welcoming Austria in 1956, Switzerland in 1963, and Cyprus and Malta in 1961 and 1965 respectively, after they became independent. Concentrating its energies in certain restricted fields, in 1950 it drew up and arranged for the signature of the European Convention for the Protection of Human Rights and Fundamental Freedoms, and this was followed by numerous other Conventions and agreements: for example on *au pair* girl placement and innkeepers' liability for guests' property, and, more importantly, a European Cultural Convention (1954) and a European Social Charter (1961). To enforce the precise legal obligations embodied in the Human Rights Convention, which has now been ratified by all member states save France and Switzerland, a Commission was set up in 1954 and a Court in 1959. This apparatus has enjoyed some practical success: for example, the British government was partly influenced by it in its 1959 settlement of the Cyprus problem, the Swedish government was persuaded to liberalise school religious instruction, the 1814 Norwegian constitution was amended in 1956 by the removal of its ban on Jesuits, and both Belgium and Austria changed their laws to avoid contravening the Human Rights Convention. The Council of Europe was also responsible for a programme of cultural cooperation which included singularly ineffective meetings of Ministers of Education, art exhibitions and, in 1961, the establishment of the Council for Cultural Cooperation (CCC) which, however, has lacked financial backing and political influence. Finally, in 1961, it endowed the European Conference of Local Authorities with a charter, and it has also kept in close contact with the Conseil des Communes d'Europe (CCE).

Needless to say, the Council of Europe continued throughout the fifties and sixties to be divided conspicuously against itself. The German deputy Karl Mommer (SPD) raised the general applause of the Consultative Assembly by his witty remark on 25 October 1955: 'Instead of making efforts to find a solution for every difficulty, the Committee of Ministers does its best to find a difficulty in the way of every solution.'

Norden – the Countries of the North

Integration in Europe during the fifties and sixties seemed to be taking place separately in three separate areas, and to be assuming a very different form in each of them. Although such loose groupings of states as the OECD and the Council of Europe extended over the west and the north of Europe and an even looser one, the ECE, embraced the west, north and east, in actual fact the west was dominated by the European Economic Community of the Six, while the north formed a separate 'club' of devotees of 'Nordic cooperation' – *nordisk samarbeid* – and the east continued on its own way. There was nothing permanent in this state of affairs, which did not survive through the seventies; none the less the Scandinavian countries did until then seem to form a separate more or less stable group, with their similarities of language and monarchical constitution, their state-subsidised Lutheran religion and their socialism, their not very dissimilar economic and political power, their long-standing preference for collaboration and harmonisation as against any form of supranationalism, the high proportion of their gross national product derived from trade – much of it intra-Nordic – and their geographical proximity. As we saw in Chapter 5, in spite of their failure to form a joint Scandinavian defence alliance in 1948-9, which drove a wedge between neutral Sweden and NATO members Norway and Denmark, the Scandinavian countries did set up the Nordic Council in 1953 and they did continue their efforts to establish a common Nordic market or customs union right through the fifties. Moreover, the transition from 'Scandinavian' to 'Nordic' by the addition of Finland, Iceland and perhaps The Faeroes and Greenland, was not a difficult one – Finland's neutrality, 'special relationship' with the Soviet Union, and language difference apart.

The notion that the 'cooperation' of the Nordic countries is somehow different in kind from the 'integration' of the Common Market, that the

Common Market embodies a 'supranational element', a 'Community spirit' or 'method' absent in Norden, is a misleading myth. It takes a legal expert to discern supranationalism in ECSC procedures, and whatever traces of it were enshrined in the Treaty of Rome were soon erased in practice. The EEC, as we have seen, rapidly and decisively moved away, in the sixties, from supranationalism towards intergovernmental collaboration, and many of its procedures approximated more and more to those of Nordic cooperation — always excepting its Court and Commission, and its commitment to 'ever closer union'.

On the other hand, there was at least one important respect in which Nordic cooperation differed from EEC 'integration'. While the Six made innovations and took initiatives, made political decisions to go ahead and left the experts to sort out details, 'made the running', in fact, the Nordic countries remained largely passive. After all, they were small powers: their foreign policies tended to be somewhat negative, based on responses to others' initiatives. It has been said that Finland never acts without first consulting Russia; Norway never acts without consulting America; and Sweden sounds them both out before any foreign policy move. The Nordic countries did invariably discuss Nordic solutions, but these were usually deferred while the broader European alternative was considered. As Danish Foreign Minister Per Haekkerup said of the Nordic common market discussions in the fifties, 'while we were discussing and elaborating these problems from every conceivable angle, developments in Europe passed us by.' In the event, the more widely based alternative on that occasion was EFTA, which did in fact revitalise Nordic cooperation and probably did increase intra-Nordic trade: by the end of 1966 it had created a Nordic free-trade area which affected over 80 per cent of industrial goods.

Just as, at the end of the fifties, the much-talked-of Nordic customs union was overtaken by EFTA, so, at the end of the sixties, that same customs union, still under discussion but by then apparently nearer fruition, was overtaken by the further evolution of the EEC after de Gaulle's departure. The extended Nordic economic cooperation which newly elected Danish Prime Minister Hilmar Baunsgaard originally proposed in the Nordic Council's Oslo session on 17 February 1968 went considerably further than the creation of a customs union; it led to the formulation of something amounting to a Nordic economic union, which was given the name Nordek, although the draft treaty setting it up, dated 17 July 1969, was entitled *Treaty establishing the Organization for Nordic Economic Cooperation* and the phrase 'Nordic Economic Union' was not used. The cause of this renewed effort of Nordic cooperation in 1968-9 was complex. Prime Minister Baunsgaard needed a foreign policy or Nordic initiative of some kind to launch his new right-wing coalition government. De Gaulle's second 'No!' in 1967 to British membership of the EEC had convinced the Nordic governments that all possibility of their joining or associating themselves with the EEC would be deferred for years. They were likewise convinced that there was little possibility of expanding economic activities within EFTA which had, however, by increasing intra-Nordic trade and otherwise, had the effect of removing some of the obstacles which had stood in the way of a Nordic customs union in the 1950s. Moreover, in the recently completed Kennedy Round negotiations for the lowering of tariffs (GATT), the four Nordic countries had demonstrated their solidarity in a remarkable way in November 1966 by signing a treaty which created a single Nordic delegation at Geneva out of the four national ones, to be led by the Swede Nils Montan. Thereafter, they negotiated as a single unit and this encouraged the belief that they were ready for further economic cooperation.

Although in 1968-9 all four Nordic governments were fully committed to Nordek which, all agreed, was to be based on a Nordic customs union, there were substantial difficulties to be overcome. One of the most insuperable was the very nature of Nordek. Although it originated as a response to the exclusion of the Nordic countries from EEC, it was never supposed to be an alternative to the EEC; it was rather an eventual bridge to it, a complement to it, a parallel development which might later be merged with it in some way. Other difficulties were the delicate position of Finland *vis-à-vis* Russia, which meant that, for the Finns, Nordek could not open the way towards EEC membership, Swedish enthusiasm for a common external tariff not shared by Norway and Denmark, and Danish insistence on the creation of a common market for agriculture as well as in industrial goods, which would create problems, especially for Norway. These difficulties accounted for some serious gaps in the draft Nordek treaty of July 1969 which, however, embodied a substantial agreed programme. Like EFTA, but unlike the EEC as defined by the Treaty of Rome, the institutional arrangements for Nordek were intergovernmental and not at all supranational — there was a Council of Ministers deciding unanimously but no Commission; like the EEC but unlike EFTA, there was to be a customs union, a common agricultural policy and fund, and the other traditional trappings of a common market as outlined in the Treaty of Rome: economic, industrial, energy and social policies developed in common, abolition of restrictions on capital movements, development of a common (Nordic) labour market, and so on.

Why was it then that Nordek — the Nordic Organization for Economic Cooperation — was abandoned in March 1970 just as the final difficulties in the way of its realisation had been resolved? Chiefly because, following the disappearance of General de Gaulle from the political scene in May 1969, at the EEC summit in The Hague in December 1969 the Common Market heads of government 'indicated their agreement to the opening of negotiations between the Community on the one hand and the applicant states on the other. They agreed that. . .the preparations would take place in a most positive spirit.' Thus the road to Brussels was open, and Denmark, followed by Norway, was glad to take it. They had little objection, in these new circumstances, to abandoning a project about which the Finns had all along been doubtful, and which, as Prime Minister Mauno Koivisto announced on 24 March 1970, they could not now bring themselves to accept. Instead, like the Swedes, they would seek an arrangement with the EEC, short of the full membership favoured by the governments of Denmark and Norway. Thus Nordek collapsed, victim of Nordic hesitations and the renewed dynamic of the post-de Gaulle EEC.

While Nordic cooperation thus sometimes suffered through the Nordic countries' sensitivity to developments elsewhere, it was at other times stepped up to compensate for these and other setbacks to Nordic solidarity. Thus the Nordic Council was set up to reaffirm Nordic solidarity after the failure of the defence union had divided Sweden from the others, and early difficulties in the Nordic common market talks had put Norway on one side. This pattern was repeated in 1961-2, when a certain disarray in the Nordic ranks became evident as Norway and Denmark applied for membership of the EEC, Sweden hung back but sought association, and Finland seemed increasingly isolated. In November 1961 the Prime Ministers agreed to draw up a convention setting out the aims and importance of Nordic cooperation, and this puff of Nordic hot air, which became known as the Helsinki Treaty, was approved by the Nordic Council at Helsinki and was signed by the governments, in March 1962. 'It was watered down, it was altogether too general, it was not binding,' said former Finnish Prime Minister and President of the Nordic Council K.A. Fagerholm, but it was better than nothing. The same pattern was repeated in the years after 1970 when efforts were made to reinforce Nordic cooperation after the collapse of Nordek — but these developments of the seventies will be noted in their place in Chapter 11.

Nordic cooperation, at least until the seventies, has never been highly institutionalised. Most of it took the form of informal contacts between government departments, top civil servants, lawyers and all kinds of private organisation. The best-known but least effective Nordic institution was the Nordic Council, itself so little institutionalised that it had no fixed headquarters and its secretariat numbered under 100 persons, divided between Stockholm, Oslo and Copenhagen — as against Comecon's 1,500 and the EEC's 10,000 or so. Dealing in the main with vague generalities or minute trivia, its 700-odd recommendations between 1953 and 1970 concerned cultural matters (209), transport (145), the law (121) and social affairs (115); only 91 related to economic matters. The fact that 60 per cent of these recommendations have been implemented or accepted by the governments does not reflect the importance of the Nordic Council. Time and again the governments simply have not put important matters to the Nordic Council; they have gone along with it but without encouraging or developing it. Norwegian dislike of it was reflected in the fourth annual session at Copenhagen in 1956, when Norwegian Prime Minister Einar Gerhardsen suggested that it might meet only every other year. It was at this session, in January 1956, that Finland joined the Nordic Council, after President J.K. Paasikivi and Prime Minister Urho Kekkonen had made soundings in Moscow in autumn 1955 and found the Russians not unfavourable, provided that defence and foreign policy were not discussed.

Between 1945 and 1970 some seventy joint Nordic organisations to promote cooperation in different fields were set up — over fifty of them in the 1960s. They included the Nordic Committee for the Labour Market (1954), which administered the Nordic Labour Market set up at that time, the Nordic Committee for Social Policy (1946 and 1951), and the Nordic Committee for Economic Cooperation (1954-71). The very successful Nordel was established in 1963 to supervise the distribution of electricity through the interconnected national power grids. Before the creation of the Nordic Council, in July 1951, the Nordic Parliamentary Committee for Freer Communications had been set up, which was superseded in 1957-63 by the Nordic Council's Communications or Traffic Committee (Nordisk Samfärdselkomité).

It was the earlier of these committees which proposed, in 1953, that the Swedes should switch over to driving on the right-hand side of the road. It calculated that well over one-third of traffic accidents were due to the Swedish rule of driving on the left. However, the Swedes themselves were determined to stay on the left: in a referendum on 16 September 1955 83 per cent of them said no to their government's proposal to drive on the right (*högertrafik*). Years later, when the Swedish Riksdag decided on 10 May 1963 to change to *högertrafik* without consulting the people, this was said to be more a demonstration of Swedish solidarity with the rest of Europe than an example of Nordic cooperation — though the Nordic Council had made representations in favour of *högertrafik* in 1961. The change-over was successfully achieved at last on Sunday 3 September 1967 at a cost of some 200 million Swedish crowns paid for partly by a special motor-car tax. A dramatic fall in the accident rate resulted: on the first day of *högertrafik* the only casualty in the whole of Sweden was an apparently inebriated cyclist who inadvertently collided with a tree. Road deaths were down 20 per cent in the first year. In 1969, Iceland followed suit, saving money by re-using the Swedish road-signs and posters; surely this at least was a gesture of Nordic solidarity? However, if road traffic in all Nordic countries thereafter went on the right, it certainly did not go at the same speed. While Danish experiments suggested that speed limits were of no use whatsoever, the Swedes had a system of variable speed limits so complicated that a Swedish judge once said in public that it was nearly impossible to drive a car in Sweden without breaking the rules. The result: a quite different system of speed limits and traffic regulations persisted in each Nordic country.

One of the more notable achievements of Nordic cooperation in the fifties and sixties was the abolition of 'internal' passports, that is, the creation of a Nordic Passport Union, in spite of the somwhat absurd fears expressed in some quarters that this might lead to an influx of spies! The project was initiated by the Nordic Parliamentary Committee for Freer Communications and came into force, after years of discussion, on 1 May 1958. In this respect the Nordic countries were in the van of progress, though Benelux followed close on their heels. Not that 'progress' is the most apt word in this context, for the Passport Union only re-created the situation before the First World War!

Limited space has meant that much Nordic cooperation — for instance a wide range of successful activities in the legal and cultural spheres — has had to be omitted from the foregoing all too brief account of developments up to 1970. In conclusion, it may be useful to pin point some of the differences between the achievements of Nordic cooperation and those of integration within the EEC of the Six. In the harmonisation of laws, in their labour market, in developing joint social policies, in cultural collaboration and in certain other fields Nordic countries had progressed further than the EEC along the road to integration. But they had fallen far behind in economic cooperation: no customs union, no common external tariffs, no common trade policy with third countries, no common agricultural policy. Their aims and methods, too, differed substantially from those of the EEC: they were not interested in political union, not prepared to develop a unified Nordic bureaucracy, and not really ready — in spite of Nordek — to merge their economies to any significant degree. But Nordic cooperation was by no means a static, unchanging phenomenon; its transformation in the seventies, however, must be taken up in Chapter 11.

Eastern Europe: Integration Among the People's Democracies

We have already discussed, in Chapter 4, the division of Europe into East and West which was part of the Cold War, and, in that context, the origins and early years of Comecon, properly speaking the Council for Mutual Economic Assistance. The closed world of the Eastern bloc, which was only finally sealed off in the early 1950s, if then, was not however merely a political phenomenon; nor was it simply a function of Russian economic imperialism. In many ways, because of the quite radical differences between the planned socialist economies of Russia and her partners or satellites on the òne hand and the Western market economies on the other, the two groups were bound to go their own separate ways. Russia, committed to long-term state planning, withdrew in the main from world trade and developed her own system, which was based on quite different economic principles from those followed in the rest of the world.

The Eastern European countries, three of which — the Soviet Union,

Czechoslovakia and Yugoslavia – are or are supposed to be federations, share a common Marxist-Leninist ideology, similar political systems based on a single Communist or Workers' Party, and, of course, an economic system based on the collective ownership of the means of production. As regards this last, while the whole of industrial production has been taken over by the state in all the Comecon countries, agriculture has for the most part been collectivised instead, except in Russia, where rather over half of land is state-owned, and in Poland, where a mere 14 per cent of socialised agriculture is state-owned land, and collectivisation has been abandoned. The East European countries, apart from Russia, comprise a northern tier of industrialised, relatively populous states – Poland, the German Democratic Republic and Czechoslovakia – and a southern tier of less populous, more agricultural Balkan states – Bulgaria, Romania and Yugoslavia. Hungary forms a link between the two groups.

Comecon was founded in 1949 by Bulgaria, Hungary, Poland, Romania, Czechoslovakia and the Soviet Union, was joined by Albania and the German Democratic Republic in 1949-50, and subsequently admitted Yugoslavia, China, North Korea and North Vietnam as observers in 1956-8. Mongolia became a full member in 1962; Yugoslavia an associate member in 1964. Albania and China left the organisation in 1961-2 and Cuba became an observer in 1965 (full member in 1972). Thus Comecon is not, strictly speaking, a European organisation. Although we have so far emphasised the similarities amongst its European member states, Comecon was of course not at all a partnership of equals: the power of the Soviet Union was all-embracing. Whereas the surface area of each of her partners varies between 0.5 and 1.5 per cent of the area of Comecon as a whole, the Soviet Union occupies 95 per cent of the area of Comecon; and, while the populations of the smaller members vary from between 2.5 (Bulgaria) and 9.5 (Poland) per cent of Comecon as a whole, the Soviet Union has over 70 per cent of Comecon's population. The declared aim of Comecon was economic cooperation; it was a sort of lop-sided East European version of the OEEC. Later it sometimes came to be thought of, more misleadingly still, as a Communist EEC.

It must have become increasingly clear to the Russians, from 1953 on, once Stalin's personal despotism had collapsed, that something more in the nature of a political organisation was needed, besides Comecon, to act as the framework or cloak for continued Russian dominance in Eastern Europe. In 1954 the Soviet government made repeated proposals for a European security conference, evidently in part with the aim of preventing or limiting West German re-armament. When this last was agreed to within the framework of Western European Union, and the German Federal Republic joined NATO on 5 May 1955, Russia convened her allies to a meeting in Warsaw on 11 May and the Warsaw Pact, or Treaty of Friendship, Cooperation and Mutual Assistance, was signed on 14 May by

Albania, Bulgaria, Czechoslovakia, Hungary, Poland, Romania, the GDR and the USSR, that is, by all the members of Comecon.

Thus for the Russians the Warsaw Pact was a direct counter-ploy and a necessary alternative to the failure of the Western powers to join in the formation of an all-European security system. It was useful to the Soviet Union in other ways: it could and did serve as a basis for the creation of a modern military machine composed of the armies of Russia's satellites which could be used in defence of the Soviet Union or to attack the NATO ground forces in Western Europe; it also served as a justification for the continued Soviet military occupation of Hungary and Romania, the original pretext for which, the need to safeguard Russia's line of communication with her Austrian garrisons, was removed by the Austrian State Treaty of May 1955.

Ever since 1955 the military situation in Europe has been dominated by the confrontation between NATO and the Warsaw Pact Organisation. The Warsaw Treaty seems to have been modelled on the North Atlantic Treaty, even to the extent of being valid in the first instance for twenty years. But the two organisations were in many ways poles apart. The Warsaw Pact was superimposed on, and subsequently further strengthened by, a web of bilateral Treaties of Friendship, Cooperation and Mutual Assistance; it was also consolidated in 1956-7, after the Hungarian revolt had been put down by the Soviet army, by a series of status-of-forces agreements with Poland, Hungary, Romania and the GDR. Its supreme body, the Political Consultative Committee, is believed to have met only four times in 1956-60 and only a dozen times between 1956 and 1970. All key positions in the military organisation of the Warsaw Pact, which is headed by the Soviet commander-in-chief of the Joint Armed Forces, are held by Russians. The integration, modernisation and re-equipment of the Warsaw Pact armies really only got under way in the early sixties: the first joint manoeuvres were held in 1961. Since then, the Warsaw Pact armies have apparently been more effectively integrated than those of NATO, and they enjoy a much higher degree of standardisation of military equipment.

None the less the two organisations have their parallels and their similarities. Morally, financially and in other more or less subtle ways, NATO was dominated by the USA just as, albeit more directly and crudely, the Warsaw Pact Organisation was dominated by Russia. Behind the confrontation of the two military alliance systems lay, and still lies, that between Russia and the United States. Moreover, just like NATO, the Warsaw Pact Organisation has had its share of problems with member states. In exactly the years when de Gaulle seemed intent on wrecking NATO, the Albanian dispute with Russia was brewing up. It came to a head in 1961, when the Albanians refused to pay their subscription to Comecon and Moscow severed diplomatic relations with Tirana. In 1962 the Albanians complained bitterly that they had not been invited to a meeting of the

Political Consultative Committee of the Warsaw Pact, which they therefore denounced as unconstitutional. A further protest note in 1965 alleged that the Soviet government had illegally and arbitrarily excluded Albania from the Warsaw Pact Organisation, infringed the terms of the Soviet-Albanian treaty by halting arms deliveries, applied a trade embargo to Albania, stolen eight Albanian submarines that were at Sevastopol for repair, and encouraged US imperialist puppets, Greek monarcho-Fascists, Italian reactionaries and Titoist plotters against Albania. As regards the recent meeting in Warsaw in January 1965 of the Political Consultative Committee of the Warsaw Pact Organisation, at which four empty chairs had been left to emphasise the fact that Albania had been invited, the Albanians were duly grateful to the Polish government for inviting them, but pointed out that they ought to have been consulted first about the place, time and agenda! This omission was 'in violation of the rules of the organization as laid down in the Warsaw Pact; it is a discriminatory move against the People's Republic of Albania'. After 1965, it was Nicolae Ceausescu who played de Gaulle's NATO role in the Warsaw Pact Organisation on behalf of Romania.

Soon after the creation of the Warsaw Pact Organisation, its economic counterpart Comecon, which seems to have been largely dormant during the early years of its history, was reactivated. At the seventh Session of the Council, in May 1956, twelve Standing Commissions were established, distributed around the member states: Bucharest was given oil and natural gas, Sofia agriculture, Budapest non-ferrous metals, Prague engineering, Berlin chemicals, Warsaw coal, while Moscow took energy, ferrous metals and foreign trade. Other Commissions were subsequently added to these. Moscow of course remained the headquarters of Comecon and seat of the secretariat; Russian was its working language. In the late fifties, several large-scale multinational projects were launched by Comecon, most notable among them being the 2,800 mile long 'Friendship' pipeline, agreed on at the tenth Session in 1958, to transport Soviet crude oil from Almetievsk in the Urals to refineries which were to be built in Poland, the GDR, Czechoslovakia and Hungary. Each country was responsible for financing its own section. In the decade after the oil began to flow in 1964, the Soviet Union delivered nearly 250 million tons of oil to her neighbours through this pipeline. In 1959 the construction of a joint electricity grid called 'Peace' was approved, and in 1962 its headquarters was established in Prague. By 1967 it included all Comecon countries in East Europe. The multinational East European 'specialised agencies' established in 1956-7 were parallel with Comecon but not part of it: the nuclear research institute at Dubna in the USSR, the Organization for International Railway Cooperation in Warsaw, and the Organization for the Cooperation of Socialist Countries in Telecommunications and Posts.

This substantial stepping-up of Comecon activities in 1956-7 and the succeeding years was undoubtedly in many ways a counter to the EEC, the negotiations for which were then under way. It was accompanied by a salvo of Soviet propaganda against the EEC which was fired off in January 1957 by the Institute of World Economics and International Relations in Moscow, in a document which became known as the *Seventeen Theses on the Common Market*. A more lapidary statement to the same effect was circulated by the Soviet Foreign Office in March 1957. The EEC was a capitalist organisation and a military alliance in disguise; all its members belonged to NATO. The people of each of them would be bound to suffer from the Common Market: the Germans would never be united if part of them joined a bloc; the French would find themselves faced by a re-armed, nuclear Germany; the Italians would be forced to go abroad to find work. The national sovereignty of every member state was threatened. A new form of colonialism was being evolved to exploit Africa. The Soviet government appealed for all-European economic cooperation in a blatant attempt to forestall or undermine the proposed EEC of the Six.

In further response to the creation of the Common Market, the institutional reinforcement of Comecon was continued. In 1958 it was given a new secretary in the shape of Nikolai Fadeyev, who is still in office in 1978, and at the tenth Session, held in Prague in December 1958, a statute or charter was decided on to define the aims, principles, functions and competence of Comecon, which came into force on 13 April 1960. A glance at this somewhat belated Comecon constitution underlines the differences between the EEC and Comecon, even though the aims declared in Article 1 of the statute

to facilitate, by uniting and coordinating the efforts of the Council's member countries, the planned development of the national economy, acceleration of economic and technical progress in these countries, a rise in the level of industrialization in countries with less developed industries, uninterrupted growth of labour productivity and a steady advance of the welfare of the peoples in the Council's member countries

are not, on the surface, so different from the aims declared in the Treaty of Rome. But the statute goes on to state that 'the Council for Mutual Economic Assistance is based on the principle of the sovereign equality of all member countries', whose cooperation is only to be effected with due respect for their 'sovereignty and national interests'. Thus any question of supranationalism is totally ruled out, and this is further emphasised by the rule that any 'member country may withdraw from the Council' on six months' notice, and that 'Recommendations and decisions shall not apply to countries which declare that they have no interest in the given question.' Naturally there is nothing in Comecon approaching the EEC's Commission or Court; its institutions are wholly intergovernmental: the Session of the

Council, consisting of delegations from each country whose 'membership shall be determined by the country concerned'; the Executive Committee of the Council, consisting of 'representatives of all the member countries of the Council, one from each country, at the level of the deputy head of government'; the Standing Commissions set up in 1956 and added to since; and the Secretariat.

Whereas the EEC achieved a measure of economic integration and trade by introducing its customs union between 1959 and 1968, no such device was open to Comecon members, which have neither market economies nor tariffs. Instead, intra-bloc trade has to be regulated, quantitatively, by a mesh of bilateral trade agreements, and this treaty mesh remained throughout the fifties and sixties — and still remains — the most important single instrument for the economic integration of their economies. The other vital element in the Comecon system in these two decades was the effort to achieve coordination and progress in the various sectors of the national economies through the exchange of information in the Standing Commissions. Attempts in 1957 and 1963 to add something further in the shape of a multilateral clearing system based on the 'transferable rouble' ended in near failure; the Comecon bank of 1963 — the International Bank for Economic Cooperation in Moscow — by no means lived up to expectations.

In the course of 1962 the Russians evidently became increasingly alarmed by developments in the EEC. After all, at that time it seemed probable that virtually all the Western European countries would either join or associate themselves with the EEC, and that it would be considerably strengthened both by British membership and by being transformed into a political, as well as economic, union. As against this potentially solid bloc in the West, the Eastern bloc seemed to be crumbling: Albania and China, at any rate, were in open dissent with Russia. No wonder this was the moment chosen by Nikita Khrushchev to launch a new propaganda campaign against economic integration in the West. 'The Common Market is in fact a state monopoly agreement of the financial oligarchy of Western Europe which is threatening the vital interests of all peoples,' he declared in a Kremlin speech on 30 May 1962. 'The Common Market is also directed against the Soviet Union and other socialist countries,' and, he explained, one of its principal aims was the economic exploitation of the peoples of Africa. On 26 August 1962 *Pravda* carried another anti-EEC manifesto from the Moscow Institute of World Economics and International Relations, this time taking the form of *Thirty-two Theses against the Common Market.*

The apparent onward progress of the EEC in 1961-2 was not only countered by hostile propaganda from Moscow but also by an attempt at positive developments within Comecon. The fifteenth Session, held in Warsaw in December 1961, formally adopted a document entitled *Basic principles of international socialist division of labour,* which was subsequently ratified in June 1962. The *Basic principles* proposed at least one significant move in the direction of economic integration which might serve to transform Comecon into a much more effective organ: 'Coordination of economic plans – the principal means of successfully developing and extending international socialist division of labour', ran one of the headings. The proposal seemed to be the extension of coordination from particular sectors to entire economies. It was followed up in the autumn of 1962 by Khrushchev's proposal for a central joint planning organ for Comecon, which was apparently designed to go further than mere coordination of national plans, and actually achieve a new type of socialist supranational economic integration. After all, the Standing Commissions had been trying to coordinate parts of national plans; moreover, all the Comecon member states' national plans save Bulgaria's had been chronologically aligned by 1955, and Bulgaria had fallen into step for the 1961-6 quinquennium. However, Khruschchev's ambitious project fell foul of the Romanians and a new and lasting schism was created in the Communist bloc.

'The idea of a single planning body for all CMEA countries has the most serious economic and political implications,' declared the Central Committee of the Romanian Workers' Party in April 1964. 'The planned management of the national economy is one of the fundamental, essential and inalienable attributes of the sovereignty of the socialist state. . . The state plan is one and indivisible.' Thus the integration of economic planning was firmly rejected by a Romania intent above all on the most rapid industrialisation possible, and fearful of having her own interests disregarded by a joint coordinated plan which would favour the ever faster industrialisation of the 'northern tier' countries, leaving Romania, as it were, to grow vegetables for them.

It was only toward the close of the 1960s that further serious attempts at reform were made within Comecon. This was the era of economic reform, of 'market socialism', in which even Russia joined, and it became increasingly evident that Comecon's role, aims and perhaps institutions would require adjustment to the new circumstances. The Russian invasion of Westward-looking Czechoslovakia in 1968 brought that country – and Romania along with it – firmly back into the Eastern bloc and seriously hindered any possibility of further market-orientated reforms, following on that of Hungary, within Comecon. At a Comecon 'summit' meeting in Moscow in April 1969, which was in fact a special meeting of the Session, the twenty-third, a general consensus in favour of further economic cooperation within Comecon emerged and some agreement seems to have been achieved on the introduction of limited joint planning as well as the further development of coordinated planning. After further long delays an elaborate programme of economic cooperation was eventually produced at the twenty-fifty Session in Bucharest at the end of July 1971 with the title: *Comprehensive programme for the further extension and improvement of cooperation and the development of socialist economic integration by the CMEA Member Countries.* However, in spite of this rather grandiose title, Comecon's further progress thereafter was by no means spectacular.

So far we have been examining the process whereby national states consciously, through their governments, have moved towards each other so that their interdependence has been increased through various forms of cooperation or integration. Here and there, elements of sovereignty have been ceded, sometimes perhaps involuntarily, but by and large the entire process has been willed by governments, ultimately with popular support. This is 'official' integration, in contrast to 'unofficial' integration, which is the result of private initiatives of many kinds.

It is difficult enough, in the case of 'official' integration, to measure its effects and assess its significance; for 'unofficial' integration this is virtually impossible. All the historian can do is to give some examples and suggest some possibilities. In the pages that follow an attempt will be made to pin point some of the fields in which 'unofficial' integration appears to be most important. We shall review in turn tourism and its probable effects, migrant labour and the multinational companies. Turning then to the world of politics, we shall look at the integration of political parties and trade unions. Finally, in the sphere of cultural and artistic activities, that curious phenomenon, town twinning, will claim our attention and, in the world of sport, we shall take a brief glance at football.

Tourism

Since about 1950 tourism in Europe has been increasing on average at the rate of some 12 or even 15 per cent per annum; but what has this mainly unplanned, spontaneous mass phenomenon got to do with integration, with the eventual unity of Europe? It is a kind of annual, temporary migration; it represents a modest beginning to the process of bringing people of different nations together which is one of the purposes of the European Community. It has helped to cause an interpenetration of culinary tastes – the Dutch drink more wine; the Italians take to beer. It should help to diminish prejudices and to deepen people's understanding and appreciation of each other. Above all, it is an economic affair, for the 'travel trade' has become a major European industry, and the entire economies of some regions and even countries have come to depend upon it. A recent report suggested that, by the 1980s, something like one quarter of London's income will derive from tourism. Tourism, in fact, increases the economic interdependence of the countries involved – and the member countries of the OECD together account for the greater part of world tourism.

According to the OEEC, a tourist is someone who stays more than 24 hours in a foreign country. Naturally, governments and international organisations like the OEEC and the European Travel Commission have tried hard to promote tourism. As early as 1949 the European Travel Commission undertook a joint publicity campaign in America on behalf of its member countries (OEEC members plus Spain, Finland and Yugoslavia): by 1954, US tourists were spending £350 million a year in Europe. In the sixties, the promotion of tourism within each country became increasingly discriminatory and nationalistic; devices were employed that had long been outlawed in international trade. There was scarcely a single European country which did not directly subsidise tourist developments, especially hotels. In or about 1960 the French Commissariat Général du Tourisme contracted with a publicity agency to promote French tourism to countries which sent tourists to France. In 1970 it organised a series of television programmes to persuade the French themselves to take their holidays in France. In the seventies, the French government concentrated on the development of tourism in depressed, and especially rural, areas: both the Ministry of Agriculture and the Ministry of Public Works were involved in this programme. Hotels were financed on a massive scale: 340 million francs in 1974 alone.

In Germany, the Deutsche Zentrale für Tourismus at Frankfurt has also been promoting country holidays and doing its best to sell German tourist products at home and abroad. In 1974, some 80 million marks were paid out in subventions for hotels by the federal and *Länder* governments. The Swedish Travel Association launched a campaign in 1969 to promote holidays in Sweden for Swedes, and another in 1971 to persuade foreigners to visit Sweden. It was in 1969 that the British Tourist Authority was set up under the Development of Tourism Act, with the specific aim of promoting tourism to Great Britain from overseas; in the same year the Benelux Council of Ministers set up a tourist commission with similar aims for the Benelux countries.

In the mid-1950s tourism for the first time became a major element in the economies of European states. In 1955 receipts from tourism represented 17 per cent of total receipts from exports in Switzerland, 11 per cent in Italy and Austria, and 5 per cent in France. By 1961, tourist receipts in Spain constituted over half of her total earnings from exports, and in Austria they were approaching a quarter. In Switzerland tourism was the second export industry by 1960, after machinery and before watches; in France it stood third. By the early 1960s tourism was earning more foreign exchange for the Italians than Fiats, and it was beginning to transform the economies of Spain and Yugoslavia, while remaining of the utmost importance to those of Italy, Austria, Switzerland and France, where around 5 per cent of the gross national product came from tourism. In Ireland, in 1970, tourism was the largest single export and the greatest national industry, providing 15 per cent of employment and an income of

£101 million.

The countries which principally supplied the hoards of tourists were, in 1961, West Germany, the United States, Britain and France, in that order. By 1963 West Germany and the United Kingdom were the only countries in Europe which still ran a deficit on their tourist balance of payments; Norway had just moved 'into the black'. The behaviour of Norwegian tourists exemplifies the unpredictability of patterns of tourist movement, which vary considerably from one country to another. In 1976 nearly a quarter of a million Norwegians, out of a population of four million, travelled abroad as tourists. The most popular country by far was Spain, with 121,945 Norwegian tourists. Next came Great Britain with 53,084, Greece with 21,675, Italy with 13,614 and Yugoslavia and Portugal with around 7,000 each. Tunisia, Romania and Bulgaria claimed over a thousand each, but the merest handful of Norwegians visited France and virtually none went to West Germany, Switzerland, Belgium and the Netherlands.

It has been estimated that, in July–August 1969, over 40 per cent of West Germans, Dutchmen and Frenchmen were away from home on holiday. Efforts to stagger holidays had been largely unsuccessful, and have remained so. As early as 1960 the Belgian Commissariat Général du Tourisme ran a 'Holidays in June' campaign, but this only slightly improved the situation. When it was put to the Commission of the EEC that it might do something to lessen the summer holiday congestion on Europe's main roads, it replied that this was an area in which national governments alone could act!

The drive to earn foreign currency has been one of the principal motives for the promotion of tourism; this was particularly so in the East European People's Democracies, where foreign currency to pay for expensive capital goods imported from the West was essential and where tourism has, since Yugoslavia led the way before 1960, made a dramatic breach in the Iron Curtain. Yugoslavia was credited with over a million tourists in 1961 and well over two million in 1964. By 1965, Hungary, Czechoslovakia and probably Bulgaria had apparently reached the million mark. These flows were mostly one-way; they continued to increase dramatically through the late sixties, though remaining far behind comparable figures in the West. In 1969, for example, nearly twenty million tourists entered Spain alone.

Migrant Labour

Since the close of the Second World War the industrial development of Western Europe has sucked in substantial flows of migrant labour which were either outside the control of the governments or, up to the 1970s, were encouraged by them. Indeed it was partly to promote these flows that certain governments set about trying to create larger than national labour markets. First in the field were the Scandinavians, who created a joint Nordic Labour Market (Arbetsmarknad) in 1954 and consolidated it in 1955 by equalising social benefits within it. The Nordic Labour Market was successful because the Nordic countries did form a natural labour market unit and did not attract very much labour from outside. Thus, industrialised Sweden was able to draw most of the workers she needed during the sixties from within the Nordic Labour Market, mainly from Finland (about 20,000 each year in 1961-70). Benelux, whose Labour Market followed in 1956, was not so successful: the Dutch continued to emigrate to Canada, Australia or elsewhere, the Belgians stayed at home as before or commuted over the border – mostly to France rather than Holland. Finally the EEC Labour Market, comprising a six-country unit, was more or less completed by 1968 but has proved singularly ineffective, mainly because it never formed a natural unity. Consequently, labour flows into EEC countries from outside have been more important than intra-Community flows.

The creation of a common labour market by a group of states clearly constitutes a move toward economic integration and, ultimately, unity. But here we are discussing 'unofficial' integration, which implies that the flow of immigrant labour can itself be a force acting towards integration and unity especially when, as has happened in post-war Europe, it has tended to settle permanently in the host countries. What are the main flows which have taken place in Europe?

France and Germany have been the principal importers of labour on the continent of Europe during the twentieth century. By 1930 there are said to have been some three million foreign workers in France: Poles, Czechoslovaks, Italians and others. When the Depression came, they were sent home by train. In Nazi Germany over five million foreigners – *Zwangsarbeiter* – were compulsorily put to work; after the war, between 1945 and 1961 when the Berlin Wall was built, West Germany absorbed over fourteen million German refugees from East Germany and other East European countries. In the immediate post-war years Italy was the most important exporter of labour in Europe: in 1946 she had two million unemployed. In 1947 she made bilateral arrangements whereby 50,000 Italians went to work in the Belgian coal mines, 2,000 went to Britain, and 5,000 each went to Poland and Czechoslovakia. On 21 February 1947 a treaty with labour-hungry Argentina provided for 60,000 immigrant Italian workers each year for six years, and on 21 March in the same year an Italian-French treaty permitted 200,000 Italians to emigrate to France within a year of the treaty coming into force.

By the time the Common Market came into existence the flow of Italian workers northwards had begun to be replaced or augmented by other south-north movements, and indeed, from 1956 onwards, intra-Community labour flows declined. In the mid-sixties surplus Italian labour was increasingly absorbed by the Italian economic miracle, namely by industrialisation in north Italy (though 182,000 Italians emigrated in 1969), and at the same time the image of a six-country labour unit was spoilt by massive inflows of workers from non-EEC countries: into Germany from Spain and Greece, Turkey, Morocco, Portugal, Tunisia and Yugoslavia; into France from Spain, Portugal, Algeria, Morocco, Tunisia and black Africa; into the Netherlands from Indonesia, the Antilles and Surinam, then from Spain, Turkey and Morocco. In 1969 West Germany attracted over a million immigrants, more than half of them from Turkey, Yugoslavia, Greece and Italy. The many Italians who were still leaving their country to look for work tended more and more to settle for Switzerland, which by 1970 had over a million foreign residents, many of them Italian, in a population of six million, so that nearly one-third of her total labour force was foreign. Britain recruited her immigrant labour not from Europe, but from the West Indies, from India and from Pakistan – a movement which reached its peak in the early sixties but, slowed down early on by racialist feeling, was hopelessly insufficient for her needs. Since 1945 indeed, Britain has never enjoyed net immigration so that – according to some economists – the labour-starved British economy remained largely stagnant. In 1969, 299,000 Britons emigrated, more than from any other European country. In spite of this continuing net emigration, Britain had 1.25 million coloured immigrants by 1972 – a number which was increased by 27,000 in that year after General Idi Amin expelled the Asian immigrants from Uganda.

It has been authoritatively argued that Europe's impressive economic growth between 1950 and 1970 was largely due to the industrial reserve army available in the form of immigrant labour. It was not just a matter of a quantitative reserve; certain qualities of this immigrant labour were all-important – above all, it was *flexible*. Flexible geographically, in the sense of being capable of rapid concentration wherever it was needed; flexible socially, in that immigrants gladly undertook menial tasks which were unpopular with residents, leaving the residents free to move higher up the salary scale. Immigrant labour kept wages low and profits high; everywhere it was equated with economic growth. By 1970 the foreign labour force was so large and so vital to the European economy that it could no longer be regarded as a merely temporary phenomenon. It seemed to be essential; it had come to stay.

Although at first it was thought that immigrant workers would remain for a time in their host countries and then return home, and this pattern was common, for example among the Italians in the fifties, there has been an increasing tendency for them to try to bring their families with them, and to stay. Moreover, so far, these foreign workers have for the most part not been successfully integrated into the society of their host country; indeed problems of assimilation have remained more or less insoluble. In the fifties, the Dutch successfully absorbed and integrated some 300,000 mainly Dutch-speaking Indonesian refugees (South Moluccans apart), many of them partly of Dutch descent; but they failed to do the same for the similar number of immigrant workers from southern Europe, north Africa and elsewhere which their government helped to recruit in the sixties. Nor do there seem to be any other examples in post-war Europe of the successful integration of foreign workers into the society of a host country, except perhaps a handful of French workers in West Germany, some German workers in France and the Finns in Sweden.

Problems of assimilation and adjustment became rapidly more prominent during the sixties. Public opinion polls showed that in France, Germany, Britain, Switzerland and elsewhere a majority thought there were too many foreigners. The French, who were liberal in their policy of allowing immigrants to be accompanied or followed by their families, soon found Paris and other centres ringed with *bidonvilles* or 'tin-can towns' in which these immigrant families lived in appallingly inadequate conditions. President Giscard d'Estaing responded with the entirely symbolic gesture of entertaining the Algerian garbage collectors of Paris to breakfast on one famous occasion (an example of his 'government by style'?), and he continued his predecessor's efforts to further liberalise the French immigration laws. The Germans on the whole refused entry to the families of immigrant workers and housed the workers themselves in dreary barracks or special workers' camps. In Switzerland, little or nothing has been done for immigrant workers either by federal or cantonal authorities, save to discourage them.

Long before even a start had been made in coping effectively with the education of immigrant children, in improving the pay and living conditions of foreign workers, and in stemming the tide of illegal immigrants, the economic crisis of 1973 onwards, with its surge of unemployment in Europe, exacerbated these and other problems. By the end of 1974 West Germany had over a million unemployed and Chancellor Helmut Schmidt's government, fighting for its political life, was pressured into preparing plans for a substantial cut-back in the 2.4 million foreign workers, or *Gastarbeiter* as they are euphemistically called, then in West Germany – whose recruitment had been virtually halted in 1973. An opinion poll at the end of 1972 showed that 54 per cent of Germans questioned thought that most or all foreign workers should be sent home. A report published by the Ministry of Labour of North Rhine Westphalia in May 1977 pointed out that in heavily industrialised Duisburg up to two-thirds of the younger unskilled workers in some firms were foreigners, most of them Turks. Living in derelict or substandard housing, they have so far resisted all attempts at integration. In some areas nearly a third of children under five were foreign and, by 1981, it was thought likely that one in three primary schoolchildren in Duisburg would be foreign.

A similar pattern has occurred in France, where in May 1977, faced with political pressure and over a million unemployed, the French government introduced a repatriation scheme which subsequently entailed offering a payment of ten thousand francs (£1,200), plus their fare home, to any of the two million or so foreign workers willing to leave the country. It was initially open only to the 80,000 unemployed foreigners; at the same time the issue of work permits to immigrants was suspended and their right to bring in their families abrogated. Naturally Spain, Portugal and Morocco lost little time in registering their protests: Prime Minister Mário Soares wrote to French Prime Minister Raymond Barre complaining that the new regulations were being so assiduously enforced that bus-loads of Portuguese tourists on their way to Lourdes had been turned back at the French-Spanish border. A rising tide of xenophobia had affected other countries besides France and Germany: both Britain and Switzerland have seen anti-immigrant lobbies winning increasing support in recent years. Enoch Powell has his Swiss counterpart in Jakob Schwartzenbach, leader of a movement called National Action against the Foreign Domination (*Uberfremdung*) of Nation and Home. Partly as a result of its activities the Swiss sent over a quarter of a million immigrants home between 1974 and 1976.

Nearly all West European countries now enforce a total ban on immigrants. Even though over a million *Gastarbeiter* probably went home during the four years of recession after 1973, some thirteen million remained — more than the combined populations of Sweden and Switzerland. Moreover, they were doing jobs like building roads, emptying dustbins, cleaning dishes in hotels, working shifts in motor-car factories and slaughtering pigs, which the resident workers are no longer prepared to do. In the summer of 1977 the Brussels tramway company had difficulty in filling 200 vacancies, although the unemployment rate in Belgium stood at 6.9%. The Italians had to bring in Egyptians to work in their iron foundries because they could not hire Italians. Yet one million Italians were unemployed in 1977 and another two million were working abroad.

By the end of 1977 it had become abundantly clear that the European countries were faced with limited options. There was no easy way in which they could remove the immigrant work-force which they had called into being to facilitate their own economic growth. Even if they indulged in large-scale deportations, which were politically and socially unthinkable, or in subsidised voluntary repatriation schemes, which were probably unworkable, this policy would simply lead to a slowing of economic growth and, probably, further increases in unemployment. The only way of coping with existing immigrants was to integrate them as far as possible into their host societies; a costly and difficult exercise which would entail treating immigrants in every respect exactly like natives. This has scarcely been begun anywhere in Europe at the time of writing in February 1978, although the Commission of the EEC made constructive proposals in its 1974 action programme. The only way of ensuring that the immigrant labour phenomenon does not continue or recur is to restructure the world economy so as to achieve a more rational international division of labour; this means transferring labour-intensive industries from the highly developed European countries to the main labour-exporting countries, starting with Spain, Turkey and Portugal and continuing with the rest of the Third World. It remains an open question whether these eventual solutions are likely to be facilitated or deferred by the admission of Portugal, Spain, Greece and Turkey into the EEC.

Multinational Companies

Although for most people a multinational company is thought of as a very large international business enterprise well entrenched in important markets throughout the world, probably American-owned, in fact any undertaking with production facilities in more than one country is multinational. It was in the 1860s that the first multinationals were founded: Henri Nestlé began creating baby foods at Vevey in Switzerland in 1867; in the same year the US Singer sewing machine company built its first overseas factory in Glasgow. A year before, in 1866, Alfred Nobel, the Swedish inventor of dynamite, opened an explosives factory in Hamburg. Some US multinationals, for example the International Telephone and Telegraph Corporation (ITT), were firmly established in Europe before the Second World War. ITT's European operations actually began in 1925 when it became the owner of Standard Telephones and Cables in Britain and other telecommunications businesses in Austria, Belgium, France and Italy. By 1974 ITT employed nearly a quarter of a million people in Europe alone, in sixteen countries, and sold nearly £2.5 billion worth of goods in Europe, equivalent to slightly over half its world sales. Other US multinationals were not far behind ITT. In 1969 International Business Machines Corporation (IBM), the computer giant whose European headquarters is (1977) presided over by the Frenchman Jacques Maisonrouge, owned between half and three-quarters of the computer industry in France, Germany, Italy and the Benelux countries, and getting on for one-third of computer production in Britain. Its turnover in 1968 was half as big again as the gross national product of Portugal. On the whole it is now widely accepted that these American multinationals did and still do represent an enormous penetration of American economic and political power in Europe; they also provided a great deal of employment.

European multinationals came on the scene later than the Americans but appear to be catching up with them. In 1977 two of the world's twelve largest companies — a list headed by the American corporations Exxon (formerly Standard Oil New Jersey) and General Motors — were European:

Royal Dutch Shell and British Petroleum Ltd (BP); and Unilever, IRI (Istituto per la Ricostruzione Industriale), Philips NV, Veba AG and ENI (Ente Nazionale Idrocarburi), all European, were among the nineteen companies with annual sales worth over $10 billion. BP is firmly English, and will remain that way; its Continental subsidiaries are managed for the most part by local nationals but most decisions emanate from London. Unilever, built up from a combination of English and Dutch companies starting in 1927, is less centralised; in 1970 it had several hundred businesses in fifty different countries. Nestlé Alimentana SA and Philips are among the more genuinely multinational of the multinational companies. Although Philips is presided over at Eindhoven by Fritz Philips, the Dutch electrical firm allows substantial powers to its national subsidiaries; for example Mullard, Pye and Philips Industries in Britain are, to all intents and purposes, British firms. The managing director of the chocolate and foodstuffs firm Nestlé is Pierre Liotard-Vogt, a Frenchman born in London: nearly half the executives at the firm's Vevey head-quarters are not Swiss nationals, and only 5,000 of its 110,000 employees are Swiss, but shareholding arrangements ensure that Nestlé will always be Swiss-owned.

The image of the multinational company has recently been tarnished. Since the outcry raised in the late 1960s against American investments in Europe, which increased from a book value of $16 billion dollars in 1966 to around $55 billion in 1977, the multinationals have been accused of all kinds of malpractice, including bribery, interference in politics and tax evasion. Above all, they have been criticised for daring to erode the sovereignty of the national state, even to the extent of having private foreign policies of their own. This erosion is partly a function of their sheer size: it has been claimed that half the world's hundred largest economic units are national states, and the other half are multinationals. Sixty per cent of the social product of Luxembourg derives from US concerns, which employ 26,000 people in that tiny country of 365,000 inhabitants. British Petroleum has been accused of making payments to Italian political parties or politicians in return for favourable legislation; the American Exxon oil company was said to have refused to refuel the American Seventh Fleet during the 1973 oil crisis; and national currencies have on several occasions been seriously affected by multinationals switching their funds around internally to themselves. No wonder the United Nations, the OECD and the EEC have all made efforts to produce a code of good conduct to regulate the multinationals' activities. The OECD guidelines, agreed in June 1976, recommended that multinationals should not bribe public servants, should not interfere in politics nor make contributions to candidates for public office or political parties, and that they should make public a range of information hitherto kept secret. Recently the wave of criticism, their proven misdemeanours, the world recession of 1973-5, and the progressive freeing of trade from tariff and quota restrictions, which has diminished the advantages of establishing plants in other countries, have all contributed to undermining the prestige, but probably not initiating the decline, of the multinationals.

On the Continent of Europe and, more particularly, within the Six, firms were slow to cooperate across national frontiers. Two methods were available, direct investment and agreements between firms. Direct investment was used to build plants, set up subsidiaries or to buy up firms in other countries. Agreements were used to exchange know-how, use licences and patents in common, and for the specialisation of production and sharing of markets. Some important mergers proved unsuccessful: the Fiat-Citroën link of 1968 and 1970 broke up in 1973. The only other transnational merger of two major firms, besides the 1971 Dunlop-Pirelli merger, welcomed by a *Times* leader on 5 December 1970 as 'a timely reminder that the impetus towards European integration is not solely on a political level', was that of German Agfa AG (a subsidiary of Bayer, the German chemicals gaint) at Leverkusen near Cologne, and Gevaert Photo Producten NV at Mortsel near Antwerp in Belgium, in 1964. Each took a half share in two simultaneously created companies, Gevaert-Agfa SG in Belgium and Agfa-Gevaert AG in Germany. The two boards were quite distinct although their membership was nearly the same and, after 1971, both had the same Belgian President. The firm did well; manufacturing was divided between Mortsel, Leverkusen and Munich; profits were supposed to be equally divided; and some 25,000 Belgians and Germans were employed in a total work-force of 34,000.

The explanation for Agfa-Gevaert's complicated arrangements, and for the failure of European companies to increase their size through transnational mergers and acquisitions, was the separate existence in the Community of six quite distinct legal systems. The provisions of the Treaty of Rome on freedom of 'establishment' (that is of setting up business in whatever member state one pleased), the free movement of capital and the harmonisation of taxes were inadequate for the purpose and in any case were only being implemented slowly and in part. In 1965 the French government proposed that each member state should enact identical laws governing the formation and operation of companies on a multinational or Community-wide basis. But the Commission suggested an alternative scheme in 1966: the Six should conclude a convention separate from the Treaty of Rome which would provide for the setting up of 'European' companies which could operate freely throughout the six member states. The 'European Company' is still only a dream and business in the European Community is still hampered by the parallel existence of national legal systems — nine of them now. However, the multinational enterprises continue to function and even multiply in this nationalistic world to which they have long been accustomed, and the formation of new ones in Europe was encouraged and facilitated after 1973 by the Business Cooperation Centre, or Bureau de Rapproachement des Entreprises, a special office established by the EEC Commission in Brussels, which by autumn 1976 had helped to arrange about fifty cross-frontier cooperation agreements between EEC firms.

Trade Unions

Although Europe's trade unions, which comprise anything from less than a quarter (France) to nearly three-quarters (Belgium) of the work-force of individual countries, have a long tradition of internationalism, this has never been their principal concern. Rather they have concentrated on collective bargaining for higher pay and other benefits at a local or national level; and their institutions and attitudes have tended to be adopted in response to the policies of governments. They have formed or tried to form national trade union centres or federations of varying but strictly limited powers in each country. In Britain and West Germany the Trades Union Congress (TUC) and the Deutsche Gewerkschaftsbund (DGB) have embraced the broad mass of the trade union movement; but in France and Italy the original equivalents of these bodies, the Confédération Générale du Travail (CGT) and the Confederazione Generale Italiana del Lavoro (CGIL), ceased to represent the trade union movement as a whole in those two countries after 1948, when the non-Communist unions seceded from them. In 1969-75 in the Netherlands, in 1972 in Italy, and in 1973 in France, efforts were made to weld together the main trade union organs into a national centre or confederation, but they enjoyed little success save in the Netherlands.

In their post-war attempts at internationalism, Europe's trade unions suffered for years from the effects of the profound ideological and political divisions which separated, in particular, the Christian democrats, the socialists, and the Communists. Thus after 1949 there were three distinct international trade union organisations in Europe. The European Organisation of the International Confederation of Free Trade Unions (ICFTU) comprised Western European trade unions only, and non-Communist trade unions at that. It was strongest in Britain and Germany. Second, the World Federation of Trade Unions (WFTU) had its head-quarters in Prague, and included the East European, Russian and Chinese Communist trade unions and had two outposts in the West: the already mentioned French and Italian Communist trade unions (CGT and CGIL). Third, there was the International Federation of Christian Trade Unions, later called the World Congress of Labour, which was in practice mainly Roman Catholic and was strongest in France, Belgium and the Netherlands. Like the ICFTU it, too, had a separate European organisation. Substantial progress towards unification of these movements has been made since the formation, in February 1973, of the European Trade Union Confederation

(ETUC) by ICFTU trades unions in both EEC and EFTA countries and Spain. In May 1974 the ETUC held a special congress in Copenhagen at which the Christian democrat World Congress of Labour's European organisation joined it, and its executive was empowered to negotiate with the CGIL for its adherence, which was secured that summer. Joined also by Finnish, Irish and, in October 1976, Greek trade unions, the ETUC comprised by the end of 1976 all the more important European trade unions save the French Communist CGT.

The formation of the European Trade Union Confederation, that is the creation of a single large trade union organisation at a European level, represented an important shift on the part of the trade union movement towards transnational cooperation and even integration. Within the ETUC, moreover, the principle of decision-making by majority vote was followed, even though that organ's central institutions were too weak to be capable of formulating common policies. The stimulus for this unification of the West European trade unions in the seventies was provided partly by the successes of the EEC in implementing its common agricultural policy, its provisions for the free movement of labour and so on, partly by the increased numbers of company mergers after the establishment of the EEC customs unions in 1968 and the general rise to prominence at that time of multinational companies, and partly by a change in the attitudes of the Communist unions, especially the CGIL. in part, too, it was a response to the rapid and successful unification of the employers' organisations in the EEC, especially the Union of Industries of the European Community (UNICE) and the Committee of Professional Agricultural Organizations in the European Community (COPA). However, the further evolution of a genuine multinational trade union organisation in Western Europe was hampered by the sheer size of the ETUC and the consequent diversity of its constituent members, by the differing amount of workers' participation in industrial concerns in the various countries, by the varying national legislations for the settlement of disputes and for collective bargaining procedures, and by the fact that Britain did not share the Continental system of works councils.

In spite of their extreme dislike of centralised 'supranational' trade union organs, their preference indeed for loose confederations rather than federations with any real degree of central authority, the trade unions have all along demonstrated a very positive attitude towards European integration. The ICFTU constitution, approved in December 1949, stated that one of the aims of the confederation was 'to advocate, with a view to raising the general level of prosperity, increased and properly planned economic cooperation among the nations in such a way as will encourage the development of wider economic units and freer exchange of commodities'. In August 1955, two months after the Messina Resolution, the European Regional Organisation of the ICFTU organised a special trade union conference in Brussels with the object of promoting integration and publicising the European idea. In 1957 and 1958 the trade unions of the Six came out with proposals for revising the Treaty of Paris to give the ECSC greater powers in social affairs and to give more extensive supra-national authority to its Assembly and High Authority. And they criticised the Treaty of Rome along similar lines: it was not supranational enough, nor was social policy effectively enough formulated in it. In the sixties the trades unions supported further moves towards integration in the EEC, deplored the effects of the 1965 crisis, and argued for more powers to the Commission. An important exception was the British Trades Union Congress (TUC), which adopted a hostile stance to the EEC and especially to British membership of the EEC, and indeed totally boycotted its institutions between 1971 and 1975, when it advised Britain's workers to vote 'No' in the Common Market referendum.

On the whole Europe's trade unions have been quick to establish a presence for themselves in the Europe of the Six and the Nine. The main trade unions supported further moves toward integration in the EEC, Twenty-One which, oddly enough, never had twenty-one members. It maintained a small secretariat in Luxembourg and comprised representatives of the ICFTU-affiliated unions in the six countries together with representatives of the European Regional Organization of the ICFTU, and observers from ICFTU unions outside the Six. Its Secretary-General, who kept in close touch with the High Authority of the ECSC, was the Dutch-man Harm G. Buiter. In 1958, he became Secretary-General of the Committee of Twenty-One's successor in the EEC, the European Community Trade Union Secretariat. Of course the trade unions are also directly represented in the EEC: one-third of the 101-person membership of the Community's Economic and Social Committee is made up of trade unionists, and they sit on other committees too. The attitude of the Communist trade unions to the EEC changed radically in the sixties from open hostility to cooperation; in May 1967 the French CGT and the Italian CGIL set up a joint Liaison Bureau in Brussels which was officially recognised by the Commission in 1969.

Multinational Political Parties?

Like the trade unions, Western Europe's political parties are organised on a national basis, having evolved in response to the activities and policies of national governments and within a purely national context. Communists apart, they have, however, since 1945, collaborated with each other across national frontiers, and, when the Common Assembly of the ECSC came into existence in 1952, the groups that emerged in it were based not on national boundaries but on ideological or party differences. Three political parties were formed: the Liberals, the Social Democrats and the Christian Democrats; and these were the first authentic multinational 'European' party groupings. Subsequently, in the EEC's European Parliament, they were joined by the Communists. Elected directly by the people, the European MPs of the future may eventually organise themselves into genuine European parties, though we may expect these to become real political parties only if the European Parliament becomes a real parliament, at least in the sense of gaining full control of the Community's executive and finances, if not also by acquiring legislative powers.

The Liberals have always supported European unification, with the solitary exception of the West German Free Democratic Party's fleeting opposition to the Treaty of Rome. Since its formation in 1947, the Liberal International has repeatedly debated European themes in its congresses and, from 1967, it has enthusiastically supported the enlargement of the EEC to include Britain and other EFTA countries. A regional group of the Liberal International, the Liberal Movement for a United Europe, was created in 1952 and, from the start, the Liberals formed a distinct group in the Assembly of the Six which, from 1959 to 1962 inclusive, outnumbered the Socialists there. Early in 1976, in readiness for direct elections in the Community of Nine in 1978 or 1979, the Federation of Liberal and Democratic Parties in the European Community was formed − a body which exhibited a certain supranationalism by accepting the principle of majority decisions at the congress it held in November 1977 to draw up a European electoral platform for its members.

Socialists have a long tradition of internationalism going back at least to the creation of the Socialist International in the nineteenth century; they soon added another dimension to this by urging the creation not just of 'Europe', but of a socialist Europe. And if this seemed far off in the immediate post-war years of Christian Democratic majorities, the vision loomed rapidly nearer in the sixties. By 1976 the Social Democrats or their equivalent were the largest single party in eight European countries: Denmark (with 25.7 per cent of the votes), Sweden (43.8 per cent), Finland (25.8 per cent), Norway (35.6 per cent), the German Federal Republic (45.9 per cent), the Netherlands (27.4 per cent), Switzerland (23.1 per cent) and Austria (50.0 per cent); and they were the second-largest party in Britain, Luxembourg and Belgium, with between 27 and 37 per cent of the votes. In the European Parliament they have successfully held their own while their rivals, the Christian Democrats, have seen their numbers reduced since the late sixties. They have also cooperated effectively in the Liaison Office of the Socialist Parties of the Member States of the European Community, which was founded in Paris in 1958 and transformed in 1974 into the Federation of Social Democratic Parties in the European Community. Apart from the German Social Democrats in 1950-2, when they opposed the ECSC, and apart from the British Labour Party throughout the post-war period, the socialists have been consistent supporters of European integration. But their congresses were by no means supranational; decisions binding on member parties could only be made on a unanimous proposal from the Liaison Office, in which the parties of all member countries were represented.

It was only after 1945 that the Christian Democratic parties began to be internationalist, and only in 1947 that a European organisation of Christian Democratic parties was founded, called Nouvelles Equipes Internationales (NEI), which was based first in Brussels, then in Paris, and finally, after 1964, in Rome. At the same time Georges Bidault and others organised the so-called 'Geneva talks' in which Bidault himself, Robert Schuman, Adenauer, de Gasperi and other leading Christian Democrats took part. In 1965 the NEI transformed itself into the European Union of Christian Democrats (EUCD), and in 1976 the Christian Democrats and certain affiliated parties in the Nine formed the European People's Party (EPP). The rules of its congress allow for the adoption by simple majority of a party electoral programme for the European Parliament, and this supranational structure puts the EPP way ahead of its socialist rival on the road toward the formation of an authentic 'European' political party.

In the current (1976-7) groupings of parties, which has been brought about partly with a view to the approaching direct elections to the European Parliament, we have seen that the Liberals, the Socialists, and the Christian Democrats have each aligned themselves together in a transnational electoral alliance. Of the so-called non-aligned parties, the only important ones, with the prospect of obtaining over ten seats in the new European Parliament, are the British Conservatives and the French Gaullists on the extreme right, and the French and Italian Communists on the extreme left. The prospects of the Communists joining forces seem remote; the Russians have always resisted the emergence of a specifically West European Communism. The Communists form a substantial political force in only three West European countries: Italy (34.4 per cent of the voting electorate in June 1976), France and Spain (about 20 per cent each); but there are 23 Communist Parties in all, mostly very small and far from agreeing among themselves. Although there is as yet no institutional cooperation among these West European Communist parties, they perhaps laid foundations on which to build at a congress held in Brussels in January 1974 when they proclaimed their intention of mutual collaboration in achieving the aim of a 'peaceful, democratic and independent Western Europe'. Since 1969, when the Italian Communist Party first sat in the European Parliament, and more particularly since 1973 when their French colleagues joined them there, there has been a Communist presence and latterly a distinct Communist group, in the European Parliament. Thus 'Euro-Communism' is emerging under leaders like Georges Marchais of France, Enrico Berlinguer in Italy, and Santiago Carillo of Spain. In spite of differences between them, they seem to be intent on convincing the rest of the West that Communism is no longer under Russian domination, that it is no longer subversive, and that it wishes to collaborate in creating a united Europe.

Town Twinning

Among the numerous other aspects of 'unofficial' integration which might claim a place in this chapter, that curious phenomenon, variously known as town twinning or twin towning, *jumelage, affratellamento,* and *Verschwisterung,* and described by Carl Friedrich as 'grass-roots integration', perhaps deserves special mention, though its significance has probably been exaggerated by enthusiasts. The idea of linking together towns in two or more different countries seems to have originated in Scandinavia in 1938, when two small provincial towns, one in Denmark, the other in Sweden, made special arrangements between each other to promote contacts between their inhabitants and organisations. After the war the formation of pairs and chains of friendship-towns (*vänorter* in Swedish; *vennskapskommuner* in Norwegian) throughout Norden was systematically organised and encouraged by the Norden associations, until by the 1970s at least 150 friendship-town chains were in existence there, many of them including three or four Nordic towns; the Nordic capitals, Stockholm, Helsinki, Oslo, Copenhagen and Reykjavik, formed one of them.

The idea was taken up in the rest of Continental Europe in 1951, when the French town of Troyes linked up with Belgian Tournai and the two indulged in an orgy of football matches, civic ceremonies, student exchanges and exhibitions. By the end of 1955 46 French towns were twinned with towns in different Continental European countries, apart from numerous twinnings with English towns. The twinning of Rome with Paris in January 1956 was much publicised and likened by a writer in *France-Soir* to a wedding, after a long flirtation. The civil dignitaries swore on oath, for better or for worse,

> to maintain permanent links between the authorities of our cities, and to favour in every field exchanges between their inhabitants in order to develop, by means of a better reciprocal understanding, a lively sentiment of European fraternity; and to join our forces to promote with all our powers the success of that undertaking so essential for peace and prosperity: the creation of European unity.

This oath was drawn up by the Council of European Municipalities (CCE), which did its best to encourage town twinnings, as did various other organisations, including the Council of Europe and Europa-Union in Germany. As for the French, by 1964 they were said to have undertaken 176 twinnings with German towns, 142 with British, 76 with Belgian and 68 with Italian towns.

The twinnings continued through the fifties and sixties and it seems that Franco-German links were quantitatively the most important, though they were not always forged without difficulties. Hanover, seeking a French partner in 1959, approached Bordeaux, but that city temporised; it turned to Caen, but was rejected outright; and it was subsequently disappointed by Rouen, which insisted on waiting till after the local elections. Eventually, Hanover was approached by Perpignan, and a match was made. Caen was choosy, rejecting Braunschweig (Brunswick) as well as Hanover before accepting Würzburg. The pattern of events that followed these twinnings was repeated endlessly. Between March and October 1964 22 visits were exchanged between Mâcon and Neustadt an der Weinstrasse in West Germany, of Scouts, school pupils, sports groups, folklorists, choirs, workers, Catholics, philatelists and civic officials. How far international friendship and European solidarity really were promoted by these junketings is open to question. Some of the multiple links or *Ringpartnerschaften* seemed fanciful in the extreme: Saint-Cloud, Frascati, Bad Godesberg and Maidenhead, for example, or Cesenatico (Italy), Aubenas (France), Delfzijl (the Netherlands), Schwarzenbek (Germany), Sierre (Switzerland) and Zelzate (Belgium). Did Europe really begin in the communes, as the motto of one of these unions asserted?

Twinned Universities

The twinning experiment was extended to other institutions besides the communes, notably to the universities, but it does not seem to have been wildly successful there, if one can judge from an enquiry undertaken by Professor Dusan Sidjanski of the University of Geneva in 1964. Three hundred questionnaires were sent out to European universities enquiring about twinnings, but only 49 replies were received. From Belgium, out of 19 questionnaires, only 1 was returned, from the University of Ghent, which recorded its twinning with the University of Lille and 6 other universities. Only 11 questionnaires were filled in of the 122 sent to Italian universities. Curiously enough, 4 of these came from the same university, Bologna, and two of them stated that Bologna University had decided against twinnings! But some working arrangements were unearthed: for example Lyons and Frankfurt exchanged four professors per annum during 1959-64. A similar professorial diffidence, or dislike of questionnaires, was demonstrated by the Italian professoriate in 1961 when the information office of the Commission of the EEC in Rome circulated a questionnaire on their attitudes to European integration. Only a quarter of the professors responded to this enquiry; a sample of non-repliers, when asked why they had ignored it, excused themselves on the grounds that the questionnaire was too complicated, they were not interested, they had insufficient time, they had lost the questionnaire, or even that they had never received it!

Football

In spite of the introduction of 'European' championships in a number of sports — fencing, athletics and basketball, for example — in the 1930s, nobody would deny that such contests, competed in by national teams, are intensely nationalistic. Yet the evolution of transnational sporting events has contributed in a modest way to European integration, and no single sport shows this more clearly than that most popular sport of all — football. Furthermore, no country has undergone such an extraordinary change of outlook in this connection as Britain.

In the 1930s Britain's attitude to Continental football was outrightly isolationist. In 1928 she withdrew from the International Federation of Football Associations (FIFA, after its French initials) and maintained her boycott of that organisation until 1946. Admittedly, the British did play occasional matches abroad, for example against the Germans, but that was on instructions from the Foreign Office, which also insisted on the players giving the Nazi salute at the start of the game. In 1930, when FIFA launched the World Cup, Britain refused to compete, leaving the Italians to win it. After the war British football suffered a series of catastrophic defeats at the hands of Moscow Dynamo in the autumn of 1945, the United States of America, of all people, in the World Cup of 1950, and Hungary in 1953 and 1954. Then, in 1955, the very year of the Messina Resolution, the French sporting paper *L'Equipe* convened a meeting of club officials and instituted a new all-European knock-out tournament — the European Cup. But the Football League refused to permit the English champions, Chelsea, to enter the first European club football contest in 1955-6 — officially for fear that this might interfere with their home commitments! However, Manchester United entered in the following year against the wishes of the League, and, from 1957 onwards, Britain, all hesitations overcome, has been an enthusiastic participant in European football, whether for the European Cup (1955-6 on), the European Cup-winners' Cup (1961) or the Union of European Football Associations' (UEFA) Cup (1958). From the mid-sixties the European-wide televising of these matches has further contributed to making the European cup the ultimate prize in European football.

It must be borne in mind that these contests are inter-club, not international, and that local pride and sentiment, just as much as national feeling, inspires the armies of fans who follow their teams round Europe by train or plane. Moreover, the Common Market has recently been insisting that the rules of several national football authorities, limiting the number of foreign players who may be fielded in a given team or even banning foreigners, contravene Article 48, Clause 2, of the Treaty of Rome, which prohibits 'any discrimination based on nationality between workers of the Member States', and hamper the free movement of workers (including professional footballers) which is a cardinal principle of the Common

Market. As early as February 1971, in a reply to a written question, the Commission advised that sports clubs and federations were not allowed to limit the number of foreign players in a team; this was after a Belgian club, Standard, had been fined 200 Belgian francs by the Belgian Football Union for fielding four foreign players in a match against Antwerp in October 1970. Belgian Union rules permitted only three non-Belgians in any one team. Italian rules, declared in breach of the Treaty of Rome by the European Court of Justice in a judgement of 14 July 1976 and repealed early in 1978, did not allow foreigners to play for Italian clubs at all. The Football Association, after some delay, in May 1976 abolished its rule that a foreigner must live in Britain for two years before playing for a British club. The Germans have come under pressure too. Cologne (IFC Köln), was accused by (Eintracht) Frankfurt early in 1977 of fielding three non-German players against them in breach of the German Football Association's rule allowing only two non-Germans in each team. Although in terms of Community law the Cologne club seemed clearly to be in the right, it was not prepared to argue the toss with the all-powerful German Football Association, which took the somewhat specious line that a club could certainly hire as many foreigners as it pleased; its rules merely limited the number in any one team to two. In any event Eintracht Frankfurt was unlikely to press its complaint: it had won the game in question 4–0! Perhaps the transfer in summer 1977 of the Liverpool star Kevin Keegan to SV Hamburg will encourage the development of multinational European football, as well as marking the start of a profitable export trade for Britain. In February 1978 the football associations of the Nine officially accepted the EEC's ruling prohibiting all discrimination against 'foreign' players from EEC member states.

This chapter is far too brief. Many other fields in which 'unofficial' integration is in evidence ought to be examined. But these other enquiries, into art, education, communications and many other areas would yield conclusions no more definitive than the few uncertain ones we have reached already. Firm conclusions escape us partly because 'unofficial' integration of this kind cannot easily be quantified, but even more so because nowhere in the field of 'unofficial' integration is there a decisive swing towards multinationalism or unification. At most we are trying to define a trend, a tendency, a slow shift, discernible only here and there.

THE EUROPE OF THE NINE

It was on 1 January 1973 that the history of the nine-power EEC began, with the entry of Britain, Denmark and Ireland; and it now seems likely that that history will end eight years later on 1 January 1981, when Greece becomes the tenth member state of the European Community. The world of the Nine, the world of the 1970s, was very different from the world of the Six; and the Europe of the Nine, too, differed fundamentally from the Europe of the Six. Whereas in the sixties economic growth and ever-increasing prosperity, cheap and plentiful energy and raw materials, and full employment were everywhere attained and enjoyed without serious difficulty, in the seventies, especially after the crucial oil crisis year 1973, which was the first in the history of the Nine, economic growth faltered or was even halted, natural resources seemed to be under pressure, raw materials prices soared, and the twin spectres of inflation and unemployment stalked through Europe and other parts of the world once more as they had done in the 1930s. The world of the Nine, then, was challenging and difficult; a world of economic depression and stagnation.

The EEC in the International Organisations

It was also a world in which, partly because of these economic problems, new international organisations were created alongside those already existing, and the EEC of the Nine was faced with a two-fold challenge: how to speak in these organisations with a single voice, and how to maintain a role and authority for itself so as to avoid being crowded out by other possibly more effective or influential organs. In the so-called 'Tokyo Round' of the old-established GATT tariff-reduction negotiations (Multilateral Trade Negotiations) between some hundred countries which were launched in Tokyo in September 1973 and are continuing in Geneva against a rising tide of protectionist pressures, the Commission has been negotiating for the Community, with the assistance of a standing committee of member states' representatives, under instruction from the Council. In the protracted negotiations at Geneva which led up to the Helsinki Conference on Security and Cooperation in Europe (CSCE) in July-August 1975, the Nine effectively concerted their views and negotiated with a single voice in spite of predictable protests from the delegate of that ultimate bastion of the independent sovereign state — Romania. This remarkably successful foreign policy collaboration culminated in the signature of the Final Act of the Helsinki Conference by Aldo Moro 'for Italy, and in the name of the European Community'. However, a somewhat clumsy move by the British delegation at the review conference which opened in Belgrade in June 1977 to secure the formal recognition of the European Community, Britain then holding the presidency of the Council of the EEC, was unsuccessful: the Yugoslav conference organisers refused to accept or circulate a proposal described by Britain as 'submitted by the European Community', and they turned down a British request for a nameplate in front of the combined British and EEC Commission delegation reading 'UK and President in Office of the EEC'. The Romanian delegate approved this refusal: 'we have not come here to perpetuate power blocs', he protested. Nonetheless, the EEC *was* represented at the Conference and it did continue in 1977-8 to speak there with one voice as it had done at Helsinki in 1975.

While the CSCE was organised to try to cope with the mainly political problem of the East-West division in Europe, a new world-wide Conference on International Economic Cooperation (CIEC) was called into being after the 1973 oil crisis by President Giscard d'Estaing of France to cope with the North-South economic division of the world into rich consumers and poor producers. During 1975, arrangements were made for delegations, headed by Foreign Ministers, from 27 nations to meet in Paris on 16 December for this so-called 'North-South Dialogue': seven oil-producing or OPEC states would form one group; twelve developing countries (including Argentina, India and Yugoslavia) another; and eight industrialised 'nations', namely Australia, Canada, the EEC, Spain, the United States, Japan, Sweden and Switzerland, the third. The remarkable emergence of the EEC, in this scheme, as a single industrial unit comprised of nine states, was however dramatically threatened by the attitude of one member state, Britain, who insisted − in spite of a resolution of the European Parliament of 16 October 1975, passed by a large majority, calling on national governments 'to speak with a single voice' at the coming world energy conference − on having a separate seat of her own and separate national representation. This lack of solidarity within the EEC, compounded by British insistence on a floor price for oil, to protect her North Sea oil interests, which was opposed by some other member states, was narrowly averted by a compromise reached at the Rome Summit meeting of the Nine on 1-2 December 1975: Britain abandoned her demand for a separate seat but her Foreign Minister, James Callaghan, would be allowed to make a brief two-minute speech as one of the four spokesmen of the EEC's joint delegation; the others were the President of the EEC Council Mariano Rumor, the President of the EEC Commission, François Xavier Ortoli, and the Luxembourg Minister for Economic Affairs. Thus the EEC's image in the world at large was not too badly tarnished, though in fact Mr Callaghan spoke for twelve minutes and was afterwards accused by President Giscard d'Estaing of breaking the terms of the agreement previously reached on the contents of his speech. When the CIEC reconvened in Paris at the end of May 1977 the EEC was represented by the Presidents of the Council and of the Commission, who both then happened to be British: Dr David Owen, the Foreign Secretary, and Roy Jenkins.

In another international organisation concerned with the Third World, namely the four-yearly United Nations Conference on Trade and Development (UNCTAD), the EEC was less successful in formulating a joint approach. The fourth UNCTAD, held in Nairobi during May 1976, saw initiatives being taken by the United States, Japan, Canada and, to some extent, Britain and West Germany, but no sign of an effective EEC voice — partly because the Council had failed to agree on a joint position because the Nine disagreed among themselves, particularly on the proposed fund to stabilise raw material prices.

In November 1975, shortly before the appearance of the EEC as a single unit in the North-South Dialogue, the first of a series of Western economic summit meetings was held at Rambouillet not far from Paris. On this occasion the EEC was not present; the six countries participating, represented by their heads of state, were the United States, Britain, France, West Germany, Italy and Japan. But when preparations were being made in the spring of 1977 for a third economic summit, to include the seven most powerful industrialised countries in the Western world, together representing over half the world's gross product, namely, in order of gross national product: the United States, Japan, West Germany, France, the United Kingdom, Canada and Italy, moves were made by the smaller member states of the EEC to secure the official representation of the EEC. An acrimonious dispute ensued over whether President of the EEC Commission Roy Jenkins should be present or not, a row which *cognoscenti* of English history, remembering the Anglo-Spanish 'War of Jenkin's ear' of 1739 occasioned by the alleged tearing off of an English captain's ear, one Robert Jenkins, by the Spaniards, dubbed 'the War of Jenkin's seat'. It was not only the French, but the British too, who resented and opposed the proposed Community presence. The dispute ended in a compromise: Mr Jenkins was given a seat at some of the discussions, for example those on the North-South Dialogue and trade negotiations, but excluded from the discussion on energy and the world economy. Nor was he allowed to sit at the same dinner table as the heads of government. Interviewed on television after this economic summit meeting, West German Chancellor Helmut Schmidt claimed that Mr Jenkin's part appearance represented an important step forward; progress was best made in such small steps, and the EEC had not been represented at all at the two previous Western economic summits.

Constitutional Change Within the Community

The EEC is thus contriving to hold its own among international organisations and learning, painfully, to speak in them with a single voice, in a world plagued with apparently insurmountable economic problems – the hostile, unfavourable, complicated world of the seventies, so different from its expansive, easy-going predecessor of the sixties. But the Europe of the Nine, as opposed to the world of the Nine, possessed certain positive qualities when compared with the Europe of the Six. It was much more of a 'real' Europe, for it was a significantly larger, more broadly based, more representative Europe than the 'little' Europe of the Six. The population of the Nine was 253 million, out of a total West European population of 335 million, as against the Six's 190 million. The gross national product of the Nine was $626 billion, while that of the Six had been $485 billion; and the enlarged Community's share of world trade had increased by 10 per cent from the Six's 30 to 41 per cent. Not only was it a larger Europe, but it was a less exclusive one, for the door that had been closed in November 1958 was reopened on 1 January 1973, when a start was made to the process completed in July 1977, whereby the EFTA countries were linked to the EEC in a free-trade area for industrial goods by a series of treaties which (save for that with Finland) allowed explicitly for further developments in a special 'evolutionary clause', Article 32. Thus the very nature of the European Community changed in 1973: besides becoming larger, it became expansionary and outward-looking.

Right from the start, namely the very first summit meeting of the heads of government of the enlarged Community of Nine held in Paris on 19 and 20 October 1972, it was apparent that enlargement was being accompanied by internal changes in the Community's institutions and their relationships. These changes had already begun to take shape in the late sixties; some of them had been first proposed or even foreshadowed long before then. The 1973 enlargement accelerated this process of internal transformation which future historians may be able to describe as leading from a European Community to a European Union. After all, the 1972 summit communiqué or solemn declaration ended with a statement that the heads of government had set themselves the 'major objective of transforming, before the end of the present decade and with the fullest respect for the treaties already signed, the whole complex of the relations of the member states into a European Union'.

The first and perhaps most significant of these constitutional changes had been proposed in Article 15 of the 1969 summit communiqué: the heads of government of the Six 'agreed to instruct the ministers for foreign affairs to study the best way of achieving progress in the matter of political unification'. The Director-General of Political Affairs in the Belgian Foreign Ministry, Etienne Davignon, chaired a committee which drew up a report, often called the Luxembourg Report, the main proposals of which were approved and implemented from late 1970 onwards. The outcome was regular (four per year) meetings of the Foreign Ministers of the member states for consultation on foreign policy matters; regular (nearly monthly) meetings of the political directors of the member states' Foreign Offices in a Political Committee also called the Davignon Committee; liaison between ambassadors of the member states in foreign capitals; and the issue of common instructions on certain matters to the member states' ambassadors. All this was outside the framework of the Treaty of Rome and quite independent of existing Community institutions. From the start, the applicant countries for EEC membership took part, namely Britain, Denmark, Ireland and Norway. Although it was criticised by good 'Europeans' for being international rather than supranational, the second Davignon Report of 1973 (the Copenhagen Report) recommended the continuation of this 'Davignon formula' for political cooperation in foreign policy. Since then European Political Cooperation (EPC), as it is often called, has proved enduring and successful, and in recent years 'EPC' meetings of the foreign ministers have usually been attended by a representative of the Commission.

By 1976 a substantial volume of EPC information, up to 100 telegrams in cipher each week, was being exchanged via the special Coreunet (Correspondance Européenne) network linking the Nine's Foreign Ministries. This was put to good effect in the autumn of that year, when the Nine delivered a joint protest to the Ethiopians through the Dutch ambassador in Addis Ababa against the proposed interception and censoring of diplomatic mail by the Ethiopian authorities. By 1976, too, the Nine's ambassadors to the United Nations in New York were meeting every week, though the Nine were by no means consistently voting together in the UN's general assembly — in 1977 they voted together on 61 occasions out of a total of 114 votes. In general terms, it can be said that this foreign policy cooperation or EPC has contributed substantially to the process described above, of enabling the EEC to speak with a single voice in world affairs; it has also added an effective new institutional dimension to the joint political activities of the Nine.

Just as the 1972 summit communiqué's call for a European union had been adumbrated in 1960 by de Gaulle's call for a European political union and the Six's efforts to create one in 1961-2, and just as the Davignon consultations of Foreign Ministers had been adumbrated by the Foreign Ministers' meetings of 1960, also called into being by de Gaulle, so the European Council was really a continuation of the summit conferences which de Gaulle had inaugurated at Paris and Bonn in 1961. Moreover it was a French president, Georges Pompidou, prompted by Jean Monnet, who revived the idea of a summit conference and was responsible for summoning those of 1969 and 1972, and another French president, Valéry Giscard d'Estaing, who proposed in 1974 that summit meetings should be held at regular intervals, namely three times a year. It seems also to have been Giscard d'Estaing who in his December 1974 pronouncement, 'The European Summit is dead; long live the European Council,' first popularised the phrase 'European Council', which has now become the recognised title of a new institution.

The constitutional validity of a meeting of heads of government of the member states of the EEC might be construed from the fact that the Treaty of Rome nowhere defines the membership of the Council: Article 146 simply states that 'The Council shall consist of representatives of the Member States. Each government shall delegate to it one of its members.' But in fact it has always been accepted that, like the Davignon Foreign Ministers' consultations, the summit meetings and their successor the European Council are outside the treaty framework. Indeed the European Council has always felt free to discuss non-Community matters. The constitution of the Nine has thus become a hybrid, a mixture of a written constitution of the Continental type based on the Treaties of Paris and of Rome, the treaty of 1965 merging the executives of the Communities, and the 1972 treaty concerning the accession of new members, and a British-type unwritten constitution where new institutions emerge, new procedures are developed, and new rules are made on the spot by those concerned without any prior authorisation or legal justification. As a result of this process, the EEC has since 1974 possessed what it lacked before, a single all-powerful institution which is in a position to lay down programmes of future activities, create new policies and modify old ones, and solve disputes by making compromises at the highest level. Although the President of the Commission now attends its deliberations, the European Council has no pretence at supranationality; it reflects the fact that the EEC is run by the governments of its member states. The question which in 1978 still remains open is, will this new institution really work? And if it does, shall we be talking, soon, of 'European Union' instead of 'the EEC'?

The evolution of these so-called 'para-Community' institutions and activities, especially the Davignon foreign policy discussions, have added to the responsibilities and work-load of the President in office of the Council and brought this institution into prominence. The presidency of the Council is held in rotation by the member states' governments for a period of six months. It involves primarily the Foreign Minister of the member state concerned and, during his six-month period of office, he is one of the most important and influential persons in the EEC, as well as, with the president of the Commission, being its official representative and spokesman in the world at large. The member state holding the presidency also has to chair a large number of Community committees, including for example COREPER. The presidency places a heavy burden of work not just on the Foreign Minister himself, but on the national Foreign Office, which has to help provide a presidential secretariat. The value of this evolving institution lies partly in the way it gives exactly equal weight and status to every member state of the Community, including the smaller ones, and partly in the way it brings each member state into a close relationship with the others and with the Community as a whole: this has perhaps been of special importance in the case of the presidencies of Denmark and Ireland.

The further constitutional evolution of the European Community may centre on the European Parliament, which should not be too easily dismissed as a somnolent, boring, poorly attended, virtually powerless assembly, mostly of veterans, some of whom have been there for twenty years or more. The former Common Assembly of the ECSC has grown significantly in size and is to grow further, from 142 members in 1952 and 198 from 1 July 1973, to 410 members in 1979, which will provide, on average, one Member of Parliament for every 632,000 EEC inhabitants. Early on in its history the European Parliament arrogated to itself, in a manner characteristic of parliamentary régimes, the right to meet whenever it chose, though Article 139 of the Treaty of Rome stipulated 'an annual session' starting on 'the second Tuesday in March'. It did this simply by dividing the annual session into several periods. In the sixties it sat six or eight times a year; in the seventies it sat on eight or ten occasions for a week each time.

In spite of this apparent progress in terms of size and frequency of meeting, the European Parliament has a serious problem: it has no single building or meeting-place. Its sessions are divided between the French town of Strasbourg and the capital of the Grandy Duchy of Luxembourg; its headquarters, with a staff of 1,800, is in Luxembourg; and, though their staffs are in Luxembourg, its twelve standing committees meet in Brussels, where office accommodation for its members is rented. These clumsy arrangements waste money (some £7 million in 1978, it was claimed), and make effective control of the other Community institutions by the Parliament exceedingly inconvenient, if not difficult.

In Strasbourg the European Parliament has always rented the building belonging to the Council of Europe and used by its Consultative (since 1974 Parliamentary) Assembly for its sessions. The original Maison de l'Europe there was rushed up in a matter of months, with a planned ten-year life, in 1949-50. It was replaced in 1977 by the £25 million Palais de l'Europe next door to it, and was then demolished. The new building, constructed in red Vosges sandstone aggregates, aluminium and glass, and known to locals as 'the Egyptian mausoleum', was officially opened by President Giscard d'Estaing on 28 January 1977. The European Parliament met in it for the first time on 7 March, but somewhat prematurely, for the building was by no means finished – one MP ruined a suit by sitting on wet paint; another almost electrocuted himself by trying to turn on a non-existent lavatory light switch.

No wonder that moves have been and are being made to establish the European Parliament in Brussels, close to the headquarters of the Council and the Commission — the former has to secure parliamentary approval for many of its decisions, and the latter has always acted in close concert with the Parliament. But neither the French nor the Luxembourg governments were happy about this, and in February 1978 they threatened to refuse to agree to a date for direct elections for the European Parliament until the plan for the removal of the Parliament to Brussels was abandoned. It now seems that new buildings for the Parliament may well be erected in the next few years in Brussels, Luxembourg and Strasbourg! Whatever happens, it looks as though the Parliament will remain inconveniently divided and partly separated from the rest of the Community.

The holding of direct elections for the European Parliament, that is, arranging for its members to be elected directly by the people instead of designated by national Parliaments, was, as we saw in an earlier chapter, provided for in the Treaty of Rome; it had even been envisaged in the 1951 Treaty of Paris that the European Parliament's predecessor, the Common Assembly of the ECSC, might be 'elected by direct universal suffrage'. But the introduction of direct elections was repeatedly delayed by the Council, and it was not until the 1974 summit meeting that a firm decision was made, with reservations from two new member states, Denmark and Britain, to achieve direct elections 'as soon as possible', that is 'at any time in or after 1978'. The European Council discussed the question further in 1975 and 1976, confirming the date of May or June 1978 and agreeing to a 410-member Parliament with the four larger member states — Britain, France, Italy and West Germany — each having 81 seats. This would mean substantial over-representation for the smaller states for, while in the larger four there would be around half-a-million voters per European MP, in Ireland there would only be 141,240, and in Luxembourg a mere 34,333 voters per MP. As to the regions, in some member states they will enjoy a presence in the Parliament, for example Wales will form 4 Euro-constituencies, Scotland 8, and Greenland (as a region of Denmark) 1 (by comparison with states, Luxembourg will have 6 and 'mainland' Denmark 15). But in others, for example, France, the voting will be based on national lists. Belgium's 24 seats have been divided between French-speaking (11) and Flemish-speaking areas (13). The type of electoral system employed and the question of whether a European MP should or should not also be a national MP was left to individual member states: eight of them opted for some form of proportional representation, leaving Britain alone with her traditional simple majority or 'first past the post' system.

In both France and Britain a substantial body of opinion was vociferously opposed to direct elections to the European Parliament, which were seen as a threat to national sovereignty. But the French constitutional council resolved on 30 December 1976 that direct elections would not violate the French constitution, provided that the Parliament's powers were not increased. The ex-Prime Minister and hard-line Gaullist Michel Debré nevertheless organised a Committee for the Unity and Independence of France to oppose the elections; and this was paralleled in Britain by the Safeguard Britain Campaign of Enoch Powell and others. However, it was the delaying tactics of the British Labour government of James Callaghan, who apparently wished to postpone the European elections until after the coming British general election, which eventually caused their date to be deferred until May or June 1979. A government spokesman had already pointed out in February 1977 that Britain, like the other eight, had only agreed to use her best endeavours to meet the 1978 deadline — there was no binding commitment! This same spokesman insisted in the House of Commons in November 1977 that 'The government has made it quite clear that it does not support federalism' and that the proposed European elections could not be considered a move towards a federal Europe, nor was there any proposal to increase the powers of the European Parliament. Mr Enoch Powell disagreed; for him, the Bill legalising the elections constituted a declaration of European political unity.

In spite of the voicing in Britain and France, as well as elsewhere, of fears concerning the powers of the European Parliament, the competence of that body has in fact substantially increased and is likely to increase still further. For example, it was not long before it successfully took cognisance of the new European Political Cooperation procedures evolved after the 1970 Davignon Report, even though they were outside the Treaty framework. Moreover since 1970, as the financing of the Community has shifted from member states' contributions to the Community's 'own resources', the Parliament has struggled not without success to increase its control over the budget. Since 1 June 1977 it has even had the right to reject the entire budget outright; but this is a clumsy weapon, the use of which would simply leave expenditure at the existing level. Indeed, this ultimate instrument of parliamentary authority is rather like the Parliament's power to sack the entire Commission — too cumbersome and unwieldy to be actually used. Moreover, since control of the budget prepared by the Commission is exercised jointly by the Parliament with the Council of Ministers, and the Council of Ministers controls about three-quarters of the total expenditure, chiefly that concerned with agriculture, Parliament's budgetary powers are still limited. Nevertheless, its transformation into a much larger body, elected directly by universal suffrage, will surely at the very least be accompanied or followed by further increases in the Parliament's influence.

Aims and Achievements Within the Nine

It was in October 1972, in Paris, that the heads of government of the Nine at their first meeting — led by Edward Heath, Georges Pompidou and Willy Brandt — drew up the declaration of their immediate aims which ended with the already-cited statement proudly proclaiming the creation before the end of the seventies of a 'European Union'. The same document, which was printed in full by the *Guardian* with the headline 'The future of Europe', set out the specific goals of the Community during the coming years. Among them were: economic and monetary union by 1980; a Regional Development Fund by 1973 and coordination of regional policies; a programme of action in the social field by 1974; 'the rapid adoption of a European company statute'; a Community environmental policy by July 1973; and the formulation of an energy policy for the Community. In February 1978, rather more than five years since this programme was laid down, and since the history of the Nine began, it is not inappropriate to see how far it has actually been carried out.

Progress with the much-proclaimed and indeed all-important Economic and Monetary Union (EMU) has been virtually non-existent, although what might prove to be its nucleus, the so-called European currency 'snake', has been in existence since April 1972. This curious reptile was an arrangement whereby the margins of fluctuation in the exchange rates of the member states' currencies would be reduced below the fluctuations permitted by IMF rules. This it was hoped, might be a step toward the progressive reduction and eventual removal of all fluctuations – by which time for most practical purposes there would be a single European currency. The 'snake' was said to be in a 'tunnel' because, if the currency fluctuations were plotted on a graph, the result could be likened to a snake wriggling up and down within the tunnel of the IMF currency band. The somewhat macabre concept of a worm inside the snake was provided by the even closer link which was maintained between the Dutch guilder and the Belgian/Luxembourg franc; namely the Benelux currencies. But the snake simply did not work. First of all the pound sterling fell out of it in June 1972, less than two months after Britain had joined the scheme; then, in February 1973, the lira followed suit, while at the same time the entire snake, or what was left of it, floated out of the tunnel of IMF limits. Subsequently the franc fell out of the snake in 1974, was brought back into it again a year later, but has been out of it since 1976.

By 1975 the very idea of 'EMU by 1980' seemed ridiculous; during Britain's renegotiations with the EEC her Foreign Secretary, James Callaghan, had poured scorn on the plan and her Prime Minister, Harold Wilson, claimed that it had been 'tacitly dropped'. A report to the Commission published in the spring of 1975 concluded that 'Europe is no nearer to EMU than in 1969', and the project received little further attention in spite of the fact that, in all, some dozen stage-by-stage plans for introducing it were discussed, until it was taken up by President Valéry Giscard d'Estaing and Chancellor Helmut Schmidt at a meeting in Paris in February 1977, and revived in a series of pronouncements beginning in the autumn of 1977 by Commission President Roy Jenkins. But he failed to persuade the European Council at its December 1977 meeting in Brussels to come to any firm decision on EMU, and it still looks doubtful if this major step toward European unity will be taken in the foreseeable future, though a possible significant transitional move in the direction of EMU had also been proposed in addition to the 'snake': the introduction of a new European currency, the Europa, under the control of a new common institution, at first to circulate in parallel with existing national currencies, later to replace them.

It was no coincidence that the Community's first firm decision to create an effective regional policy followed the statement about EMU in the 1972 summit communiqué. Indeed, the two were explicitly linked together: 'The Heads of State or Government agreed that a high priority should be given to the aim of correcting, in the Community, the structural and regional imbalances which might affect the realization of Economic and Monetary Union.'

Although the Six had laid down no common regional policy in the Treaty of Rome, they had recognised in a special protocol that the relatively poor, agricultural south of Italy — the so-called *mezzogiorno* — was a European problem and a European responsibility. Still, little or nothing had been done until the 1973 enlargement of the Community, when Britain and Ireland, both suffering from severe regional problems, reinforced the hitherto solo Italian voice demanding a Community regional policy. But fierce bickering between the member states followed the 1972 summit decision. Partly this was due to German, and to a lesser extent French, unwillingness to act as paymasters; partly it was due to a fairly generalised hesitation by governments to relinquish control of their own national regional policies. Hence it took the Community more than two years to act on the summit decision, and it was only in 1975 that the European Regional Development Fund and the Regional Policy Committee were actually set up, the former to augment the monies already being devoted to the regions from existing EEC funds but via the national governments: the European Investment Bank, the European Social Fund, the ECSC Fund and the Guidance Section of the European Agricultural Fund. Important new proposals were under discussion in 1977-8 but, up to then, there was no sign that these various, admittedly feeble, efforts to reinforce rather than replace national regional policies had had any more effect than the national policies themselves. The problem of regional economic imbalances remained unsolved, and the richest regions of the Community were still five or six times as wealthy as the poorest. No significant improvement had occurred since the 1974 situation when, if the average income per head in the EEC was 100, the average in the Molise in southern Italy was 36, in Donegal, Ireland, 39, in Paris 180 and in Hamburg 210.

The programme of action in the social field agreed to at the 1972 summit was formulated rather more expeditiously than the regional policy, but it suffered from the rapid rise of inflation and unemployment at just the time of its implementation, namely 1974 onwards. This Social Action Program comprised a number of measures based on the need for full employment, better working conditions, and the more effective participation of workers in the running of firms, the first two of which were by no means attainable in the economic situation of the mid-1970s. Indeed the rising tide of unemployment was more likely to force the member states to take separate measures of their own than to encourage them to develop a common policy, especially since there are virtually no social policies laid down in the Treaty of Rome and the member states in any case had very different social welfare systems. Moreover the amount of unemployment varied greatly from one member state to another. In the first nine months of 1977, for instance, it varied from West Germany's 3.5 per cent of the labour force at one extreme to Britain's 7.5 per cent at the other. Against this background, and in spite of the greatly increased resources of the European Social Fund, which had been reorganised in 1971, one can only say that the creation of effective social policies is not likely to go down in history as one of the achievements of the EEC in the seventies.

Other aims or policies proclaimed by the 1972 summit have likewise been delayed or, at best, have proved ineffective. The European company statute is still being drafted; public sector purchasing has still not been opened up and remains as 'closed' and nationalistic as ever. On the other hand, in the field of science and technology there has been a good deal of activity and some progress towards common policies has been made. Moreover the Community environmental policy, proclaimed in October 1972, partly under the influence of the United Nations Stockholm Conference on the Environment of June of that year, has slowly but surely got under way. The Commission has launched two successive Action Programs beginning in 1973 and 1977 respectively, which include directives on the disposal of waste oils, on the quality of drinking-water and of sea-water for bathing, and many proposals, including detailed recommendations for the protection of wild birds. A varied programme of environmental research is also under way, and the Commission itself has saved 20 per cent of its paper bill through recycling. Two institutions were created in 1973 to support this programme: the European Environmental Bureau (EEB), consisting in 1978 of 38 non-governmental conservation bodies from the Nine, and the Community Environment and Consumer Protection Service.

Lest this bustle of activity gives the impression that environmental pollution in the EEC is a thing of the past, it is salutary to mention Europe's largest industrial and domestic open sewer − the Rhine. In no area has the national state more abysmally failed to provide for the well-being of its subjects than in this one of pollution, and no better example of this failure can be found than the Rhine, virtually all the pollution of which is caused by EEC member states. As late as 1885 Switzerland, Germany and the Netherlands set up a Commission to regulate salmon-fishing in the Rhine; but present-day chemical and even thermal pollution is such that all forms of life are threatened, and Dutch gardeners cannot even safely water their plants with Rhine water. It is said that one can actually develop a film in it; and it has been calculated that every month the following substances enter the Netherlands, carried by the waters of the Rhine: 80 tons of arsenic, 300 tons of copper, 20 tons of cadmium and 10 tons of mercury; not to mention a host of other chemicals, mostly derived from industrial effluents, insectides, fertilisers and the Alsace potash mines. All this happens in spite of the fact that throwing or emitting harmful effluents and other noxious substances into the Rhine has long been outlawed by international agreement; for example in 1875, Baden and Switzerland banned anything 'through which fish might be harmed'; and in 1954 and 1961-2 the Central Commission for the Navigation of the Rhine banned oil and oil residues. The International Commission for the Protection of the Rhine, composed of four delegates from each member state, was set up in 1965 by France, Luxembourg, the Netherlands, the German Federal Republic and Switzerland. Since 1972, ministerial conferences of the Commission's member states have been held with the EEC Commission – under pressure from the European Parliament to do something about the Rhine – as observer. But it was only at the end of 1976 that the five member states of the Commission agreed to help the French pay for the cost of reducing the amount of chlorides dumped into the river from her Alsace potash mines, and to authorise the Commission to draw up a list of proscribed chemicals. At the same time a step was taken which was long overdue: the EEC joined the International Commission for the Protection of the Rhine as a full member.

After the environment policy, an energy policy figured in the 1972 communiqué: 'The Heads of State and Government deem it necessary to invite the Community institutions to formulate as soon as possible an energy policy guaranteeing certain and lasting supplies under satisfactory economic conditions.' Alas! This proved even more of a pipe-dream than most of the 1972 Summit's other declared objects. Here, even more than with regional and social policies, national interests have been jealously guarded and furthered and national programmes have consistently been given priority over Community programmes – to the extent, indeed, of totally undermining the latter.

In the autumn of 1973, when the OPEC countries used oil as a political weapon, attempting to apply an embargo on deliveries to the United States and the Netherlands, raising prices in so dramatic a fashion that they were doubled in a few months, and reducing deliveries, the member states of the EEC one after another took or threatened to take individual national measures in desperate attempts to save their own bacon; moves which constituted flagrant infringements of Article 34 of the Treaty of Rome, prohibiting quantitative restrictions on exports between member states. Thus Belgium, Luxembourg and Italy introduced a system of licences for oil exports and came very close to using them to limit oil exports to EEC countries; the British informed the hard-pressed Dutch, who were driven to banning Sunday motoring, on 21 November 1973, that they dared not supply them with any oil for fear of Arab reprisals; the Dutch threatened to stop natural gas deliveries to their EEC neighbours if they continued to interfere with the free flow of oil; and the French carried 'go it alone' policies to extremes by making a separate deal with the Arabs. The Commission was prepared to authorise almost any national measure provided it was duly notified. A year later, on 15 November 1974, the Nine's failure to act together in the international oil crisis was further underlined by the setting up of the International Energy Agency by the United States, Japan, Canada and other oil-consuming countries including eight of the Nine, namely the entire Community except France.

Since 1973 Europe's dependence on Arab oil, then meeting some 70 per cent of her requirements, has been greatly reduced by the rapidly increasing North Sea production; but this has brought with it a series of disputes between the EEC and Britain over Britain's insistence that all North Sea oil from her sector be landed in Britain, in breach of the EEC regulations on competition; over Britain's repeated demands for a guaranteed minimum price for her oil, rejected by the French; over her refusal to guarantee EEC countries their normal supplies of oil in the event of another energy crisis while at the same time insisting on reducing her stockpile of oil below the agreed EEC level; and over her 1978 plan to construct at least two new oil refineries, in order to make sure she has refining capacity by 1985 to process two-thirds of her North Sea oil, in spite of the fact that two-thirds of the EEC's refining capacity had had to be closed down in the previous year, and there was still excess capacity.

If the EEC has fallen so very short of the plans and projects proudly outlined by the heads of government in 1972, on the eve of its enlargement from the Six to the Nine, what success has accompanied its other policies and efforts since then?

The common agricultural policy survives with modifications and is still blamed for producing surpluses in a partly starving world. It was reported in September 1974, when the 'beef mountain' stood at 210,000 tons, that, since all freezing facilities ashore were fully taken up, two refrigeration ships would soon be anchored in Bantry Bay, loaded with 8,000 tons of frozen Irish beef. Now, in February 1978, the beef mountain weighs in at 382,000 tons and some of it has had to be stored outside the EEC in Austria and Switzerland. Unilateral national measures continue to be taken by governments in the face of demonstrations by angry farmers: in 1974 the Italians introduced systematic curbs on food imports from their

EEC neighbours, and the French introduced direct subsidies and tax rebates to help their farmers which the Commission claimed were in violation of the Treaty of Rome. Moreover, some would argue that the very essence of the CAP has been destroyed by the need, since the 1969 currency crises, and subsequent variations in member states' exchange rates, for an elaborate system of internal payments called MCAs – monetary compensatory amounts – which are paid to bridge the gap between the current exchange rate and the so-called 'green currency' rate used for EEC farm transactions. These MCAs are not very different from internal customs duties or export subsidies to the non-expert eye; their existence makes common farm prices more myth than reality.

The inadequacy of the European Community's response to difficulties caused by a dwindling natural resource is exemplified by its ʾailure to implement the common fisheries policy enunciated in 1970. This was based on the principle that, as it were, all Community fish are placed in a single pond and shared out equally; or, put in another way, all EEC fishermen should have equal access to the waters of member states.

The reaction of the world's national states to the gradual diminution of fish stocks because of over-fishing was the predictable one of creating and then extending exclusive national fishing zones, which were fixed at three miles in an 1882 convention signed by Britain, Belgium, Denmark, France, Germany and the Netherlands. When the Icelanders, more dependent on fish than any other people, unilaterally extended their limit in 1958 to 12 miles, the frustrated British fought the first 'Cod War' against them, then denounced the 1882 convention, called a European Fisheries Conference in London, and signed a new convention in 1964, along with twelve other West European countries, agreeing to a 12-mile zone. In 1972 the Icelanders extended their limits to 50 nautical miles and, in 1975, to 200 miles. The British fought the second and third 'Cod War' against them before themselves adopting the 200-mile limit, along with their EEC partners and indeed the rest of the world. The new 200-mile limits came into force in the EEC, Russia and elsewhere on or about 1 January 1977, the general concept of a universal 200-mile 'economic zone', to cover the resources of the sea and under the sea, having been accepted by the United Nations 1976 Law of the Sea Conference.

By 1976 it had become abundantly clear that the North Sea and North East Atlantic area as a whole were being drastically over-fished. The North Sea herring catch had been more than halved since the mid-sixties, and cod catches by French and German vessels were halved between 1964 and 1974. In spite of this critical situation the Nine found it impossible to agree on a management régime for their new 200-mile limit. First, the Irish introduced unilateral measures of their own, banning, from April 1977, all trawlers over 110 feet long from waters within 50 miles of their coast. Ten Dutch skippers, arrested and detained at Cork for mackerel fishing 28 miles south of the Old Head of Kinsale, refused to accept the Irish justice offered them, and the Commission appealed on their behalf to the European Court of Justice in Luxembourg which, on 16 February 1978, ruled that the Irish 50-mile limit was discriminatory and therefore illegal under agreed Community rules. It was adjudged discriminatory even though, according to the Irish, it applied to trawlers of *all* nationalities over 100 feet in length; apparently the Irish possessed only two such vessels. Next, the British followed suit, with a unilateral ban in summer 1977 on all herring fishing in the North Sea which provoked Dutch and Danish protests, though the EEC Commission supported it.

Meanwhile, as from 1 January 1977, along with the newly-established EEC 200-mile limit, the Nine had agreed that all negotiations with non-member states for fishing rights within the limit should be the responsibility of the Community and not be undertaken by individual member states. In the early months of 1977, while several East European countries were allotted temporary catch-quotas by the Commission, and others were banned from fishing in EEC waters, the Russians and others tacitly accepted this situation, even though the EEC Commission had refused to make trade agreements with Comecon. In mid-February the Soviet Fisheries Minister Alexander Ishkov led a delegation to Brussels for preliminary negotiations with British Foreign Office Minister of State David Owen, who led the EEC delegation because Britain held the presidency of the Council in the first half of 1977, and Finn Olav Gundelach, the (Danish) Commissioner responsible for fisheries. These talks had no immediate sequel; and hopes for a genuine Community régime for the control of third-country fishing in EEC waters were somewhat undermined by subsequent British insistence on a 'dominant preference' for her own fishermen within a fifty-mile zone. Thus, early in 1978, the Commission's proposals for fish catch-quotas, other conservation and control measures, modernisation plans for fishing fleets and the like were all held up by British intransigence, and the common fisheries policy was still far from being effectively implemented. On the other hand, negotiations with third countries continued: in February 1978 an agreement was initialled with The Faeroes and it was expected that those with Norway and Sweden would follow soon, though early in April 1978 British Minister of Agriculture and Fisheries John Silkin insisted that Britain would not approve these agreements until her demands had been met.

Unlike some of the policies so far discussed, a common transport policy was mentioned in the Treaty of Rome. Article 75 instructed the Council to lay down 'common rules applicable to international transport to or from the territory of a Member State or passing across the territory of one or more Member States'. But the Council has found it impossible to agree on many of the rules proposed by the Commission. Up to 1968, virtually no progress was made. In 1969 and 1970 the Council agreed on regulations for drivers' hours and for the installation and use of tachographs in their cabs, which would record their driving behaviour, speed and hours of driving. However, the British Transport and General Workers' Union opposed this 'spy in the cab', which it regarded as 'an infringement of the personal liberty and integrity of the drivers' – even though in West Germany it was warmly supported by the unions and has been credited with reducing accidents and saving fuel. In 1977-8 Britain was in danger of being hauled before the European Court of Justice for not having tachographs fitted in all new lorries, as well as for refusing or failing to implement the Community regulations limiting drivers' hours.

It seemed incredible that, in 1977, twenty years after the signature of the Treaty of Rome, road haulage traffic between the member states of the Community was still regulated by a wasteful, inconvenient and anti-quated system of bilateral quota agreements totally out of keeping with the spirit of the Treaty of Rome. Yet such was the case. In June 1976 this quota system nearly caused Dutch lorry-drivers to blockade the frontier with West Germany; they had requested 60,000 'round trips' per year into Germany and back from the Netherlands and been offered only 45,000 by the West Germans. In 1976 the Brenner Pass was still the scene of long delays for lorries carrying goods between Germany and Italy because of the inadequacies of the twenty-year-old bilateral agreement fixing the 'transport quotas' between the two countries. This agreement permitted a mere 770 round trips on either side. Once this diminutive quota was exhausted, a singular procedure was resorted to whereby a German lorry could only cross the border and enter Italy when an Italian lorry arrived from Italy to enter Germany! The result of this lunatic system was lengthy delays. Nor could a waiting lorry-driver leave his cab and relax; he might be released from the queue at a moment's notice, even in the middle of the night. Admittedly the Community had introduced a system of Community licences in 1962 which made it possible for a holder to make a round trip anywhere in the Community, but these only covered 15 per cent of the trade; the rest was regulated by the bilateral quota agreements. At the end of 1977, the Ministers of Transport of the Nine managed with difficulty to agree to increase the number of these Community licences by 20 per cent.

This near-ludicrous situation calls in question the entire credibility of the Community. Yet the failure of the Six and the Nine to create a common transport policy for road haulage traffic has been caused by real difficulties. Railway interests have consistently and universally opposed any further opening up of road goods traffic. Throughout the sixties, while nobody was desperately in favour of a transport policy, the Dutch were solidly opposed as standing to lose heavily from the introduction of any joint scheme which would almost certainly have the effect of eroding their very competitive position as the Community's most efficient road hauliers, with far more than their 'proper' share of the market. Furthermore, it was difficult for the Community to shoulder its way into an existing system which had been working more or less effectively. Nor must it be forgotten that great efforts were already being made in the field of road traffic by several well established international organs which, with their wider membership, were often better qualified than the EEC to cope with international traffic problems, notably the OECD, the United Nations ECE at Geneva, and the Conference of European Transport Ministers (CEMT), with its Paris secretariat.

Other EEC efforts in the transport field in the seventies have enjoyed mixed success. In 1972-4 the Community led the way in creating a 'green card common market' by abolishing the compulsory use of green insurance cards for motorists crossing frontiers. This was joined by Sweden, Norway, Finland, Switzerland, the German Democratic Republic, Czechoslovakia, Hungary and Austria. Although the European Council, meeting in Rome in December 1975, agreed on the introduction of a European Passport for 1978, the Council of Ministers has so far been unable to implement this decision; apparently there have been disagreements about the languages in which the document will be printed. Finally, efforts have been made, so far without any success, to end the confusion caused by the introduction and ending of summer time on different dates by the member states using it: Britain, Ireland, the Benelux countries, Italy and, since 1976, France. They found it quite impossible to accept the Commission's recommendation that they should all apply summer time during the same period. It was claimed in March 1976, when summer time was introduced in France, that nearly 100 French timetable planners had been taken to hospital with nervous breakdowns; one of them was supposed to have had a pulse of 60 in the left wrist, of 80 in the right, while his heart was beating at 70! At Basel-Mulhouse airport passengers were confused by three clocks, one showing French time, one Swiss time and the third Greenwich Mean Time. In 1977 the Nine were still divided into three 'summer time units': Belgium, Holland, Luxembourg, France and Italy all ended summer time on the same date; Britain and Ireland ended theirs four days later; West Germany and Denmark remained on Greenwich Mean Time plus one hour throughout the year.

If the EEC has failed, in recent years, to implement some of its policies, it has achieved at least one unqualified success: the foundation of the European University Institute at Florence. Not that it is strictly a Community affair, because it was set up by the governments of the Nine, and is funded through their contributions; nor is it a 'real' university, but rather a graduate school only — hence the official title 'European University Institute'. It opened its doors to seventy research students in a fifteenth-century monastery overlooking Florence, the Badia Fiesolana, donated by the Italian government, in October 1976. So far it is limited to four departments: history and civilisation, economics, law and political and social sciences.

A European University had been first suggested in 1949 in the Consultative Assembly of the Council of Europe in Strasbourg by André Philip. In 1950 the Committee of Ministers was asked to study this proposal, but nothing was done. It was indirectly as a result of Walter Hallstein's revival of the idea at Messina in 1955 that it was included in the Euratom Treaty, Article 9 of which stated that 'An institution of university status shall be established.' While the Italian government consistently favoured the project, obtaining agreement at the February 1961 EEC summit for Florence as its site, the French were opposed to a university taking undergraduate students and opposed to an autonomous institution; they preferred a graduate school firmly under the control of the governments. After lengthy delays and further controversies, a Convention was finally drawn up and signed by the Six in 1972, which after the three new members had acceded to it, came into force in 1975. The extra-Community nature of the European University Institute is emphasised by its constitution: its governing body is the High Council, composed of two representatives from each of the member states, and each state has a single vote. There is nothing supranational about this arrangement and nothing autonomous.

The Problem of Britain

The principal reason for the slow progress of the EEC in recent years, at any rate insofar as internal developments are concerned, has remained almost unchanged from the 1960s: it is the nationalism of the member states. Not one of them has been prepared to make serious concessions of sovereignty to the Community, nor to commit itself any distance along the road toward federation; nor, more importantly, has any member state been prepared to permit national policies – whether regional, social, monetary or whatever – to be replaced, rather than merely reinforced, by Community policies. The only difference between the two decades was that whereas, in the sixties, France was usually the scapegoat, in the seventies Britain increasingly took over the role, which had traditionally been assigned to de Gaulle, of throwing a succession of spanners into the Community's works. We may perhaps excuse Britain, with enormous reserves of oil and 60 per cent of the Community's fish within her 200-mile waters, for being somewhat possessive in respect of these important natural resources. We may also forgive her, plagued as she is by severe regional problems, mainly in urban areas of declining industries, for bludgeoning her partners into giving her a major share of the available Community funds. After all, she was undubitably one of the poorest member states, ranking with Ireland and Italy as in most need of help of every kind, and the Treasury was not the only government department to see EEC membership partly as an accounting exercise, in which the essential requirement was that Britain should emerge as a net beneficiary.

On the other hand, what did seem totally inexcusable, especially to the outside observer not too well aware of the internal problems of the Labour Party, was the cynical and unscrupulous way in which, after one British government had accepted the terms of entry into the Common Market in 1971-2, another, in 1974, threatened to withdraw from the Community altogether unless those terms of entry were renegotiated in her favour, and even had the effrontery to submit the question of continuing British membership to a popular referendum.

It was Britain's newly appointed Labour Foreign Secretary, James Callaghan, who in 1974 startled and dismayed the eight at a Council meeting in Luxembourg on the unfortunate date of 1 April. Criticising the common agricultural policy, the plans for Economic and Monetary Union, and Britain's alleged over-large contribution to the Community budget, and calling into question the concept of a European Union enunciated at the 1972 summit, and the EEC's policy toward the United States, which he implied was unfriendly, Mr Callaghan said that, if the British government failed to renegotiate the terms so as to remove these and other objections, 'we shall submit to the British people the reason why we find the terms unacceptable and consult them on the advisability of negotiating the withdrawal of the United Kingdom from the Community.' Asked at his press conference after the meeting about the propriety of breaking a solemn international treaty engagement, Mr Callaghan blithely remarked that, in a democracy, 'even a treaty must rest on popular consent and this one does not.' Not a scrap of sympathy for Britain's position was voiced by her partners, all of whom insisted that there could be no question of revising the Treaty of Accession. The West German paper *Die Welt,* in an article entitled 'The British cold front', claimed that 'Today Europe for the British means something different from what it means to the other eight,' and suggested that the most alarming EEC crisis of the last ten years had begun. *La Stampa* detected a 'serious threat for the future of Europe'. The new Labour government had made a most unfortunate impression, and Britain had placed herself in a position of isolation from which, in many ways, she has still not emerged at the time of writing.

In the event, Britain's demands, suitably moderated, were met without serious difficulty, and Prime Minister Harold Wilson was able to tell the House of Commons on 18 March 1975 that 'Her Majesty's Government have decided to recommend to the British people to vote for staying in the Community.' Asked the question, 'Do you think that the United Kingdom should stay in the European Community? Yes? or No?,' nearly two-thirds (around 63 per cent; by contrast, over 90 per cent of Danes voted in the 2 October 1972 EEC referendum in that country) of the British people turned out to vote: 67.2 per cent of those voting were in favour, 32.8 per cent against. The other one-third stayed at home, so that in fact less than half (43 per cent) of the population of Britain registered a positive vote for Europe (but only 20.9 per cent voted no).

This favourable decision of the British people on 5 June 1975 was by no means accompanied or followed by a more 'European' policy on the part of the government; far from it. Substantial elements in the Labour Party, led by two Cabinet Ministers, Tony Benn and Peter Shore, remained firmly opposed to the EEC; both belonged to the Labour Common Market Safeguards Committee, comprising over sixty MPs, which was against direct elections to the European Parliament, against Economic and Monetary Union, and in favour of radical reforms to Britain's advantage of the CAP and the Community budget. Moreover James Callaghan, now Prime Minister, in a letter of 30 September 1977 to the Labour Party's National Executive Committee, stated that 'The government has never accepted that the Community should develop into a federation. It is our policy to continue to uphold the rights of national governments and parliaments.' At the end of 1977 and in the early months of 1978 Britain continued to make herself extremely unpopular among her EEC partners, including those traditionally friendly like Holland. She seemed more isolated than ever.

Nationalism among the Nine

It would, however, be a gross distortion of the truth to suggest that Britain alone was holding up progress in the Common Market, just as it would be to attribute all the crises of the sixties to France. The same nationalism — or Gaullism — that has inspired recent British 'European' policy, has made it difficult for the EEC to settle several serious internal disputes between some of Britain's Continental neighbours.

The so-called 'wine war', for example, exacerbated Franco-Italian relations in 1975-6. The Community 'wine lake', a massive surplus which became a major problem in 1975, was caused in part by the exceptionally abundant harvests of 1973 and 1974, in part by a tiny 1 per cent annual reduction in the huge French consumption which could not begin to be offset by the relatively enormous (50 per cent) increases in wine consumption in countries like Britain. The French farmers reacted violently against imports of Italian wine, with demonstrations, road blocks and attacks on wine ships and lorries. In the spring of 1975, violating Community rules, the French government closed the frontier against Italian wine, then relented and imposed an equally illegal frontier tax, of about 12 per cent, on imported wine, which was not removed until the following spring after its denunciation by the Commission.

The economically hard-pressed Italians have likewise been guilty of nationalistic moves which have been criticised for being in flagrant breach of the Community spirit. On 5 May 1976, fearful of a further devaluation of the lira, Prime Minister Aldo Moro announced sweeping import restrictions on virtually all goods except grains; the scheme was much more extensive than the similar import deposit scheme which had been introduced in 1974. The EEC Commission reluctantly agreed to the 1976 scheme — for a period of three months only. A year later, in the summer of 1977, the Italian government was reported to be launching a 'buy Italian' campaign which was surely a breach of the Community spirit. The object was to cut down on the import of luxury goods like the 83 Rolls-Royces ordered by Italians so far that year, costing £3.1 million; but in fact it was foodstuffs, and above all, oil, which was causing the Italian balance of trade deficit, and her best hope lay in an export drive rather than in import curbs.

On 1 October 1977 *The Economist* published an article entitled 'Nine naughty boys' which pointed out that every one of the member states was subject to investigation by the Commission for infringing Community regulations. At that time 179 separate cases were under investigation and another 200 were suspected. The French and Italians came out of this worst, with 41 and 35 cases respectively; West Germany, Belgium and the Netherlands had 17, 20 and 21; Britain and Denmark each had 12, Luxembourg 11, and Ireland was the best-behaved member state with a mere 10 violations of rules to its discredit. This misbehaviour ranged from unfair subsidised rail freight rates for French farmers to a British import ban on potatoes, and included the failure of five member states to apply a 1965 (!) Community directive on the pharmaceutical industry, and the illicit holding of less than the minimum level of crude oil stocks agreed by the Council of Ministers in 1972, by Italy, Ireland and the Netherlands.

Expansion in Europe

Even though the EEC, faced as it is with the 'British problem' and with the continued nationalism of its member states, has had difficulties in speaking with a single voice in world affairs, in acting as a single unit in international crises, and even in achieving effective 'internal' policies, nevertheless all the available evidence points to its persistence and to its further enlargement and development. Crystal-gazing apart, it has during the seventies not only greatly increased its stature and influence inside Europe; it has also so extended its system of world-wide trading connections that it is tempting to think in terms of a new kind of European imperialism, a new European conquest of the rest of the world. In the old days, this would have been called aggrandisement.

More than anything else it was the enlargement of the EEC on 1 January 1973 that made possible, and in many ways positively stimulated, the further extension of its power and influence in non-Community Europe. This point is nicely illustrated by developments within the Council of Europe, a body to which all the Nine belong. From 1973 onwards, the Council of Europe's Committee of Ministers came to be dominated by the Nine. At that time it consisted of the Foreign Ministers (or their deputies) of 17 states, and it is hardly surprising that a discernible split occurred inside the Committee of Ministers between the Nine on the one hand, and the 'non-Nine' or the Eight, on the other. In effect, the Committee of Ministers of the Council of Europe was 'taken over' by the EEC. Perhaps even more striking is the way in which the parliamentary assembly of the Six and the Nine has established itself firmly as *the* European Parliament and will doubtless consolidate its position still further after the direct European elections of 1979. Meanwhile, it has completely overshadowed the once proud and, in 1949-50, momentarily influential Consultative Assembly of the Council of Europe, which, whatever it chooses to call itself, can clearly never now become a European Parliament.

Expansion in Europe: the EFTA Countries

Unlike the Council of Europe, the European Free Trade Association (EFTA) is quite distinct in membership, as in most other ways, from the EEC. Its size and status were much reduced in 1973, when Britain and Denmark left it to join the EEC. Since then, a network of agreements signed between each individual EFTA member state and the EEC, and administered by Joint Committees, each comprising a delegation from the EFTA country concerned headed by its ambassador to the Community and a delegation from the Commission's foreign affairs department (Directorate-General I: External relations), had, by 1 July 1977, brought about an enlarged free-trade area for industrial goods including the Nine EEC member states and the Seven EFTA member states: namely Belgium, Britain, Denmark, France, the Netherlands, Ireland, Italy, Luxembourg and West Germany on the one hand and Austria, Finland, Iceland, Norway, Portugal, Sweden and Switzerland on the other.

Thus, weakened by the EEC in 1973 and subsequently transformed, in a sense, into a sort of appendage of that body, peripheral, dispersed EFTA – though numbering among its member states three of the richest countries in the world, Norway, Sweden and Switzerland – is apparently in the process of being increasingly attracted into the orbit of its larger, more tightly knit and more centrally placed neighbour. For the closer cooperation between the EEC and EFTA, which is being widely advocated, especially in EFTA countries, seems likely to lead to a gradual assimilation of EFTA into the EEC. The 'pull' that the EEC exerts on her neighbours was illustrated at a meeting of the Switzerland-EEC Joint Committee in November 1976, when the Swiss, though by no means obliged to do so, submitted to the EEC details of their proposed legislation against pollution by cars. According to the *EFTA Bulletin* for January/February 1977, 'the Swiss authorities were interested in seeing that there was not too great a difference between the regulations applied in various countries and they therefore wished to give the EEC an opportunity to make any observations on the Swiss measures.'

Some of the EEC's policies have had a powerful influence on her EFTA neighbours. Although in 1972 Norway decided after a referendum not to join the EEC as a full member, but signed a free-trade agreement with her instead, nevertheless she kept her crown inside the EEC currency 'snake' which she had joined earlier in 1972 in anticipation of membership. In March 1973 the Swedes joined the snake too, so that, since the franc finally dropped out in March 1976, this rather lop-sided reptile, dominated by the German mark, has also included the three Scandinavian (until Sweden left in August 1977) and the two Benelux currencies. In the field of scientific and technological research the EEC launched a programme in 1971, which was shared by up to ten non-EEC countries, run by the Committee on European Cooperation in the Field of Scientific and Technical Research (COST). From 1977 COST countries were also being given the opportunity of participating in various Community programmes. Significantly, a Commission publication, the *Bulletin of the European Communities. Supplement 3/77,* recorded that 'With regard to the possible enlargement of the Community, COST furthermore offers the advantage of early collaboration with the potential candidates.' Virtually all the EFTA countries belong to COST. Finally, the thrust of the EEC toward EFTA is clearly apparent in the common fisheries policy, for Iceland and Norway are now faced with the need to negotiate with the EEC for fishing rights within the new 200-mile EEC 'economic zone' off the coasts of Britain, Ireland, West Germany, Denmark and (for the time being, at least) Greenland.

Quite apart from the rather generalised effect of these EEC activities and policies on the EFTA countries, individual member states of EFTA have become increasingly involved with the EEC, even to the extent of seeking membership. Norway is an obvious candidate, though only in the fairly distant future. Switzerland, whose government in summer 1977 announced its intention to join the United Nations, may sooner or later consider joining the EEC as well. Portuguese Prime Minister Dr Mário Soares toured the capitals of the Nine early in 1977 and persuaded their governments and the Commission to look with favour on Portugal's application for membership. Austria, in April 1976, considered the possibility of applying for observer status in the European Parliament; and Sweden has been a member, from the start in 1973, of the Nine's Joint European Torus (JET) project for research into nuclear fusion which, after long delays due to a display of petty nationalism in the EEC Council, was eventually sited at Culham near Oxford by a decision of October 1977. In 1976, too, the Swedes signed an agreement which had the effect of incorporating Sweden, via her National Board for Energy Source Development, into the EEC's programme of research and training in thermonuclear fusion. Portugal has already decided to leave EFTA for the EEC; could other defections follow?

Expansion in Europe: the EEC and Nordic Cooperation

Since 1973 the EEC has also made a remarkable impact on Nordic cooperation which, however, still retains its essential autonomy and character, in spite of the fact that one of its participants, Denmark, joined the EEC in 1972, all of them belong to EFTA and signed free-trade agreements with the EEC in 1972-3, and one of them, Finland, also signed a treaty with Comecon in May 1973.

The immediate response in Norden to the 1972 'Nordic splits', when Denmark joined the EEC, varied from country to country, but there were important constants. All the Nordic governments reacted predictably by paying even more than the customary lip-service to Nordic cooperation, which had indeed been used in both the Danish and Norwegian referendum campaigns, by a minority of the opponents of EEC membership, as an argument against joining. The Danes in particular insisted that they would continue to be firm supporters of Nordic cooperation. The day after the referendum in Denmark, Prime Minister Jens Otto Krag said, 'Being the only Nordic country in the European Community will increase our Nordic responsbility... Nordic cooperation can and must be continued and developed under the new conditions.' Denmark was thought of by the Danes themselves as a bridge between the EEC and Norden, though some observers have wondered how they could contrive to be on both sides of the negotiating table at once. A notable intensification and elaboration of Nordic cooperation accompanied the verbal declarations of governments and interested parties. In practical institutional terms much of this was rescued from the wreckage of Nordek. By far and away the most important development was the establishment in 1971 of a new institution, the Nordic Council of Ministers, with a permanent secretariat in Oslo which began to function on 1 July 1973. In this bureaucratic consolidation the venerable Nordic Council did not lag far behind: a Swedish delegate to the 1975 session in Reykjavik wondered what on earth the point was in flying 400 people and two tons of paper to Iceland; it was also claimed that the main achievement of Nordic cooperation was a steady increase in the number of persons involved in it. In 1976 another institution was set up, in Helsinki – the Nordic Investment Bank, which had originally been considered in 1957 and recommended by the Nordic Council in 1964.

On the face of it, Denmark's membership of the EEC since 1973 appeared to have made little difference to Nordic cooperation, but a closer scrutiny reveals growing shortcomings. In the first place, Nordic solidarity on the global stage, if it ever really existed, has been weakened. Compare the much-vaunted achievement of the Nordic countries during the Kennedy Round of

GATT negotiations in 1966, in negotiating as a single unit with a single delegation, with the situation now, where, inevitably, Denmark's voice in GATT affairs is with the EEC, and there is an EEC delegation but no Nordic one. It is true, however, that the Nordic countries do act as a single group and are accepted as a group, within the International Monetary Fund; whereas the EEC on the whole does not and is not. Moreover, the influence of the EEC has recently been making itself felt, albeit uncertainly, in the far north-west of Norden, above all in Greenland, which is still part of the kingdom of Denmark. It is fifty times larger than 'mainland' Denmark in area, but has only 1 per cent of the combined population. In this part of the world, Nordic solidarity seems a long way off, and disintegrative tendencies are more to the fore than integration. The Faeroes, granted home rule by Denmark back in 1948, requested a three-year moratorium on EEC entry from 1 January 1973, when Denmark joined. But it took the 26 members of the Faeroese parliament or Lagting a year only to decide unanimously to stay out of the EEC, apparently because they wanted to keep their own fish for themselves. They asked for a trade agreement instead, and, since then, they have signed an agreement on fishing rights with the EEC. It is often forgotten that, on the very same day that the people of Denmark voted themselves into the EEC, the Greenlanders voted against membership by 9,386 votes to 3,905, the turn-out being a modest 55.7% of the electorate. Partly, ignorance and confusion may have caused this lack of interest and adverse vote. Public debate both in Denmark and Greenland had not been facilitated by the fact that one of the two Greenland members of the Danish Parliament or Folketing spoke in favour of Greenland's membership and the other against. In any event, Greenland was brought by Denmark willy-nilly into the EEC, and, since then large sums of EEC money have been pumped into her from the Social Fund, the Regional Fund and the Agricultural Fund. She has also received a substantial loan from the EEC's Investment Bank, and may find that the Danes manage to get special terms in Brussels for her share of the 200-mile fishing zone. Not until after Greenland has achieved home rule in 1979 will the possibility of her continuing membership of the EEC be raised again. The question is whether the new hospital and airport at Godthaab and the other EEC goodies will persuade her to remain in the European fold; or will the 1977-founded nationalist party, the Siumut, succeed in keeping her out?

Since 1973, while the EEC has been modified in a way that seems to make it more acceptable to the Nordic countries, namely less supranational, more intergovernmental, Nordic cooperation has increasingly approached the EEC in its mechanism and institutions. Both are now run by a Council of Ministers and a subordinate bureaucracy. They are by no means any longer two quite different animals. Will Nordic cooperation remain a distinct entity, a way of life, or will the tentacles of the EEC strangle it?

Expansion in Europe: the East

Although in the 1970s there has been a fitfully continuing and many-sided amelioration in East-West relations, so that the Eastern Europe of the state trading countries has become less of a world apart from the West, nevertheless it shows no real signs of imminent disintegration or even significant penetration from the West. Naturally, it will be our concern here to indicate the increasing role which the EEC is playing in Eastern bloc affairs, but against these developments must be set the still very strong links which group together Russia and her smaller East European neighbours. Both Comecon and the Warsaw Pact Organisation still flourish. The latter seems recently to have evolved two new institutions: a Foreign Ministers' Committee, which officially met for the first time on 25-6 May 1977 in Moscow although it had been preceded by a meeting in Moscow in December 1975 of the Foreign Ministers of the Warsaw Pact member states; and a 'Parliamentary Consultative Assembly' which first met in Leningrad on 5 July 1977. Comecon is now in process of completing one of its characteristically spectacular joint projects, the 1,720-mile natural gas pipeline from Orenburg in the Urals to the Czechoslovakian border, but it has fallen behind the timetable of its 1971 *Comprehensive programme* of integration, and has still not succeeded in producing a single centrally determined Comecon plan.

Alongside the 'positive' solidarity encouraged by the Warsaw Pact, by Comecon, and by Soviet policy in general, a certain 'negative' solidarity has been engendered in the East in recent years. Western monetary instability after 1969 and soaring inflation after 1973 have demonstrated the value of the East bloc's non-convertible rouble in providing it with a distinct monetary system. In spite of the new Adria oil pipeline, which will pump OPEC oil from the Yugoslav Adriatic coast to Hungary and Czechoslovakia, and in spite of a recent US Central Intelligence Agency report that Russia might be short of oil by the 1980s (could this be wishful thinking?), Comecon in Europe has become, and is likely to remain for some time, a single energy unit, in surplus at the moment, nearly all the supplies for which come from the Soviet Union. The smaller Comecon countries, apart from Romania, which has her own (dwindling) oil supplies, and to some extent Poland, which has some coal, are locked into this system partly because they are short of hard currency with which to purchase oil on world markets, and partly because they are compelled to participate in the cost of the pipelines and to accept payment in oil or gas. Thus Bulgaria, Hungary, East Germany and Czechoslovakia will each receive 2.8 billion cubic metres of gas between 1980 and 1990 through the Orenburg pipeline they are helping to build. Finally, Eastern bloc solidarity has tended to be increased in recent years by its growing deficit with the West: by 1977 Comecon countries' debts with the West were thought to total nearly $50 billion. They are faced here with a common problem which may demand a joint solution, part of which might take the form of increased intra-Comecon trade, for which the transferable rouble could be used.

What has been said thus far seems to confirm the continuing solidarity of the Eastern bloc, nor have developments in East-West relations as a whole done much to undermine it. Instead of encouraging all-European economic cooperation, the Helsinki Conference on Security and Cooperation in Europe led only to a confrontation on human rights. West German *Ostpolitik* has brought about an improvement in relations between the Federal and Democratic German Republics, but it has not produced the faintest sign of any detachment of the GDR from her Comecon neighbours. As to the countries which, in the fifties or sixties, gave a certain impression of rebelliousness or separatism *vis-à-vis* Russia, or even openly revolted against her, they have not in the seventies shown signs of wishing or daring to move away further. Albania has remained no more solitary and taciturn than before; Yugoslavia participates as an observer in Comecon, and in 1976 in particular Romania stepped up her contacts with Soviet leaders and increased her trade with Eastern Europe at the expense of that with the West. Nor does the fact that, in 1966-73, five Comecon member states associated themselves with the GATT imply any serious split in the Communist ranks; still less a desire on the part of those countries to join the West.

On the other hand, the EEC has made an undeniable impact on Eastern Europe since the much-quoted 1972 summit communiqué affirmed the Nine's determination 'to follow a common commercial policy towards the countries of Eastern Europe with effect from 1 January 1973' and to pursue a 'policy of détente and peace with the countries of Eastern Europe'. But the first initiative came from the East: at the June 1973 twenty-seventh session of Comecon, Secretary Nikolai Fadeyev was instructed to make contact with the EEC. Applying to the Council, he was cold-shouldered and advised to consult the Commission. He did this in September 1973 by inviting Commission President F.X. Ortoli to visit Comecon headquarters in Moscow. Instead, the Commission sent a delegation led by the Director-General of External Relations (Community jargon for foreign economic affairs), Edmond Wellenstein, which got nowhere. The EEC, having itself recently, after many delays and difficulties, contrived to introduce a joint commercial policy to coincide with the expiry of virtually all existing bilateral trade agreements between EEC member states and individual East European countries, was quite unwilling to see Comecon behave in the same way. Instead, in November 1974, it sent a copy of a modest trade agreement, between itself on the one hand and an individual East European state on the other, to each state trading country, and urged them all to sign bilateral agreements with itself. They refused; and after 1 January 1975 there were no valid trade agreements in existence between West and East European countries. None the less, trade continued, and is still continuing, without them. At the same time the member states of the EEC, deprived of the right to sign their own trade agreements with Comecon member states, signed cooperation agreements instead. A typical one was the ten-year Soviet-Danish Agreement on Economic, Industrial and Technical Cooperation signed on 28 August 1975 in Moscow, which envisaged cooperation in shipbuilding, building, building materials production, milk, meat, chemical production, environmental protection and the peaceful use of atomic energy. It was to be implemented by an intergovernmental Soviet-Danish Committee for Economic, Scientific and Technical Cooperation. Less typical was a Franco-Romanian agreement of December 1976: Citroën, one of France's biggest capitalist firms, actually run by Peugeot, was to take a 36 per cent interest in a Romanian state-owned industry and invest 2.5 billion francs in a factory in which, from 1980 onwards, 130,000 cars would be built annually, half to be sold in Eastern Europe, the other half to be marketed in the West.

Against the background of this nationalistic scramble by EEC member states for East bloc goodies, Comecon made another approach to the EEC early in 1976 for a 'framework' agreement or agreement on the lines along which Comecon member states might make bilateral treaties with EEC member states. Again the EEC stalled; the Council managed to take nine months to reply to this invitation. It was, in fact, quite unwilling to discuss matters of trade with Comecon, only with that organisation's individual member states, and even now, early in 1978, the two sides are still only conducting talks about talks. The creation of the EEC's 200-mile fishing zone from 1 January 1977 induced Russia, Poland and the GDR to begin discussions for a framework agreement between themselves and the EEC regulating reciprocal fishing rights within the 200-mile zones. Here, too, progress has been slow and nothing has yet been signed.

In spite of the oft-repeated assertion that both Comecon and the Soviet Union have consistently refused to recognise the EEC, the truth is that, since 1973, Russia has made repeated efforts to enhance the status of Comecon by involving it in negotiations with the EEC. But the EEC has held out firmly against this, fearful of in any way facilitating the Russian hold over East Europe and hopeful of somehow penetrating and breaking up the solid Communist front there. Some Comecon member states, too, notably Romania, have been suspicious and resentful of any extension of that organisation's powers. Since 1974 Romania has been included in the EEC's generalised preferences scheme, and in 1976 she signed a textile agreement with the EEC. As to Yugoslavia, she has had a trade agreement with the Community since 1970 which is administered by an EEC-Yugoslavia Joint Committee; she has benefited since 1972 from the EEC's generalised preferences scheme; and since May 1971 she has, as a member of COST, participated in various Community projects of scientific and technical cooperation. In 1977-8 talks were in progress with the aim of renewing the existing agreement and forging closer links between Yugoslavia and the Community and it does not seem beyond the bounds of possibility that she may one day negotiate associate or even full membership. The interests of the Nine were avowedly political: especially because Greece was likely to join the Community, some buttressing of Yugoslavia against the uncertainties likely to follow the approaching departure of the elderly President Josip Broz Tito would certainly be desirable.

Expansion in Europe: the Mediterranean

It is perhaps when we turn to look at southern Europe and the Mediterranean that the expanding influence of the EEC is most apparent. The 1972 summit communiqué referred to 'the fulfilment of commitments to the countries of the Mediterranean Basin with which agreements have been or will be concluded, agreements which should be the subject of an overall and balanced approach'. So far as southern Europe is concerned, the agreements referred to were, in chronological order, those with Greece (1962) and Turkey (1964), in both of which the Six virtually promised ultimate full membership, Spain (1970), Malta (1971) and Cyprus (1973). Although the Nine have only slowly developed what they call their 'Mediterranean policy', and no attempt has been made to create a Mediterranean 'sphere of influence' for the EEC, it does seem that the gradual assimilation of the European Mediterranean countries into the EEC as full members will be the eventual outcome. We have already mentioned, when discussing the EEC's impact on EFTA in the seventies, that Portugal received assurances on this score in 1977. Since the fall of the right-wing military régime in Greece in 1974 the negotiations for her entry as a full member have made progress which can only be described as 'rapid' in EEC terms, in spite of the hesitations of the Council of Ministers in 1977-8. This speed has been due, in the main, to Prime Minister Konstantinos Karamanlis, a determined European who is faced with some opposition to EEC membership within his own country.

The long-expected Spanish application for EEC membership was delivered in Brussels by Foreign Minister Marcellino Oreja on 28 July 1977. Here too the EEC's moral obligation is strong. During Franco's régime membership was rejected on the grounds that Spain was a dictatorship; now, under Adolfo Suarez's democratically elected government, EEC attitudes will be different and the negotiations could well take place in 1979-80, perhaps permitting Spanish entry on 1 January 1982, a year after that of Greece. Spain, of course, is a very different kettle of fish from Portugal or Greece. She is a major industrial power — tenth biggest in the world — with a growth rate over the last decade much above the EEC average; her income per head is now close to Italy's and her 34 million inhabitants (roughly the same population as Turkey's) place her not far behind the EEC's 'big four', which in 1972 had populations ranging from 52 (France) to 62 (West Germany) million. As for Turkey, full membership prospects are still remote, but revision of the 1970 Additional Protocol, which allowed for a twelve-year transition period before the completion of her customs union with the EEC, may be in the offing.

Political motivations are paramount in the case for EEC entry of every one of these Mediterranean countries. On both sides an element of urgency is felt on this score: namely, the need to support democratic régimes which have recently rejected dictatorships or, in the case of Turkey, to keep her within NATO and the Western orbit in general. The cost of the operation to the member states of the Nine, it is admitted, will be very substantial. An important lead within the EEC has been taken on this subject by Britain who, though she may be dragging her feet in other respects, has been and is a firm supporter of the admission of these Mediterranean countries to the EEC. As Foreign Secretary Anthony Crosland put it in the European Parliament in January 1977, 'enlargement is an investment in the democratic future of Europe.'

The EEC as a World Trading power

So far, we have confined our discussions of the EEC's expansion to Europe, but the 'overall and balanced approach' to the Mediterranean announced at the 1972 summit, which is now regarded as marking the start of the Community's 'global Mediterranean policy', naturally implied a relationship with the Asian and African countries bordering that sea. In November 1972 the Council stated that the Mediterranean policy would also include the 1969 agreements with Morocco and Tunisia and preferential agreements with Israel, Egypt and Lebanon as well as the agreements with the European Mediterranean countries already mentioned. The policy was supposed to aim at creating by 1 July 1977 a Mediterranean free-trade area in industrial goods to complement the one being created in northern Europe with the EFTA states, the gradual freeing from EEC duties of up to 80 per cent of imported agricultural goods, and a programme of cooperation designed to foster the social and economic development of the Mediterranean countries. The very long delays in the negotiation of new agreements to implement this policy were almost entirely due to the EEC. On the one hand there were fundamental differences of approach between the member states, especially between the consumer-orientated British who welcomed the possibility of obtaining cheap food from the Mediterranean region, and producer-orientated France and Italy who regarded this as a threat to their own agriculture. On the other hand, because of the absence of firm general guidelines, much time was wasted discussing trivial matters such as the question of whether an EEC customs duty reduction of 55 per cent should apply only to tinned fruit salads weighing over a kilo, or also to those weighing under a kilo. Success came in the end with the signature, in April 1976, of cooperation or, more accurately, trade and aid agreements with the Maghreb countries — Algeria, Morocco and Tunisia — and, early in 1977, of similar agreements with Israel, Jordan, Lebanon and Syria. These agreements are an important advance on earlier ones: most of them are for an unlimited period of time, provide for a 'permanent dialogue' in the form of a Joint Committee of management, include provisions for various types of cooperation and financial assistance, abolish EEC tariffs on raw materials and industrial goods while substantially lowering those on agricultural imports, and in some cases provide for the free movement of, and prohibit discrimination against, immigrants from the Mediterranean countries wishing to work in Europe.

The EEC's Mediterranean policy has been complemented, since 1973, by the Euro-Arab dialogue between the EEC and the Arab League. Initiated in 1974-5 with a series of talks between experts, this was institutionalised in May 1976 when the Euro-Arab General Commission met for the first time in Luxembourg, comprising the President of the Arab League's Council and the Secretary of the Arab League on the one side, and representatives of the EEC on the other.

The above-mentioned agreements with the Mediterranean countries represent only one of the ways in which the EEC disburses aid to and promotes trade with the world's less developed countries. However, while trade policy is largely in the hands of the Commission in Brussels, aid is for the most part an instrument of the national governments. In fact, EEC aid constitutes only 13 per cent of all the aid given by the Nine member states. The Community has organised a successful programme of food aid since 1970: in 1975-6 it donated 708,000 tons of cereals, 150,000 tons of powdered milk and 45,000 tons of butteroil — a valuable use for some of those much criticised CAP surpluses. As to trade, the Commission pioneered a new type of trade privilege open to every Third World country, the 'generalized system of preferences' (GSP), which came into force on 1 July 1971. This system, which requires no negotiation and entails no reciprocity, simply allows goods imported under it to enter the EEC duty-free, up to certain maximum quantities. By 1977 one hundred and eleven countries were benefiting from the scheme, which has been extended every year since its inception, and nine industrialised countries, including Japan and the USA, have launched schemes of their own modelled on the EEC's. Finally, the EEC has played an important role in the recent world-wide attempts to regulate the textile industry. It was a signatory to the GATT multifibres agreement (MFA) of 1974, otherwise known as the Arrangement regarding Trade in Textiles, and has since then negotiated bilateral agreements with a number of textile exporting countries throughout the world.

The growing world stature of the EEC was demonstrated by United

States President Jimmy Carter's visit to the Commission in Brussels on 6 January 1978, when relations between the EEC, Japan and the United States, the North-South Dialogue, the GATT negotiations, the energy question and other world problems were all discussed. It is also reflected in the development of relations between the EEC and Japan. From June 1973 the Commission started twice-yearly top-level discussions with Japan on the same lines as those already held with the USA; in November 1974 it set up a permanent delegation in Tokyo; and since then contacts and discussions have become increasingly frequent, as the need to curb Japanese exports to EEC countries became felt in 1976-7. By February 1978 the EEC was insisting that the Japanese must take steps to reduce their enormous trade surplus with the Nine and they had accepted this and agreed, for example, to purchase some European aeroplanes. The EEC also entered into relations with China. In September 1975 the Chinese opened a delegations in Brussels and on 3 February 1978 a five-year non-preferential trade agreement was initialled which should come into force in June 1978. Premier Chou En-lai had said in Peking on 13 January 1975 that the Chinese would 'help the Western European countries in their attempts at unification'. As a matter of fact the Chinese had for years been expressing their friendship and approval towards the EEC: it was their second-biggest trading partner after Japan, and they saw it as a possible counterweight to the world dominance of the two imperialist superpowers, Russia and America.

In Latin America the EEC has been slow to act. In spite of the 1970 declaration of Buenos Aires by the Latin American countries expressing a wish for relations with the EEC, only four agreements had been signed by 1976, with Argentina (1971), Uruguay and Brazil (1973), and Mexico (1976). On the other hand, on three occasions since 1974 a European Parliament delegation has conferred with representatives of various Latin American Parliaments. Spanish and Portuguese entry into the EEC may be expected to stimulate and transform its relations with Latin America.

By far and away the most significant event in the EEC's history as a world trading power was Britain's entry. This is true even though the EEC of the Six was already the world's largest importer. By 1973 the trade of the Nine was three times that of the USA and well over twice that of the USA and Russia combined. But the impact of British membership was not merely quantitative. The British had rampaged through the world for centuries; they were still outward-looking; they still had multifarious world-wide contacts and connections; London was still an incomparably greater city, in global terms, than Paris or Rome, a world financial and insurance centre, hub of the world's commodity markets, and Heathrow had substantially more international air traffic than Paris or, for that matter, any other airport in the world. Added to this was the arrival in

Brussels of the only authentic world language.*

The world trading connections of the EEC were greatly expanded as a direct result of British entry. The nineteen mainly ex-French African and Malagasy signatories of the 1964 and 1971 Yaoundé Conventions plus the three East African signatories of the 1971 Arusha Agreement were now joined by eighteen ex-British states in Africa, the Caribbean and the Pacific, as well as six other African States. These 46 African, Caribbean and Pacific (ACP) states joined with the Nine in signing the Lomé Convention in the West African republic of Togo on 28 February 1975. This agreement was based on the principle of the duty-free entry into Europe of raw materials and industrial goods from the non-European signatories and of preferential treatment for their agricultural exports to Europe. It set up a system of stabilisation of export earnings for a number of primary products, called Stabex; included special agreements for sugar, bananas and rum; and provided for industrial cooperation, financial aid and institutional arrangements. It is due to be renegotiated (with 53 countries) in 1978-9 before it runs out at the end of 1979. Other direct or indirect results of British entry into the EEC were the development of relations between the EEC and the five members of the Association of South-East Asian Nations (ASEAN), the signing of Commercial Cooperation Agreements with India and Pakistan in 1973 and 1976 respectively, regular consultations between the EEC and Australia and New Zealand, and the signature of a Framework Agreement for Commercial and Economic Cooperation with Canada in July 1976.

Is there anywhere in the world which does not have contacts with the EEC? Iran, not hitherto mentioned, has had a trade agreement since 1963 which allowed Persian carpets, dried apricots and caviar into the EEC duty-free. As to South Africa, in September 1977 the Foreign Ministers of the Nine approved a code of conduct for EEC firms operating in that country or with branches there; nor have the Nine experienced any difficulty in achieving unanimity in condemning apartheid.

Conclusion

There can be no real conclusion to a history that is still under way; every comment is provisional only. But the events we have traced so far do point in a certain direction. The régime of totally independent national states has, in Europe, been substantially modified by the evolution of all kinds of interconnection between them, many of which have been discussed in this book. The political and economic map of Europe does have a new dimension, in addition to the national states: that of inter-state organisations varying in significance, in terms of an eventual European unity, from OECD and NATO on the one extreme to the EEC on the other. Europe

---

* It was said that Valéry Giscard d'Estaing and Helmut Schmidt got on well because they both spoke the same language – English.

has moved nearer to unity since 1945; some parts are nearer than others. But progress has seemed extraordinarily slow, mainly because national sovereignties have been defended to the last ditch on even the most trivial matters. At one time it seemed as if a 'little' Europe, a close association or federation of the Six, might serve as a tightly knit nucleus for further integration, while other centres of integration seemed to be developing independently in Northern and Eastern Europe. But in the last ten years this situation has been transformed. Progress towards unity in the north and east either has not materialised or has been slowed almost to a stand-still, and regional integration in both areas has even to some some extent been penetrated by the EEC. Meanwhile the EEC, abandoning, perhaps temporarily, more likely for ever, federation and supranationalism, indeed casting off the entire theology of 'little' Europe, has embarked on a process of enlargement and internal change which looks like giving more weight to cooperation between governments. In recent years, in spite of efforts, especially on the part of the Commission, which has by no means lost its position of central importance among Community institutions, to create and implement effective common policies to cope with problems vital to all which cannot easily be solved individually, the jealous protection of national interests has still stood in the way. On the other hand, the EEC has moved towards its loudly proclaimed goal of 'European Union' by breaking out of the treaty framework and creating institutions and policies not prescribed in the Treaty of Rome; it has thus acquired a new momentum of its own. Moreover, its continued and, since 1973, rapidly increasing, role in the world at large seems to point to its development as an effective vehicle of European influence outside Europe. However it changes its name, its size or its function, the EEC has demonstrated its ability to transform itself, to survive and to extend it influence. It has undubitably come to stay, and if Europe continues to move, however haltingly, towards unity, if integration continues, then any such further activities will surely be centred on the EEC.

INDEX

F6